Jean-Pierre Rives

A Modern Corinthian

PETER BILLS

JEAN-PIERRE RIVES

A Modern Corinthian

Translations by Averil Craven

London
ALLEN & UNWIN
Boston   Sydney

George Allen & Unwin (Publishers) Ltd,
40 Museum Street, London WC1A 1LU, UK

George Allen & Unwin (Publishers) Ltd,
Park Lane, Hemel Hempstead, Herts HP2 4TE, UK

Allen & Unwin Inc.,
9 Winchester Terrace, Winchester, Mass 01890, USA

George Allen & Unwin Australia Pty Ltd,
8 Napier Street, North Sydney, NSW 2060, Australia

George Allen & Unwin with the
Port Nicholson Press
PO Box 11-838 Wellington, New Zealand

First published 1986

British Library Cataloguing in Publication Data

Bills, Peter
  Jean-Pierre Rives: a modern Corinthian.
1. Rives, Jean-Pierre   2. Rugby football players
– France – Biography
I. Title
796.33'3'0924   GV944.9.R5/
ISBN 0–04–796123–6

Set in 11 on 13 point Palatino
by Nene Phototypesetters Ltd, Northampton
and printed in Great Britain
by Butler and Tanner Ltd, Frome

To my mother, for suffering a journalist's whims so graciously – and to my father, for showing me the way . . .

"If you want to interest a Frenchman in a game, you tell him it's a war. But if you want to interest an Englishman in a war, you tell him it's a game."

Contents

Illustrations

Author's Acknowledgements

Jean-Pierre Rives is known and respected across the world. Hence any portrait of him has to contain the thoughts of rugby players and friends from a variety of nations and continents. All of them, without exception, I found courteous, helpful and kind; a tribute to the characters who play in and administer the game of Rugby Union.

First, my thanks to Jean-Pierre Rives himself who allowed me to live in his Paris apartment during the writing and researching of this book, sharing his life, buying me meals and newspapers from England and generally making known to me that anything which was his, was mine too. I shall not forget such generosity.

Elsewhere in France, I drove 4,000 miles talking to people who welcomed Averil Craven and myself into their homes, offices and places of work with a warmth of friendship which belied, for all time in my mind, the claims of some Englishmen that the French and English simply cannot get along together.

Jo Maso in Perpignan was a sage counsellor; Michel Palmié (Beziers), Jean-Pierre Bastiat and Claude Dourthe (Dax), Roland Bertranne (Bagnères), Jerome Gallion (in Marseille), Jacques Fouroux (in Paris), Jean-Claude Skrela (in Bordeaux), Jean Salut, Pierre Villepreux and Walter Spanghero (all in Toulouse) offered guidance and words of wisdom and experience as well as friendship. Also in Toulouse I recall gratefully the help of Jean-Pierre Rives' parents and grandfather; while his close friend, Robert Paparemborde, assisted me in Paris.

Jean Michel Aguirre drove more than fifty miles to keep a rendezvous in Tarbes and then provided, in splendid English, a valuable insight into his friend and former playing colleague.

In Australia, my thanks to Andrew Slack, captain of those wonderful 1984 Wallabies and a man of great manners and humility. Also, Mark Loane was invaluable in recalling times playing with and against Rives.

In New Zealand, Andy Haden, Stu Wilson, Andy Dalton and

Bryan 'Beegee' Williams, that wonderful ambassador for his fine country, provided much help. My business colleague, Trevor Harris, is to be thanked for his work in this area.

Near home in the British Isles and Ireland, I received assistance from some of the greatest names in the game. In Wales, Gareth Edwards provided humorous recollections of Rives, Graham Price was a friendly host at his home in the hills above Pontypool on a warm summer's afternoon and John Scott, that Englishman turned Welsh import, helped me in his office. I would also like to thank Clive Rees, the London Welsh and Wales wing, and John Kennedy, of the *South Wales Echo*, for their assistance.

In Scotland, John Rutherford and Colin Deans, two of the pleasantest men in the game, were also of great assistance while in Ireland Fergus Slattery provided thoughtful words on Rives in a thoroughly friendly and objective manner. Tony Neary, of Lancashire and England, also contributed and John Reason, rugby correspondent of the *Sunday Telegraph*, helped me with research from his files. David Lawrenson, a friend more than business colleague, was also of great assistance to me.

Jean-Pierre Rives' friends, Albert Feraud and Maurice Arnal, were helpful as well as being excellent company. I should like to thank too my editor, John Bright-Holmes, for his help and advice, and also my publisher, Derek Wyatt.

To all the people mentioned and any others I have unintentionally omitted, I should like to express my grateful thanks, but particularly to Averil, my great companion in France, and in life, for all her help.

Certainly, to the people of France who made us so welcome in their beautiful country, my eternal gratitude.

> 'Vive le rugby,
> Vive la France.'

PETER BILLS
Royal Tunbridge Wells
September 1985

"If I search for something solid or secure around me, I see neither walls nor furniture, only people. Friendship or love of others has been my cloak and my house.

"I hope to have given them, in exchange, the satisfaction I owe them but I fear I have disappointed them in many ways.

"I hate nothing as much as deceiving people. I cannot bear hearing the sound of a door or a heart closing.

"And if you ask me what life's direction should be I would tell you that he who embarks on the route of a one way street risks a lot in making it a no entry."

The thoughts of Jean-Pierre Rives,
as conveyed by his friend, Antoine Blondin.

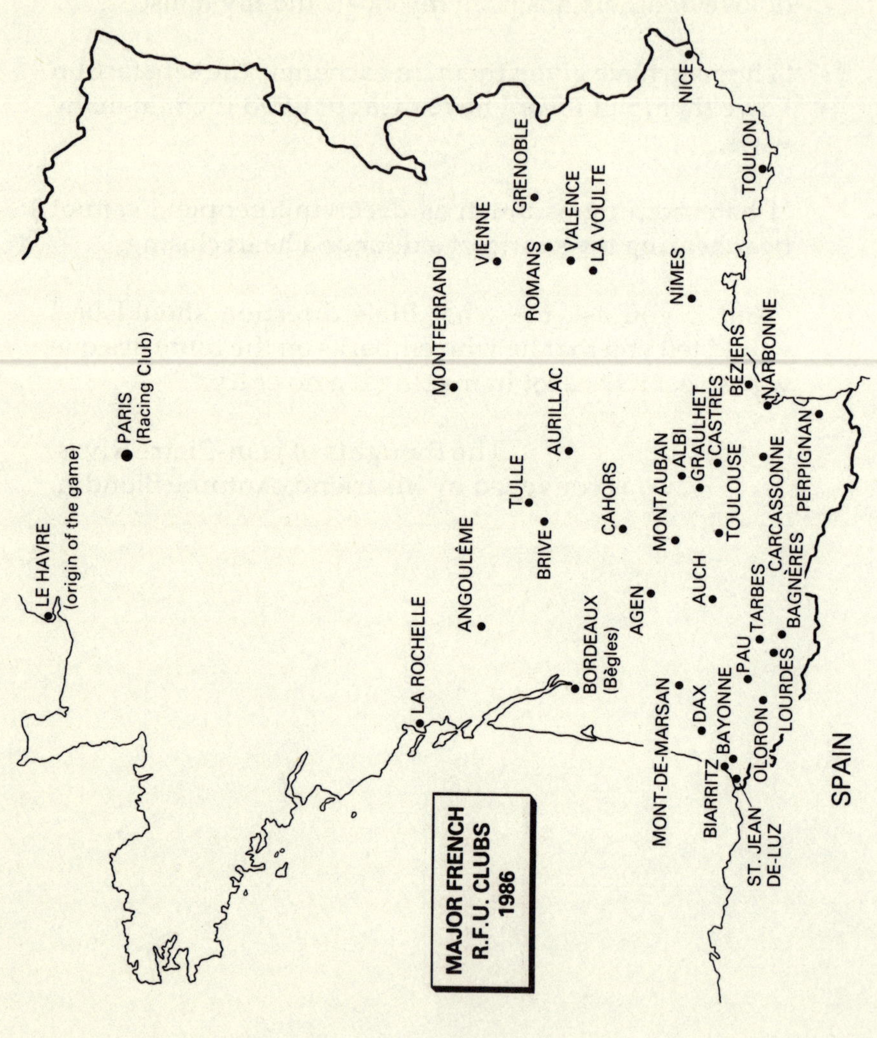

MAJOR FRENCH R.F.U. CLUBS 1986
LE HAVRE (origin of the game)
PARIS (Racing Club)
LA ROCHELLE
ANGOULÊME
BORDEAUX (Bègles)
AGEN
MONT-DE-MARSAN
DAX
BAYONNE
BIARRITZ
ST. JEAN DE-LUZ
OLORON
PAU
TARBES
LOURDES
BAGNÈRES
AUCH
TULLE
BRIVE
CAHORS
MONTAUBAN
TOULOUSE
ALBI
GRAULHET
CASTRES
CARCASSONNE
PERPIGNAN
NARBONNE
BÉZIERS
MONTFERRAND
AURILLAC
VIENNE
GRENOBLE
ROMANS
VALENCE
LA VOULTE
NÎMES
NICE
TOULON
SPAIN

Captain Courageous

*"Detested sport, that owes
its pleasures to another's pain."*
——WILLIAM COWPER——
1731–1800

The eyes were glazed, not through the blood which had almost become his trademark, rather with the mist of emotion which caused a slight twitching of his body, as though it were being subjected to electronic stimulus. Half a dozen injections, administered as an antidote to the stabbing pain he felt at each movement, had been scarcely more effective than aspirin.

We all knew his face well enough; and the blond hair, hanging soaked and dank on a wet rugby afternoon, had already been a rallying sight to the youth of rugby for some six years or more. And yet, it seemed, nothing could have prepared us for the appearance of this man now as he stood at the top of the pavilion steps contemplating the arena like the infantryman his killing ground.

His body quivered with adrenalin, and the muscles tightened. Jean-Pierre Rives, France's captain, understood what was at stake: he knew that a physical nightmare, an afternoon of unremitting agony, lay before him. Thus, even the slightest mental preparation that was calculated to block, at least partially, the worst of the physical torture from his mind was a valuable medicine for him that day.

And yet Rives was not alone. Other men had stood at these steps steeling their muscles and nerves against the torment they knew confronted them. Almost exactly fifty years earlier the cream of Australia's cricketers had to walk through the white wicker gate to face the challenge of 'Bodyline'.

So here we now were, beneath the green tin roof of the old stand, a structure which epitomised the days of Empire if ever a building told of Commonwealth and history. This was Sydney; home of the strine accent, and playground for a thousand tilting cans of beer. Yet the battle Rives was waging with his own conscience and emotions was a new experience for a man who had epitomised the laid-back, cool, apparently uninterested approach to major sport and its singular demands; the blond-haired flank forward of whom his fellow Frenchmen would tell one after another of humorous anecdotes.

Rives' predecessor as leader of the French national team, Jean-Pierre Bastiat, used to joke: "At two o'clock in the afternoon, you wouldn't give him ten years to live, he would be so lethargic. But at three o'clock, he would come to life. I have seen him broken, knees demolished, bandaged up, but still he would go on."

This time it was different. For only fourteen days earlier Rives had dislocated his shoulder four times, an injury which was to cause him physical pain even five years later. The absurdity of the challenge before him was to play and survive a major Test match against the Australians with only one arm of any use. The other hung limp at his side, lifeless and useless. It was a handicap few sane men would have contemplated, still less accepted. But by his action in taking up the gauntlet as best he still could, maintaining all the while his classically Corinthian sporting attitude, Rives revealed the core of his character.

Corinthian? Certainly, a throwback to a bygone age; a man still in love with that era of true sportsmanship, with its close friendships with adversaries; a romanticist of sorts, a complex character who was destined to become the greatest sporting attraction France had seen in decades.

Rives, trapped at the bottom of a ruck in an earlier match at Sydney, against New South Wales, had hissed in pain through clenched teeth, as a rogue boot disfigured his shoulder bone. Of course, rugby men see such things the world over, like the New Zealander raking studs down J. P. R. Williams' face at Bridgend, coolly cutting open the skin almost like some abattoir worker about his trade. The trick, so they tell you, is to get up with a grin, and bound off to the next confrontation. Is it, or should it, be so? Should men like Phil Bennett, captain of the British Lions, 'Benny' to his friends, lie squashed under bodies on a New Zealand tour and feel boots driving like sledge hammers into his body and neck?

As Rives was helped away from Sydney that day, his shoulder bone grotesquely twisted out of position and threatening to burst through the skin, his shrewd, calculating mind had no time for feelings of retribution. The Test match, at Brisbane's colonial style Ballymore ground, lay only eight days away. And France, infected by injuries, was facing major problems.

Bravely as Rives had played all through his career, this was a serious worry. Rives, to his friends, was a man in love with humour. What was the joke he told about himself of a match he played against Romania, a few seasons earlier? "I took a punch," he recounted, "my god, what a punch. It caught me close to my kidneys. I could not move. I said to Jean-Claude Skrela, who was playing on the other flank, 'I cannot walk. I cannot stay on the field'. And do you know what Skrela said to me? 'Why do you want to go off. It does not matter if you cannot walk. You should be running. Stay where you are'."

And the little fellow, with the grappling arm power of a mechanical scoop and short, scuttling legs which revved almost to danger point when he smelt a whiff of his prey, stayed exactly where he was, playing on in agony. Not much seemed to worry Rives on the rugby field. Even the seriousness inherent in some horrific injuries he incurred left him undaunted.

I recalled a story he had told me late one night about his tour with the French team in South Africa, the previous year. Early in the tour, Rives had tackled Mark Loane, the huge Australian then playing for Natal, the province which Tommy Bedford, of Oxford University and South Africa, once termed "the last outpost of the British Empire".

Rives suffered a heavy blow in the tackle, but stood up after brief treatment. What followed almost threatened to give Mark Loane, a surgeon, some months' work sewing up split sides.

Rives: "I did not know where I was. I said 'Where are we?' "

French colleague: "South Africa."

Rives: "Which town?"

Colleague: "Durban."

Rives: "What are we doing."

Colleague: "We're playing rugby."

Rives: "Is it fun? Am I playing well. What is it like."

Roland Bertranne, one of the French centres: "We are playing a rugby match. Be serious, Jean-Pierre. You know what is going on."

Laughter, amused grins from players on both sides, as the conversation progressed.

Rives: "Where did you say we were?"

Bertranne (tired of the nonsense): "We are in the country – we are playing cowboys and Indians."

Rives: "Oh, I want to play that with you."

Bertranne: "But you *are* playing that with us, cowboy."

Rives: "Am I a cowboy?"

Bertranne: "You are a cowboy, yes."

Rives: "Oh, I am really happy then."

Another colleague: "You have already killed three Indians."

Rives: "Oh, oh, I am so happy."

Four hours later, Rives sat in his bathtub back at the hotel. He got out, dried himself, and told astonished colleagues: "Are we ready? We have to go to the match now."

His colleagues: "Oh no, you have already played in it."

Rives: "Really, when? It cannot be. Because I didn't play, I didn't leave the hotel."

Colleague: "You did play."

French journalist, Jean Denis: "Jean-Pierre, what is wrong. You played perhaps the best rugby match of your life."

Rives: "But I cannot have done. I am not tired, nothing. I don't feel anything – I am sure I didn't play."

Colleague: "But you scored a try."

Another friend: "And you passed the ball for two more tries."

Rives: "There is something funny here."

Next day, with a king-size hangover-style headache, Rives watched the TV replay of the match – and learned all about his missing afternoon. As blows on the head go, and their often surprising side-effects, it was a hair-raising few hours for the French captain and his colleagues.

At least it was a simple matter of black and white that time. But bravely as Rives now tried to utter comforting words in the daily medical bulletins on his shoulder, the coach, Jacques Fouroux, knew his captain had not a scent of a chance of appearing in Brisbane. Indeed, but for his personal knowledge of an exceptional man who always had a brutal disregard for his own safety, Fouroux would have ruled out Rives for the remainder of the short, nine-match tour.

But Rives was at his peak. France had gone to Australia as

Champions of Europe, a title secured the previous winter when his inspirational leadership, and driving, selfless play, inspired a modest side to win an unexpected Grand Slam.

The lure of the great 'Grand Chelem', as it is known in France, had been only a moderate motivational force for Rives. As befitted a modern hero of folklore, titles and formal accolades were of little interest to him. The competition, the contest was what inspired Rives; win or lose, the playing of the game was what counted. Winners were winners, losers were losers; all of them, merely passing phases. Friendship, the gauge Rives used to measure his success on the sporting field, was the greater value, the true currency.

Yet for all that, there was no mistaking the locking of horns between the two gladiators from the Northern and Southern hemispheres, to decide the unofficial title of 'World Champions'. A year earlier, the Australians had tamed the feared New Zealanders 2–1 in a three-match Test series. France, then, as kings in Europe, could meet no stronger opposition currently playing the world game, for South Africa was absent from the picture.

In Brisbane French hearts, always good value for a romantic splurge, had been inspired by the sight of that genial but iron-man prop forward, Robert Paparemborde, leading his young side out on to the brown, scrub-like turf of the Ballymore ground. It was a rare moment for the man known as 'Papa' or 'Patou' to his friends. The strong, often silent prop, one of the game's great gentlemen, revealed the emotion he felt by a crack in his voice as he made his dressing-room speech. It spoke volumes for the honour he experienced that day.

It was early July, the Australian mid-winter. 12,000 miles away, at home in France, locals would sniff testily and wonder when summer would break. Here, on Australia's eastern seaboard, a little south of the Tropic of Capricorn, the sun shone handsomely, so that we needed only to drape light sweaters around our shoulders as we strolled through the picturesque old colonial sidestreets towards the tree-lined ground.

Australian rugby followers usually travel without the paraphernalia of their European counterparts: Englishmen in duffelcoats, lugging the claret and port towards Twickenham on the train; Welsh supporters carting giant paper leeks around the British Isles on their jaunts; Scotsmen, packing the tartan travelling rug in the car, and the wee dram for the inside pocket.

In Queensland a colonial atmosphere pervades even the tarmac at Brisbane airport. The modern image, if you want to further the myth, portrays all Australians as men of bursting beer guts, abusive language and pom baiters; but Brisbane, unlike Sydney, is hardly a cosmopolitan centre; it is, rather, a city caught up in its own parochial little squabbles and disputes; and Queensland's premier, the bombastic Joh Bjelke-Petersen, lords it over his fellow citizens like some current-day Cecil Rhodes.

Ballymore, unlike the Sydney Cricket Ground (or SCG), is a compact little ground, cramped when the Test match circus arrives. Rugby union in Australia is dominated by two States, New South Wales and Queensland. In Sydney, they use the cricket ground for the main rugby arena. In Brisbane, a 25,000 crowd forces the local youngsters up the blue gum trees to get a decent view.

Considering the size of the continent, the game has made only moderate strides in influencing just two States. Australian Rules football, to many people little more than a version of grievous bodily harm with a ball, dominates in Victoria while the other States seem scarcely aware of rugger at all.

France, then, shorn of the experienced nucleus of her Grand Slam side, knew that the portents were hardly propitious as her blue-shirted heroes stepped on to the old ground. Durable and experienced threequarters like Bertranne and Laporte, and for-midable forwards such as Imbernon (from Perpignan), Joinel and the Basque, Dospital, had all declined the trip. Furthermore, injuries in the build-up through six provincial games, had condemned at least five others to the sidelines; the flankers Rives and the late Pierre Lacans; the young bull from Beziers, Wolff, from the front row and, behind the scrum, Berbizier at scrum half and the quicksilver Codorniou, a player of intuitive skills.

If the French had ever been naive about their intended reception, two or three games prior to the first Test dispelled any such hopes. Then, four days before the Brisbane Test, Michel Cremaschi, the loose head prop, had been too slow to remove his head out of the way of a punch by an over-enthusiastic foe which shattered his jaw. Earlier still, in the first match at Brisbane against Queensland, the scrum half Berbizier had also been pitched out of the tour by a boot which ripped open his right ear, leaving a wound which would require thirty-eight stitches to mend. The sight of Berbizier, blood pouring from his wounds, leaving the field at Ballymore, was a reminder to any Frenchman of the rigours of Australian rugby.

Yet for all that, France in the Test reached half time 14–9 to the good. Brisbane's crowd, bedecked in the yellow hats offered freely by the local brewery, had been hushed; but neither the score nor the silence could last.

Paparemborde, the 15½-stone farmer's boy from Laruns, a village in the hills above Pau in the south of France's rugby heartland, was quietly stroking his black, droopy moustache at half-time. He, more than most, understood the loss of Rives, his playing compatriot and friend for six years. But as Rives was to say later: "I felt so happy, such pride for Papa when he led out France in Australia. It was an honour he so much deserved."

'Patou' was a man in the Rives mould, honest, brave, a character who led from the front. The coach, Fouroux, some hours later called his patched-up side "France's 2nd XV", but by then, French optimism, the spirit which oils a nation's wheels, had been cruelly dashed by an Australian side stung into a second-half revival, as if a swarm of bees had launched an infantry assault.

Mark Loane, that storming giant of a man at No. 8, had burst away from a line-out, brushing aside challenges with the disdain of a holidaymaker flicking flies off his skin. Loane's pulsating run created a try on a plate for Poidevin, his back row colleague who had faithfully kept pace with him, and Australian spirit flared decisively.

The Australians scrambled home, 17–14, a result to break the hearts of Frenchmen. More than a few compassionate locals raised a glass to Patou and his brave boys. Some, chancing upon these curious looking blokes in funny flat, black caps who wandered around the car park looking for a suitable spot to indulge in a time-honoured, traditional French past-time, even downed their cans of beer to taste the Frenchmen's wine. Parties which start like that tend to develop – and these were no exception to the rule.

And so to Sydney, and a week of rumour, innuendo and denial. Would Rives appear on Saturday? Had he been ruled out already? Has he gone home? Can he still stand up properly?

In the days and hours approaching the second Test, Rives

created, deep in his own mind, the resolution he would need to withstand a rugby match sure to give him such pain as he had never experienced before.

For Rives, pain was no stranger. In the first, overtly physical encounter with Queensland, France's captain had suffered hideous punishment, as he sacrificed his personal safety for the sake of his team's first victory on the tour.

Loane, No. 8 on that day too, conceded Rives was a man who would willingly endure personal agonies for the benefit of his side: "That match between Queensland and France was a very physical game. Queensland had never beaten the French and, late in that game, trailed 18–15 with a few minutes remaining. At least twice, we had the French pinned on their own line and probably only needed the ball to make the winning score. But Rives buried himself on that ball to prevent us winning it. He took the consequences and they were pretty severe. We needed a try to win but we lost. Rives took some real punishment to stop that try being scored – the boots were going in and they weren't treading carefully. But he never let go of that damned ball."

Loane knew his subject. A rugby player of renown, and esteemed in his profession, Loane explored new ground in assessing Rives, a player he faced and played alongside in a career spanning almost a decade. "Rives," he reflected, "took punishment all his career but he seemed impervious to pain. Some guys are like that – Willie Duggan, of Ireland and the British Lions, was another. He seemed to enjoy a physical mauling. I was in South Africa, working, when the French toured there in 1980. It was obvious on that tour how the French players had so much respect for Rives because, in France, to go down on the ball at all is to risk being maimed.

"It's absolutely terrible over there. No-one goes on the ground because you get your head kicked in. But here was a guy who spent hours of his rugby life on the ground, taking the treatment. Rives took that bravery too far at times. It is not possible, no matter how much your heart is willing, to contribute fully to a match with a busted shoulder joint."

Yet here was Jean-Pierre Rives, treading cautiously as he shepherded his side out into Sydney's sunshine. Even to appear was magnificent; to play the entire game, injured as he was, bordered on lunacy.

His appearance brought gasps of disbelief from the French supporters, decked out, quite incongruously in the Australian city, in black berets, and carrying baguettes of French bread. Australians murmured in astonishment or roared with laughter.

Rives' straw-coloured hair tumbled down on to shoulders which resembled a monster's. Heaps of padding, strapping and protection for the damaged shoulder had built the top of the Frenchman's torso into a figure more suited to American football. His protection was almost obscene, hideous on a field of supposed sportsmanship. What place had he here, why this ridiculous charade, of going through the motions simply to get on to the field?

Loane, as amazed as anyone else in the 42,000 crowd, said: "I was staggered he tried to take on the game, let alone finish it. It was bravery to the point of insanity. OK, the French were running out of players because of injuries. And Rives always led from the front. Perhaps all rugby is folly in the end. But I certainly would have found it impossible to play with that.

"He could not tackle but he tried to take the ball off players several times. It made me think of Napoleon's troops bravely retreating from Moscow. Battered and beaten but still attempting to make a contest of it."

Battered and eventually beaten, Rives was – but not bowed. And his appearance at Sydney, sustained as it was in the main by sheer will-power, revealed a side of the man his closest acquaintances would come to regard as crucial.

Rives himself said: "Maybe I should not have played that day. But I did so because on tours there is a special spirit and to know that is to understand these decisions. We were in the same boat that day – and what a boat! So many injuries. The players asked me if I would play and I said 'OK'. I wanted to be together with them. Everyone knew before the game I could not play very well. But they wanted me with them and that was a great compliment to me."

That was it; for the boys, for comradeship! The personal honour was superfluous. Rives played because close friends, colleagues, had asked. That old colonial spirit flourished in the mind of France's romantic captain!

Rives tried to explain it thus, "It is the spirit – l'esprit. Somewhere, something happens. I don't know. Maybe I should not have played, but I don't regret my decision because it was good for the spirit. I was with all my friends in the team.''

Starting the match was remarkable. Finishing it, defied logic as well as medical expectation. The French defence in Brisbane, particularly in midfield, had been as secure as wet sellotape. But with Rives playing, in mind if not body, and Lacans tightening the other flank, France made a brave fist of it for a long time.

Australia 9, France 6, at half-time; the French contingent took off their berets, wiped their foreheads and dared to contemplate a minor miracle.

Alas, that was too much to expect. Thereafter Mark Ella, Australia's creative Aborigine half back, plucked a jewel of a try from the bag, looping around Hawker with a scuttling dash, to surge past Rives' ineffective challenge and find the gap. Slashing through the defence, Ella timed his delivery to perfection by sending in O'Connor for the try. Australia were away.

Rives, his damaged arm hanging limp the whole time, could only lean with a gesture on the side of scrums. His challenges were diluted from their normal potency; yet still he managed to delay some Australian movements. As Australia's second-half control tightened, Rives' effectiveness dissipated further. Yet the man stayed there, reasoning later: ''Maybe I should not have entered the field. But when you say 'yes' and you play, you have to fight and try and finish the match. That was the reason why I stayed on the field, even if I didn't play very well. I could not move much – it was above all a feeling of frustration.''

Not a frustration, but a basic mistake according to Jean-Pierre Bastiat, the back row international, now retired. He said: ''In France, Jean-Pierre's action in playing with such a severe handicap, was seen in two ways. Firstly, it was seen by us, knowing rugby, in a difficult way because we knew Rives but we knew rugby. We felt it was wrong because he did a disservice to his team, to his friends, to the French side. But by ordinary people, it was received with the contrary view. People said 'what courage, he's a martyr', and 'It's amazing, how could he do it? It's unthinkable'. We felt he must have been a bit mad. At the same time, we recognised his great courage.''

And the Australian Loane: ''I couldn't believe he would actually take the field to play. He was obviously in great pain and difficulty and he didn't contribute much to the game physically because you need at least two arms to play rugby. But there was no doubting his bravery and sincerity. It had the right effect on the morale of the French side that day, although I felt they were not as dangerous a team as at Brisbane. They might have done better to choose a player who was fully fit. But the longer the tour had gone on, the more injuries the French had suffered. And the less sure they seemed of their own ability without Rives. Conditions were hard and play was pretty physical.''

Years later, Rives was to reflect: "It wasn't a good tour. We never had the feeling within the team which you should have on a tour. Maybe that was because we had left too many good players at home. You cannot build a successful side on one tour – it takes two or three years. It wasn't a tour I remembered with much pleasure.

"We lost in Sydney and it was a pity because when you do your best and you lose, it's difficult. But when you lose without fighting really . . . and all the tour was a little like that. When we left, the team wasn't really fixed and we had to work on it. To go on tour, you have to be ready before and we were not. You cannot build up a new team like that."

France's coach, Jacques Fouroux, a small figure cast in the Napoleonic mould, was to reflect at the end of the affair: "It was madness for Jean-Pierre to play. But as I shared his madness, I was just as mad as he was. It was mad because it didn't change anything. It only accentuated the seriousness of the injury.

"When I was a player myself, I often played with injuries and fractures. You are unconscious of it in the game usually, and I believe you recognise the great player at times like that. But it was not playing with that one serious injury that showed Jean-Pierre's courage. He was always hurt somewhere on his body. The manner in which he played meant that he was hurt every time in some way or another. But he always rose above the pain. That was his great courage, his No. 1 quality. It was fantastic courage."

Behind a powerful pack of forwards, and at the receiving end of scrum half John Hipwell's crafty, experienced service, Mark Ella had plotted Australia's victory. How we marvelled at his deft hands, neat little scuffling chip kicks into space, and deceptive pace and strength. His run to create O'Connor's try had the stamp of a genius: the rush through the gap, like a pheasant startled by beaters scampering off in search of safety.

It was the end of an era for Australia. Four years later, when they ruthlessly exposed the inadequacies of British rugby by winning the Grand Slam on their major tour of the British Isles, only three of the fifteen men who played in Sydney against Rives and his side played a sustained role.

For purists intent upon assessing the darting, elusive Ella in direct combat with Rives, a dynamic hardened flank forward, the damaged shoulder made a mockery of the encounter. But Rives understood the value of the Aborigine to Australian rugby; and he criticised British sides, years later, for not recognising the player who was the fulcrum of the Wallaby team. "The Australians are more entertaining than other southern-hemisphere nations because they always play attacking rugby," Rives said. "They are physical, but they play a certain open style of rugby. Mark Ella was very important in that system because everything revolved around him. And I am not sure that, without Mark, it was possible for the Australians to be the same. They will have a hard job to find someone like him, now that he is retired. If British sides could have defended more against him, maybe the Australians would have had more problems in winning that 1984 Grand Slam. You had to put pressure on him; he was the key. If he was kept quiet, it was so much harder for them to attack because he could touch a ball two or three times in one attack.

"I don't think the British teams appreciated that enough. They did not put sufficient pressure on him, at every moment of a match. Ella was very strong, so strong on his feet and clever and fast. Very good. He made the other players play and he really organised everything."

With a whirr and a whine of its engines, the 747 jumbo jet climbed out of Sydney, its gleaming white livery shining against the blotchy clouds and deep blue of an Australian sky. High over the top of Botany Bay it soared, tipping gently as it banked away and set course for Europe. Inside, squashed uncomfortably amid the bawling babies, pestering kids and harassed stewardesses, a weary rugby man stretched his aching frame. Twenty-four hours earlier Australia and the world had witnessed one of the bravest acts known on the rugby field. Now the gambler who lost had to meet his debts; and the pain of defeat would linger long in his mind and body.

Jean-Pierre Rives slouched in his seat, eyes closed, mind

searching for inner sanctuary, tie loosened at the neck and askew. The French cockerel on his blazer pocket, the proud creature which had set out from Europe as a king crow four weeks earlier, looked more like a skinned, mangy bird.

Behind his appearance of resting, Rives' mind raced. The occasional flicker of the eyelids gave the clue; this was not a man at peace with himself. His mind was back-tracking – to how different it had all been two years earlier, in this same part of the world.

New Zealand, 1979, had been the zenith of Rives' achievement hitherto as French captain. True, it had been a brief tenure up to that stage, for the Toulouse flanker had assumed control when Bastiat, the big Dax No. 8, had been ruled out through injury. But one man's loss is another's gain and Rives had seized his opportunity with alacrity. Only some wayward goalkicking by Aguirre, their full-back, against England at Twickenham, had cost the Frenchmen the Championship. The Bagnères man, in all four penalty attempts, had failed to line up his sights accurately like a good soldier, and a typically hotch-potch England side, with personnel changing as if it were a bus, scraped home by a single point, 7–6; but it was enough to rob France of the Championship and save England from another wooden spoon.

Now, with the European winter finished back home, Rives was thinking of New Zealand, and the rigours of a nine-match tour, spanning just four weeks. It was a trip which was to see a drawn Test series, with one victory apiece, but the manner of France's success in the final match, contributed one of the most glorious chapters in French sporting history.

New Zealand; land of cold, wet winters where rugbymen suffer the worst that the heavens and All Black boots can inflict; a land where the people harbour a fanatical fervour for the game, bordering on paranoia. Where else, I wondered, after one trip, could you go to dinner and hear three businessmen dissecting, assessing and picking over the whys and wherefores of a recently selected All Black side, like vultures burrowing into every cranny of the corpse? Not just for half an hour; rather, during pre-dinner drinks, throughout a lengthy meal, and over coffee afterwards. My companion, steeped in more civilised, more feminine pursuits, shook her head in bewilderment.

"That Hewson's a fairy, I'd have him out."

"But who else are you going for. There's a lad at Manawatu, but his defence isn't as good as his goalkicking. And remember, the Lions fly half has a fine boot on him; he'll expose the lad with his garryowens, if we pick him.''

''What about the Auckland fellow – he could do a job for you?''

''No – his positional play isn't hot. Campbell's kicking would crucify him.''

And so they went on, right through the daylight hours and far into the night. They probably turned round in bed to face the second half into the wind!

Caught in a remote part of the South Island, tired, depressed and wearing a melancholic expression when the conversation turned to home, Rives sought an unusual ally to plot one of his sport's most remarkable comebacks of recent times.

French stock had faltered, very nearly calamitously, after a soured encounter at Hamilton against the Waikato region. The absence of the French squad's only two English-speaking players, Rives and Aguirre, captain and vice-captain respectively, created a void which the local referee found as cavernous as the nearby Waitomo caves. France lost 18–15 in a display which heightened the need for Rives to appear, both to ensure greater fluidity in communication and to adhere to the discipline the young man had instilled among his charges.

Things improved, to a degree, with three substantial successes as a prelude to the first Test meeting with the All Blacks, at Christchurch's vast, rambling Lancaster Park. But such moments of prosperity seemed as fleeting as the sun, as France was crushed 23–9 in the International. Mesny's beautifully constructed try for France in the second half was one solitary jewel in a crown of thorns for the Frenchmen.

The same scenario was to be witnessed two years later in Australia, only this time there was a crucial difference. In the New Zealand captain Graham Mourie, a quiet, withdrawn yet intense and extremely intelligent young farmer from the Taranaki province in the North Island, Rives discovered a man his parallel in sporting approach, and in insistence on discipline and fair play, allied to the idealistic spirit.

Mourie consoled his friend in Christchurch that night, telling him: ''You never know what may happen in rugby. Don't dismiss your chances, your hopes for the second Test match, Jean-Pierre. Nothing is certain in this great game.''

Rives was sceptical, yet grateful for his friend's counsel. "It made me think maybe we could do something in Auckland but I knew the chances were against us."

There was further encouragement the next day when the Frenchmen studied the video recording of the first test. Aguirre, by far the most experienced of the back-line, said: "We knew we had given far too many points to New Zealand. We said to ourselves 'this is not possible'. No side can give points to New Zealand in their own country. So for one week, we trained hard and kept on saying to the young players 'it is possible, we can win. We are going to win.'

"We trained as Jean-Pierre had never done before or after that match. We trained so hard; very quickly, always very hard and committed. Jean-Pierre did not like training very much – he arrived very late in the sessions at normal times, usually when the running was finished and the ball work was about to begin. But in Auckland that week, it was different. And the young players respected Rives so very much on that tour."

It would have been a revelation to the giant, affable Bastiat at home in France. Bastiat remembered tours in Canada and Japan when he had roomed with Rives – and ended up becoming a sort of mother-figure cum secretary cum cleaner-up and bottle washer for the disorganised, blond-haired young man.

Bastiat said: "Jean-Pierre was priceless, a law unto himself. When the plane was about to take off, he remembered he had left his trousers and jacket in the hotel. When everyone else was leaving for training, he would want to have breakfast. When everyone else was going to bed, that's when Jean-Pierre wanted to go out. At midday, he wanted to go to sleep.

"Jean-Pierre is the perfect boy who never wants to say no. He would give you three meeting places on the same day at the same time in ten different places.

"With Jean-Pierre, I didn't pass one single day at the hotel without arranging his things, or finishing his packing because every time I left our room last, I had to pick up all the things he had left behind. It was the same stage by stage, town by town."

But Bastiat smiled genially as he talked of his former colleague, years afterwards. "Always, it was very amusing sharing a room with him, sharing your life with him. Jean-Pierre was a person who could have several fiancées. But to have a wife all his life?

I don't think there is one woman on earth who could actually tolerate him unless he changes.''

But for one week, in faraway New Zealand, Rives pulled his act together; he toed the line. Ready for training on time, a hard grafter during the sessions in the build-up to that final Saturday – even his social life had its wings clipped for seven vital days. It was a transformed Rives, a man bent on fulfilling a destiny, reaching for the crock of gold which seemed, mysteriously, almost magically, to have come within sight.

Yet even Rives' new-found optimism was tested to the limit during that momentous final week of the New Zealand tour. Between the two Tests, in the last midweek game, his French side lost by a single point, 12–11, to a moderate Southland team down at Invercargill, on the southern tip of South Island. It was hardly the result required but was at least commensurate with the harsh surroundings.

As the days moved closer to Auckland and the final Test, Rives drew heavily on the inspirational content of Mourie's words. He was to say much later: ''But for Graham's encouragement, his words of hope to me, I do not think I could have lifted up the players in their mental approach. His optimism changed my mind.''

Aguirre, a worthy lieutenant, remembers clearly that splendid, sunny winter's day in Auckland. ''We were concentrating hard but we were not afraid of the game. We thought we could win or certainly give problems to the All Blacks; more problems than in the first Test. By giving more support in the back row, helping each other and backing up every player with the ball, we felt we could improve considerably. Our forwards could run well and in our threequarters we had speed, true speed.

''I remember when I saw the stadium at Eden Park, there was a small ground beside the main pitch. I told the threequarters we would go there to warm up with the ball. I said to Jean-Pierre, 'I want to take the threequarters', and he said 'OK, you do what you want'. He stayed with the forwards in the dressing-room.

''In this warm-up, we had running, tackling and really hard work. Yes, it was unusual to see proper tackling but one or two players in the team had some problems with defence and I made sure they tackled hard in the practice. My belief was that if we wanted to use our threequarters in the game, we had to warm up thoroughly."

The Frenchmen astonished Eden Park's gnarled, wise old locals with the fervency of their training, just before a major international. It was a new dimension for New Zealanders hardly accustomed to the sight of threequarters going flat out in preparation.

The warm-up lasted forty-five minutes before an enthralled gallery. At the end, Aguirre drew his young colleagues around him and said simply: "Good, now we will do the same here on the main ground".

The Frenchmen had uncovered the key to the series in one, ephemeral moment during the first Test. Mesny's fine try had capped a long flowing movement involving Laffarge and Averous from the backs and Rives and Dintrans as support players. If the backs could be released to run freely, argued the French hierarchy, then the All Blacks might find problems establishing a tight hold on the game. Parity up front, missing in Christchurch, was a further essential ingredient, for the French scrum had been rocked back in the first three clashes of the Test. This time those early bone-shuddering meetings of the men up front, saw a transformation; far from being heaved back, the French eight squeezed their famed rivals to an extent that the mighty Blacks had to give ground. It was a psychological boost which played a vital role in the match.

There followed one of the great rugby Tests encompassing an extraordinary turn around of fortunes. The Frenchmen ran the ball as though their lives depended upon it. Caussade, a tall gaunt man who bore a haunted expression after the first Test, was a reformed character with the introduction of Gallion, the little Toulon scrum half.

Caussade, his jet black hair streaming in the wind, flowed into space it had seemed impossible the Frenchmen could find. But with the All Black forwards under much greater pressure up front, the roaming Mourie had his licence to destroy revoked. More pressing matters had to be attended to up front – and Caussade, especially, used his space to great profit.

Gallion had shed tears of frustration and sadness at his exclusion from the first Test team. All his splendid work in the early part of the tour had borne scant reward. But the selectors now acknowledged their error and Gallion, like his half-back partner, became inspired, a man with a mission. Outside his crisp, lengthy service, Caussade's pacey breaks created the gaps. The fleet-footed Codorniou and Mesny, the craftsman beside his shoulder at centre, exacted a chilling revenge.

Caussade scored a try, Gallion got another by charging down a bemused New Zealander's kick, Averous and Codorniou scored other tries, and Caussade converted one and dropped a neat goal. Aguirre, the perfect foil for his tearaway young backs, added a penalty goal – and France's lead at half-time was 11–7. In the second half Costes, an arrow of a wing, wrought havoc with his penetrative, silky running, yet it was with a final piece of perceptive defence that he saved his side, crossing from his own flank to catch and clear a dangerous New Zealand kick, high to the French line, in the final minute.

With that one act Costes revealed the commitment which had personified the French display; and Rives, the man regarded as immortal by his colleagues, was the master hand behind it all. The French had won 24–19.

Aguirre's tribute to his captain was handsome. "Jean-Pierre was everywhere; in with the forwards, helping and supporting the threequarters. Encouraging, coaxing, assisting, but most of all leading. Everyone in our side played well but the All Blacks were surprised at our form. However, at the end of the match, they were happy to have played in such a good game."

Aguirre recalls the Auckland public for their generosity, despite defeat. "The people were so good; they were applauding us all the way. It was a fantastic day."

Aguirre believes victory in Auckland was perhaps the most prestigious of Rives' entire career. Rives, too, understood the importance of the performance, preferring to talk, with typical modesty, of his players' quality more than his own contribution.

"All the players were inspired – it was a wonderful day. I recalled Graham's words at the end and I knew their importance. But Graham had spoken first, telling me to remember the lesson. I was grateful to him and I told him so. He had said to me 'Do not forget that anything is possible in this game, Jean-Pierre'.

"Afterwards, there was silence in our dressing-room. No noise of celebrations, nothing.

"Normally, you have players moving into the shower at intervals to wash and get dressed. This time, I remember, there was nothing; no-one moved. We all felt a deep satisfaction but we were drained mentally as much as physically. It had been a very hard week."

Jerome Gallion recalled: "Jean-Pierre was the basis of our success in Auckland because he took hold of the team. We were near the end of the tour, we had lost the previous match before the second Test and I would say the morale of the troops was at its lowest. Even certain directors were beginning to make a negative evaluation of the tour.

"But Jean-Pierre allowed the revolt or rebellion, if you like, of the team but he refused to submit to this point. He asked each player to think and to begin to question this view of the tour as a whole, before it was over.

"Even on the field, he allowed the team to rebel and that is why we were successful."

Robert Paparemborde remembers: "It was a fabulous win in Auckland and for Jean-Pierre and myself the best souvenir of rugby. It was extraordinary because we had a team which was not special. But everything went well for us that day; all the kicks succeeded, all the passes were taken. It was as though magic was part of it.

"I remember Jean-Pierre talking to us before the game. He told us to be proud, have pride and faith because it was 14 July, our national day. As we had lost a Test already, we had to believe in ourselves. I think it all went well because everybody took heed of his words.

"For me, South African rugby is the hardest of all but the rugby I really like is the rugby of New Zealand. Because the players like to enjoy themselves – but they do not reproach themselves as much as the French players. They go out to win and enjoy themselves and they are the ones who most resemble the French players."

A cancelled flight allowed Rives to discuss the whole occasion at greater length with Mourie that same night. If Rives was a romanticist, Mourie was more of a pragmatist; yet the two men bore similar ideals on to the sporting fields of the world. It is not surprising that they became such close friends in later years, particularly when the New Zealander went to Paris to work and the two men played together for the Paris club, Racing Club de France.

But back in Auckland, 1979, no-one understood better than

Rives the romantic value inherent in the Bastille Day victory, and how it had proved an appropriate celebration. For Rives, the rugby player, was never as important, never as real a man as Rives the quixotic character who created an artificial shell around his real self. Rives, the authentic Rives, was to come to hate the image which Rives, the public man, attracted to himself during a career which spanned nine years at the top of the world game. Captain courageous, he became, to millions the world over; a classic Corinthian of rugby in France, to an entire nation. But only to a precious few friends did he reveal his true self. It was a secret person whom he fought ferociously to guard, so secret, perhaps, that he is still struggling to find it for himself. The story of that battle, as much of his brilliant career as a rugby player, is the special fascination of this biography.

"They gave me a jersey and said 'Play'"

*"No sleep till morn,
when Youth and Pleasure meet,
to chase the glowing hours
with flying feet."*
—— LORD BYRON ——
1788–1824

The little boy with blond hair, his short trousers flapping against chubby knees and the sleeves of his woolly sweater rolled halfway up his arms, was grappling with a rifle. Hardly tall for his age, he heaved the barrel of the weapon into position and lined up its sights. His pink cheek pressed against the metal.

Across the back yard of the house, just beside a large tree, two rabbits were playing in the sun. Carefully, just as his father and grandfather had taught him, the youngster adjusted the direction of the barrel, settled as comfortably as he could, and squeezed the trigger. One rabbit fled, the other limped away, caught by the blast, mortally wounded. Somewhere beneath a nearby hedge it died quietly, the silence broken by the applause of the two men, who smiled affably at the boy.

But Jean-Pierre Rives, aged only eight, was struggling to contain his tears. He fled into the house, his mother anxiously watching him. As the men of the family sought further prey, the youngster buried his head in his hands, no longer able to mask his feelings.

It is the kind of mental anguish experienced by most humans, in their formative years at least, when they first experience the power of the gun. But on Jean-Pierre Rives, already a quietly determined boy if excessively shy, the incident was to have a lasting effect. Many Frenchmen, even to this day, have a great love for shooting;

out in the countryside, even just beyond Paris where the magnificent, remote woods of Versailles, Fontainebleau and Ermernonville offer the first retreat from the city, it is a popular recreation. In the grand hills of the Burgogne or in the villages of the south, men out walking their dogs, guns half-cocked with the barrel broken, are a regular sight.

Deer, wild boar which still roam the lonelier woods of France, and a variety of other game, are shot. But never by Rives. For a man with friends in every stratum of society, in each region of the country, he has more chance than most to indulge in the sport, yet he rejects shooting as a recreation. He refuses to countenance cruelty to animals, saying simply: "Their right to life is as strong as ours".

And he has similar feelings about flying. "I do not want to trouble birds – to disturb them in the sky, is not very fair. The sky is for birds, not man."

Rives knew the old village house well; he had been born there, on the eve of the New Year, 31 December 1952. In a darkened room overlooking the back yard, his life had begun, and there it continued through his early years, whenever his parents were in France. The house, dating back to the 1800s, was in the centre of old St Simon village, a few miles from Toulouse. Like with Blackheath, Dulwich or Hampstead around London, inner-city sprawl has all but swallowed much of the quaintness of the old place. For most of its inhabitants, Toulouse is a convenient fifteen-minute drive away, a suitable compromise for those who prefer to spend summer days in the countryside but, alas, must work in the city.

Jean-Pierre's grandfather, Raymond, was also born in the house, eight years after the Treaty of Paris had, in 1898, concluded the short but eventful war between Spain and the United States. The two-storey house, with turquoise blue shutters at every window, stands behind rusting iron railings from which the paint is flaking away.

Raymond Rives, nodding like an approving schoolmaster as he recalls the exploits of Jean-Pierre's rugby life, has an astonishing collection with which to revive his memories. On the walls of every room in the lower floor of the house, pictures virtually cover the wallpaper: portraits of Rives from team photographs, action shots; Rives in the national shirt of France, in the club colours of

Stade Toulousain. Even at eighty the old man remains a fully paid-up member of the Stade Toulousain club. The membership card he proudly takes from a wallet proves his sporting pedigree. With a shortened stride, and slightly hunched shoulders similar to his famous grandson, the old man still attends Toulouse club games. But the international matches, he reflects, are different these days. He finds the fireworks too much; a reasonable reflection for an elderly man, even one who had been a well-known cycle pursuit racer. Now, since the death of his wife ten years ago, he lives alone with his memories and the inspiring pictures of Jean-Pierre's deeds on the rugby fields of the world.

Proudly, he will lead you into a smaller, side room off the main living-room. Here rugby programmes, books, newspaper cuttings and other memorabilia are crammed on to a moderately sized old wooden table in the centre of the room. The old man approaches the collection like a banker his prized safe.

Suddenly, it seems, the trace of a stoop vanishes, the weary eyes instantly light up, the voice lifts and grows in strength; both body and mind seem inspired. Raymond, after all, knows about scaling the peaks of sporting achievement.

In 1928 he became a Champion cyclist, winning 400 francs at the velodrome D'Anfa, Casablanca, and earning a little ribbon of honour which he still possesses, the colour faded though its meaning is still vivid. But he never played rugby. Nor did his son, Jo, to any extent. He became an Air Force officer, and a pilot of such high esteem that for several years he flew the Sultan of Morocco's personal aircraft.

Jean-Pierre, older than his brother Philippe, has inherited the blond colouring of his mother's father, who was Austrian. He had met his Italian wife-to-be close to the Austrian-Italian border, but their daughter, Lydia, Jean-Pierre's mother, was to follow more in her mother's dark, attractive Italian looks. Jo, Jean-Pierre's father, has a round, chubby face of great warmth and joviality, liquid brown eyes smiling with welcome and friendship. Lydia, an elegant, well-dressed woman, perhaps reveals a trace of the shyness of her elder son.

Jean-Pierre spent several of his early years in North Africa, travelling with his parents wherever they were stationed. Duties took Jo and his family to Araba in Nigeria, to Abidjan on the Ivory Coast; and to Marrakesh, Morocco. There was a tour of five years in Araba, two years in the Moroccan city, and another spell at Abidjan. Rugby was largely unknown in such countries, apart from the friendly games arranged by French expatriates, but tennis was a popular sport, especially for French men and women a long way from home and with time to spare. Thus Jean-Pierre took up tennis as a boy, reaching as far as a junior final at the French Championships at Roland Garros before losing in the final of the boys' doubles competition.

Both his parents were enthusiastic tennis players, and Jean-Pierre fell in love with the game. On visits to Africa, there would be tennis in the morning, a brief break for lunch, and more tennis in the afternoon. Almost every spare moment of the young man's life was devoted to the game in which, his parents felt, he might progress far. They recognised their son's natural ability at ball games. At tennis, he excelled.

His mother recalls: "Jean-Pierre was always very thorough; most things he did, he did well. He wasn't a boy who just mucked about. I think he would have been successful in anything because he was that sort of a person. He wanted to win all the time. Although he was timid and shy, he had a very strong personality.

"Even now he is still a timid person, but the strong personality masks that. He is different to what people can see."

For all his son's skills at tennis, however, Jo was concerned about the boy's future. He remembers: "Tennis is fine, but it is not really a physical game and I felt Jean-Pierre needed to play in a sport with much greater physical contact. We all play tennis, almost every day even now. Jean-Pierre still loves it, but I saw it then as a hobby for him, as a pastime; not a sport for a young man growing up."

What followed invokes one of the earliest memories in Jean-Pierre's own mind. As a child, he recalls wanting to become a fireman, "to wear one of those lovely helmets". But although he was often in aeroplanes, there was scant chance of a career in aviation. For one thing, he retains his dislike of air travel. In addition, his eyesight is not first-class, a factor which would have almost certainly prohibited any chance of becoming a pilot.

His father's antidote to the lack of physical contact in his son's sporting life, was to suggest Rugby union. He says now: "We wanted something to bring Jean-Pierre out. Tennis is lacking in something – for example, I only played tennis for pleasure.

I played football for more physical sport. I had played rugby only a few times but I watched it in later years and enjoyed doing so."

Rives himself brings a humorous, self-deprecating note to the story of his first taste of rugby. "At the start, it was not my fault. I am sorry," he says, tongue ever so slightly in cheek. "I was playing tennis, and was very calm and slow and quiet. One day my father said to me 'Come along, you are to play rugby because you need some physical exercise'. He said I needed to take some pushes, some confrontation; he said maybe it would waken me up a little.

"He took me in a car and we arrived on a field where there were other small boys. I was twelve years old. They gave me a jersey and said 'play'. But I had never thought about rugby before, I knew nothing about it. They said you have to put the ball over the line. So I played. But I did not understand or know at all what I should do. And, I have to say, for my father the idea failed because I slept just as much after I played rugby. I played rugby, OK, but I didn't wake up much more. The idea did not succeed."

Rives played in any position available in the early stages of his career. But his lack of size meant that he was, more often than not, put into a threequarter position. The timid, shy boy was by no means certain what the sudden injection of urgency and vitality was all about, nor the reason for it. His father, a military man and very correct, understood the need for the boy to be built up physically but his mother was to admit years afterwards: "I still wish he had gone into tennis as a sporting career".

No matter, Rives became a rugby player. Not at the centre threequarter position he desired ("France lost another Jo Maso, perhaps" he used to joke later) but at wing forward, "because I was told I could tackle".

The essence of tackling was a curious, new phenomenon to Rives. But, typically, for a boy who showed great commitment in all he did from an early age, his enthusiasm and desire to do it well, put him apart from others of his age. At tennis, he had been classified as a fifteen-year-old when he was still only twelve because he kept beating opponents of his own age and the two years above him. At rugby, too, he showed the courage which was to become his hallmark, like a young tree displaying the fine greenery it is to amass later in life.

Curiously, it might all have been so different. A few years earlier, while living in Abidjan with his parents, Rives was taken to see a rugby match and returned, predicting: "Tennis is for me – rugby is at an end".

But the determination and personality which seems inherent in the family, was displayed by both sons, Philippe as well as Jean-Pierre, who were both healthy and strong.

Philippe, the younger by five years, became a Champion of France at his chosen sport, rowing, when he was twenty-seven. He also competed in the World Championships. Their father had a great influence over both boys. Thus, sporting achievement was to follow, to the great pride not only of the parents but also of the sons, each happy to see the other succeed in his own sport.

Jean-Pierre moved from junior school to the Lycée Technique for three years followed by the Lycée Berthelot for one year. Afterwards, he was to go to the University of Toulouse, but by then he had made an auspicious start to his rugby career.

Typically, Rives' parents followed the growing success of their son's sporting career by charting his progress from newspaper cuttings sent to them when they were back in Africa. But Jean-Pierre, having stayed at home in France to continue his studies, was far too reticent and modest to send his parents any of the stories which were appearing as his career expanded. Rives looks back, with only ephemeral interest, and says wearily: "I did not come from a rugby background, so I did not bother to tell my parents when I had some stories in the newspapers at the start of my career."

In fact, Rives became a schoolboy international, and a player good enough for his father to say: "You watch, one day he will be in the international team". But his mother paid little interest to the hard world of rugby: "When I was playing at Toulouse for the University team, my mother came to the University sports centre to look for me and watch a match. But she looked for me on the soccer field!"

Instilled within his mind was the desire to be apart from the pack, to do what he wanted regardless of expectation. His mother says: "Jean-Pierre did everything by contraries. He went to bed late and went through a period when he constantly did the opposite of what he should have done. Perhaps he still retains that, today."

Rives' forceful play, however, helped the Lycée Technique team to become Champions of rugby, at their level, in the period 1966–8.

But his parents seldom saw him in action. "We felt it was too much of a distraction for him to have us there and even when there was a rare chance to watch, only my wife would go," says his father.

As Rives grew, so his game developed, acquiring the compelling combination of speed and skill, mainly in creative play.

"I believe I played my best rugby at that time," he says, "from age 17–20. I played differently in those days. Everywhere, at every moment, I was attacking. That was my role – I never thought about defence. No-one defended. I had already been influenced by Jean Salut in the way of attack." Jean Salut, the TOEC (Toulouse Olympique Etudiants Club) and French international flank forward, was his great hero and the man who became his mentor in the game throughout his senior career.

"But later, I played for the Beaumont club when it was a side which was very weak in the front five of the scrum. Also, with the national side and a first-class club like Stade Toulousain, you must do all things, not only attack."

At nineteen Rives, already gaining a high reputation by his play for the University at Toulouse, astonished the French rugby selectors when they chose him to appear in a trial match, France 'A' against France 'B'. He replied to the offer of a national trial: "No, thanks. I am playing for my University".

Rives relates the story as though oblivious to the effect it might have had on his career. "I didn't know anything about the trial match, or the set-up. My mind was not just on rugby at that time; in fact, I was playing it only for pleasure. After rugby matches, I would go off and play tennis. My life was not simply rugby.

"I played in the University side just for fun. I loved so much the game between 3 and 4.30, but after that the life did not mean much. For me, rugby is not a monopoly of friendship or anything else. It is a great, great place to find all things. Some people say if you are not playing rugby, you are not great. That is ridiculous.

"I told the selectors who wanted me for the trial match, I was sorry, I was not free to play. I said 'I am already playing and would prefer to be with my University'."

The snub was received with astonishment. It was the first impression the selectors received of a very different type of young man from Toulouse who, in the main, enjoyed every moment of his life and did precisely what he wanted, showing little respect or time for conventional methods.

His mother recalls: "The selectors at first didn't believe Jean-Pierre was really like he is. They thought it was some act. But to us he is still like the boy he always was. Some people did not understand him but for us he was always the same. Perhaps his music showed him really as he was, and still is. He likes to play the piano particularly when he is sad. That touches me very much. He can play good classical pieces and he plays with his heart. The nights before he took his examinations for music, he could not sleep. He was very nervous; whenever he had to give recitals, he was very unhappy and worried about it. He was so conscientious. Before rugby matches, he did not suffer from nerves. But he liked to concentrate hard so we didn't worry him with anything; he was quite on his own."

The loner, pondering his fate uncertainly, questioningly, in his own mind; exploring the labyrinth of possibilities before him. Even now, Rives still enjoys spells of solitude, as remote as the general plotting his charts in the final hours before the launch of a campaign.

Through his childhood, and on into his teens, the young man had shown an ability to decipher his own problems. Close as he was to his family, Rives still sought the explanations, and answers to his dilemmas, within his own mind. He was, and still is, very much his own man.

Humour forms an integral part of the man's character; it has always done so. Jean-Michel Aguirre, his colleague in the French international team, knew Rives at Toulouse University and played for the French Universities on a tour of Romania which both players made at the start of the 1970s. This tour was to become known as the "Rives passport tour".

"Jean-Pierre arrived at the airport without his passport – he always forgot something," said Aguirre. "There was no time to return home to collect it, but another player who had been in doubt for the tour because of injury, found he could not travel when he reached the airport. So Jean-Pierre said 'No problem – I will take his spare passport'."

Pierre Villepreux, the brilliant full-back who played thirty-four times for France from 1967 to 1972, was coach to the French Universities side for that tour. He takes up the story: "No-one thought it would be possible for Rives to use this other passport. The problem was, the other player, Morlaès, who was with the

Begles club, was a tall man and had very dark hair. Also, it was short. Jean-Pierre looked as different as it was possible to look – he had long, blond hair. But he said 'not to worry; it is no problem'. When Jean-Pierre reached passport control at Bucharest airport, the man studied the passport. He looked strangely at him, but waved him through. We could not believe it."

So for an entire tour, Rives became a player from the Begles club, named Morlaès. The ruse was maintained all the way back to passport control, prior to the departure for France, at which stage even Rives became a shade sceptical: "To enter the country is nothing – to leave the country is more important".

This time, the passport control staff were not so easily convinced. A swarthy, dark man, gruff voice working in tandem with an interpreter, asked Rives: "Your hair – what happened?"

"Oh, it is nothing. I change it. This picture is old."

A grunt. "Uh."

A stamp on the passport. And freedom.

Villepreux added: "The team thought it was incredible".

The story had an amusing sequel when the Romanians sent a side to tour in France two years later. Rives was outstanding in one match against the tourists, and afterwards was approached by the Romanian coach. In broken, hesitant French, the trainer said to Rives: "Monsieur Rives, you are a fine player. In my country, two years ago, I see another player, so like you. He was the player from Begles, Morlaès." And, tugging playfully at Rives' blond locks, the coach added: "But he was called Morlaès. Funny, he was so much like you!"

Absorbed now by rugby to an increasing extent, Rives was uncertain about the path his career outside the game should take. His impish humour was apparent once more when, on his final day at school, prior to University, he was asked to nominate the occupation for which he would train.

Rives explains: "We were asked to choose a subject, and our names were called in alphabetical order. A girl with the same name as me, was very nice; oh, she was lovely. They asked her, 'What are you going to do after school'.

" 'I am going into pharmacie'.

" 'And you, Jean-Pierre Rives, where are you going?'

" 'Oh, me, I want to go into pharmacie too.' "

For one splendid year, Rives worked in the world of 'pharmacie'; "spending my time helping this girl with her work". But at the end of the year, the girl moved on to the next stage, and Rives quit. "I changed jobs and I changed girl-friends – I was not in love with her anymore," he added mischievously.

Holding his attention had been difficult for the girl, and it was not surprising. Rives showed distinct signs of impetuosity, losing interest in regular or routine events. He endured that life like a tiger stalking in its cage.

"At the Lycée Technique, we had to do drawing so much of the time. There was much industrial drawing. There was an English measure we used and although I have nothing against English measures, we always had to translate inches into centimetres. For me, it was a lot of time and trouble to do that. So I took days to do simple drawings – always there was two days delay. I was like Air France!"

Although ill-at-ease he lasted three years. Finally, he changed again, this time to law studies. He said in later years: "All my life I changed. I like many different things in my life, nothing too much the same".

Another factor now became constant and continued throughout his career; his notorious unpunctuality and unreliability. "Always my worst dream was that I would arrive for a match at half-time," he says. "I would call out 'Wait for me, wait for me'.

"When I was a young boy, I was always very absent-minded, always late. And often I lost my way to the ground.

"I arrived late for one match but I could blame my father for he was driving the car. He lost his way. Afterwards, however, I would know the way to the cakeshop. I stopped after every match to buy cakes; I eat them all the time. That is my vice. The sort with a lot of cream. Any sort.

"Once I was in a hotel with the French 'B' team, and one morning I missed training completely. They left the hotel to train without me because I was so late. I said 'Where are they', but no-one knew; they had gone. It was a big problem for me in my career for I was always late."

Rives has no doubts as to the rightness of his decision to concentrate on rugby, reducing tennis to the status of a mere hobby. "I never regretted not taking up tennis for a career. I played it for the spirit, for the pleasure. But I was not good enough to play the game as a professional."

For the spirit, for the pleasure; these words reveal the inner core of the man. Throughout his career he was to demonstrate his belief, his passion for such qualities. And without doubt the man who influenced him in such views was Jean Salut.

Salut was a man of enormous charisma, spirit and character, like Rives, the quintessential individualist. Salut was his own man, his success created by his own diligence and beliefs. Frenchmen who assessed him solely as a rugby player believed seven national caps for a man of such natural talent was an absurd waste of ability. But Salut was a man disliked by some, especially those in officialdom. He went his own way, spoke his own mind and did not suffer fools gladly, particularly if they were selectors.

Once, at a training session before an international for which he had been chosen, Salut was spoken to by a selector who was standing on the touchline. "No, Salut, do not do it that way, but in this way," ordered the official.

"Do it your own – – – – way" barked the chunky, blond-haired flanker, before storming away. It may have been commendable but hardly endeared him to the selectors.

Rives says of Salut: "For me, he was the best rugby player ever. He had the greatest spirit you could find, and he played the best rugby I have seen on the field. If I could have been ten per cent of Jean Salut, I could have been a great player. He was never an automatic choice for France probably because he was too much like a rebel. Unorthodox as a player and as a man. He had too big a temper. He said many things selectors did not like.

"But Salut's rugby was like Barbarians' rugby. I fought for a long time for that kind of rugby to come to France, for people to embrace it once again. Open rugby with every possibility tried."

Rives watched spellbound when, as a youngster, he first saw 'Jeannot' Salut play. Rives, too, was with TOEC and they played a club match against Mont-de-Marsan, the club of the Boniface brothers. "Jeannot could make André Boniface angry. He would say to him 'Now I make a little drop goal for you'. Boniface said 'Oh, yes', hardly believing, but Jeannot would do it.

"Then he would pass, then he would kick; he could play like Jo Maso, or like Jean Prat. I have this image in my mind of Salut. He reached the full-back in one match and was close to the try-line. When he was one metre from him and the line, the full-back tried to make a tackle but Salut jumped clean over him to score the try. It was incredible; he went right over the top of the man."

Rives, palpably influenced by the exploits of this extraordinary, unconventional man and rugby player, played with Salut in that same TOEC team: "I still consider it one of the greatest moments of my life. I had dreamed so many times of playing with Jeannot, that I don't know if I played or not, in that match. I just dreamed so often about playing many games with him that I don't know if it was true or not, when we did finally play in the same match.

"Then I went to Beaumont and played against him – oh, what a hard player to face. And then, finally, when I went to Stade Toulousain, I played with him again, very briefly." In one match Stade Toulousain had a backrow of Salut, Walter Spanghero and Rives. The Don, the junior godfather, and the young protégé.

Rives blames his own timidity for a failure to learn enough lessons from Salut. "I learned some things but not as much as I should. But it is difficult to learn from your hero. I would have liked to have played like Salut, but I don't believe I did. I was not good enough.

"Always, my dream was to play like Jean Salut or Jo Maso and I consider I failed in that respect. I could tackle and fight and work hard but to be quick, to jump high and to be different, you need special qualities. But I was never desperate to jump one metre more and become a great jumper in the line-out; to run a yard or two faster, or such things. Rugby was never the most important thing in my life. For me, life is when you try to be happy, try to do something, to be well in your mind and healthy in your body. Rugby or work should create enthusiasm; it should make you happy, make you feel great and want to go for something in it.

"Rugby is a means to an end, a way to happiness. It is a way to express yourself but it is never something as important as life. For me, to be is to do; you have to find yourself, to be creative. But also, you learn to share with people; share experiences, share things. Loving what you do and sharing with people you love. That is great.

"I don't know whether people take rugby too seriously but perhaps they take it for motivation, whatever that is. I don't like that word; I prefer enjoyment, emotion. You should never be ashamed of emotion – laugh, smile, cry. It is life. The heart is swelling.

"It is like the Welsh. Rugby and religion is in their life. Rugby expression is for them a way to say we are alive – and why not? It is something inherent in their history. It is the same in South Africa but maybe that is where we enter the political side of it, because then it means something more than just enjoyment. We should let politicians play their own games; rugby should be as simple as the pleasure it creates."

For Jeannot Salut, there was, in his own mind, a clear sign, a firm link between the young blond-haired Rives and the player he had been himself, as a youngster. Salut says: "At the beginning, I predicted Rives would be an international. He was very gifted. I knew him when he was a boy with TOEC; I was his friend above all and maybe I inspired him a little. But he didn't model himself on anyone. He was himself, an individual player.

"We were very, very good friends, despite the gap in our ages. But already he liked to associate with people older than himself. That's the first thing. It was because he was more grown up, more mature than the others. He was very intelligent and liked the company of older people more than those of his own age.

"Also, he was blond, like me, but more so; he played in the same position as me . . . we had many similarities. He liked me, he often came to see me. We were friends from very early on."

At that time, few men could hold a candle to the mercurial gifts of the French international centre, Jo Maso. The silky running, free-flowing style of which Maso was the essence, seemed to epitomise the greatest qualities of traditional French rugby: sheer joie de vivre, uncomplicated by rigid team patterns; the expression of talented players, taking rugby away from a drab, dour image to the verge of poetry – in motion. It was heady stuff, especially when it came off.

Poor, shell-shocked England, on their 1970 visit to Paris, discovered the lethal concoction that could create. Six tries rattled past the English defence, like West Indian quick bowlers clean bowling English batsmen; uncertain, pusillanimous defence ruthlessly punished. Maso was not playing that day, his international career in temporary abeyance for two years. But his stamp, that special pedigree, was readily apparent in the play of men like Trillo, Lux, Villepreux, the Stade Toulousain wings, Bonal and Bourgarel, plus Berot, the architect who created much of their harmony. Berot, too, was a member of the Toulouse club. The young Rives, at an impressionable age, was witnessing the quality of rugby which was to become his crusade in the later years of his career.

Jo Maso provides a rare glimpse of Rives in the early stages of his career. "One day, I played for Perpignan against TOEC and I saw Jean-Pierre Rives play with the juniors. I thought, who is this blond boy? Because he resembled Salut, so much. Someone said to me, 'You will see. He will be a good player'. I knew it also – he had all the basic qualities then; the speed, vision and physical qualities.

"I believe Salut was an example for Jean-Pierre because when he began, Jean-Pierre was so much an attacking player, just like Salut. He was so strong and fast, good in attack, for his age."

Maso, known as the prince of French threequarters for his elegant genius, was not to know it but the two were to become close friends, through their rugby connections. Maso, invited to play by the English Barbarians, inspired in the young Rives so much of the love for rugby of that ilk.

No-one, certainly not Rives himself, missed the significance of Maso's part in another shattering defeat for the English in Paris, in 1972. It was the final match France were to play at the old Colombes stadium, which had been built for the 1924 Olympics. Maso's was a virtuoso display, even though it was devoid of a try among the six that were scored; yet it was rich in quality, poise, control and timing. It was one of the finest exhibitions of play by a creative threequarter ever seen in that era. Its like was to vanish, tragically, off the face of the European game, within a few, short years.

For England, crushed 37–12, it was an afternoon of humiliation. For Jean-Pierre Rives, watching the match, it provided irrefutable evidence of the rugby he desired; the open, attacking, entertaining game which made the sport almost unequalled in attraction, and which produced rugby of spirit, of freedom; the rugby favoured by the British Barbarians club; the true, sporting rugby of Rives the Corinthian.

From Toulouse to France...
The man of attack

*"Mon centre cède, ma droite recule,
situation excellente. J'attaque."*
——— MARSHAL FOCH ———
1851–1929

The errant schoolboy, William Webb Ellis, the young man who is credited with the birth of rugby football, had picked up the ball and run off towards immortality, as long ago as 1823. Yet rugby took its time to reach Toulouse, on the banks of the meandering Garonne, in the south of France.

Paradoxically, the regions of France where it first took root, Le Havre on the French channel coast, and Paris, are no longer the strongholds of the game. It is almost exclusively in the south of the country, in the area from Biarritz and Bordeaux on the Atlantic coast, to Nice and the port of Toulon on the Mediterranean, that the game's strength is now concentrated. Indeed, the geographical restriction the first-class game imposes in France, curiously parallels the pocket of major Rugby League clubs in the North of England. Rarely does either area find its walls breached. (See the map on page xvi.)

It took the game the greater part of the nineteenth century to reach the south of the country. The first club in Toulouse was the 'Ligue Athlétique de Lycée de Toulouse', formed in 1890. Two years later, the 'Sans Souci' club was established by two devotees who had known the game in the north, Mercade at Lycée Michelet in Paris, and Tallavignes, a pupil at the Lycée de Reims. The 'Sans Souci' club recruited its new members from the Lycée de Toulouse; but as the game flourished they were to face increasing competition for players.

Two more clubs became established, Stade Toulousain, and Stade Olympique des Etudiants de Toulouse, now the TOEC club. Jean Salut and Elie Cester, both French internationals in the 1960s, represented TOEC, which was formed in 1896. Teams from Toulouse and Narbonne were in competition from as early as 1894; that year, the Lycée de Narbonne played and beat their Toulouse counterparts, 5–3, in Narbonne. No matter, the Toulouse men took their revenge the following year, winning 13–0. The seed had been sown; its roots were taking to the favourable soil of the south.

In the region, the game certainly had a phenomenal baptism. In 1896 the Lycée de Toulouse faced the renowned Stade Bordelais side, at the 'Prairie des Filtres'. Bordelais were the 'grand favourites', so the record books relate, but the men of Toulouse, solid and inspired, kept the score to 0–0 at half time. That was considered a surprise; heroic is the word favoured by the rugby historians to describe the second half which was again scoreless. By common consent, both teams then decided that a further ten minutes should be played and the referee, a Monsier Shearer, an official from the south-west, agreed. But the period of 'extra time' was never played; the spectators, too enthusiastic say the accounts, had invaded the pitch and ruled out any possibility of further play. A pitch invasion in 1896!

In 1903 the 'Stade Olympique des Etudiants de Toulouse' contested the French Championship final with the Stade Français club of Paris. The Toulouse team was forced to start the final with only fourteen players; Fabregat, the missing man, arrived late. He got changed on the touchline, entrusted his watch to a spectator and launched himself into the game with his team surprisingly leading 5–0.

Perhaps he should not have bothered. Mysteriously, Toulouse were not as effective with their full complement of players, and lost the match 8–16. Poor Fabregat; he deserved a better fate for striking so elegant a pose as the latecomer. A bearded gentleman, who resembled slightly the English cricketer Dr W. G. Grace, he took the field with a belt strapped around the waist of his knee-length trousers, his ankles engulfed in boots which resembled those of a hiker.

The SOE club of Toulouse had the honour of providing the first Toulouse player for the French national team. Some privilege! Pujol, the left wing, played on New Year's Day 1906 for France against New Zealand, at the old Parc des Princes ground, near St Cloud, on the western outskirts of Paris. Watched by a crowd of 3,000, the New Zealanders scored ten tries and won the match 38–6, and poor Pujol, who hardly saw the ball throughout the game, was promptly dropped for France's next match. He never again represented his country.

But the Toulouse man no doubt offered a silent prayer of gratitude for missing France's next two games. The same year, on March 22, England went to the Parc des Princes and overwhelmed the French 35–8. That time the home side yielded nine tries – the same number they were to surrender when they played England, at Richmond, the next year. This, another heavy French defeat, 41–13, made a total of 28 tries conceded by France in her first three international games!

In 1908, the Stade Toulousain half back, Mayssonie, earned selection for France, and enjoyed a greater degree of success; France only conceded five tries against England in Paris, losing 19–0.

The French game was certainly experiencing its teething problems on the international stage but, at club level, Stade Toulousain was on the verge of making a major impact. The club's lower sides, the reserves, third team and fourth team, had brought back to Toulouse the trophies of their respective divisions, in 1909, 1910, 1911 and 1912. Now, also in 1912, Stade Toulousain was facing the might of the Racing Club de France, in the Championship final, played in Toulouse.

One Racing Club wing, Faillot, was Champion of France in the 400 metres; the other, Geo André, was the complete athlete who became a French international rugby player in 1913 and 1914. André had a magnificent physique; he threw the weight, participated in the high jump, 110-metres hurdles and, in spare time when the mood took him, ran the 100 metres in 11 seconds.

The Racing Club side justified its reputation by capturing an early 6–0 lead. All Toulouse waited with uncertainty. 12,000 spectators had crammed into the stadium at Ponts-Jumeaux; now they saw the scrum half Mayssonnie put Toulouse back in the game, with a clever try, which the full-back, Dutour, converted. 6–5 – Le Stade within a point!

Toulouse possessed great spirit and determination, but they also had the inspirational qualities of their captain, Mouniq, who played nine times for France between 1911 and 1913. Behind the scrum, their wings were scarcely as celebrated as their Paris counterparts, but in Moulines they possessed one of the finest centres never to win a cap for France. Mariette and Servat, both Toulouse forwards, suffered injuries yet they continued, the former with his forehead covered in blood, a Jean-Pierre Rives before his time. And then, the great moment. Mouniq won the ball and found his right wing, Pierre Jaureguy, who ran clear, and scored the decisive try between the posts. Stade Toulousain had won, 8–6, and were Champions for the first time.

That night they sang their favourite song, 'La Toulousaine', right through the town; and in the weeks which followed, a special postcard was produced to mark the event.

Stade Toulousain were to become Champions seven more times, in the years 1922, 1923, 1924, 1926, 1927, 1947 and 1985. But no Championship was celebrated with greater excitement in the city than that first one in 1912. Alas, within barely two years, the bloody battles of the First World War would erupt over France but, before then, there were witnessed the first vestiges of unsavoury play which stains the French game at club level even today. In 1913, Stade Toulousain, as Champions, went to Bordeaux to play the Bordeaux UC club in a qualifying match. Initially, the atmosphere was unhealthily intense; Bordeaux had been Champions in six of the past nine years, but had seen Toulouse take the title in 1912. They sought revenge.

In the event, retribution was severe. The Toulouse prop Bergé found himself treated as a doormat by the Bordeaux forwards, and his forehead was badly cut; by no means the only example of excessive aggression in the match.

The Toulouse captain, Mouniq, deciding that his team was at a clear disadvantage in such an atmosphere away from home, took drastic action. A dapper little man with a neat, short haircut and clipped moustache, Mouniq had a very slight frame, giving him the look of a small boy. The contemporary pictures show him clutching a rugby ball which seems to cover most of his chest. But his reputation as a player, and charisma as leader, was unquestioned. Thus, when he decided to lead his players off the field at Bordeaux, the whole side followed without a murmur of disapproval.

The match was lost; the trophy gone. Stade Toulousain would

not take the French Championship for another ten years, although the Cup itself was replaced in the war years by the 'Coupe de l'Esperance'. Stade Toulousain won that in 1916, beating Stade Français 8–0 in the final. But it was a grievous time for all France, not just its rugbymen. The Toulouse club lost 79 of its members, players and supporters, in the war, compared with only six in the 1939–45 conflict and one – Claude Pech – in the Algerian war of 1957.

Thus, the young Jean-Pierre Rives as he approached the Stade Toulousain ground in 1973, with a trace of trepidation, was walking towards a club steeped in history. He was scarcely twenty-one, and by no means convinced as to his pedigree for a place at such a distinguished club.

Pierre Villepreux, a physical education teacher, knew Rives through his contacts with Toulouse University: "Jean Pierre was not a big player, but an interesting one. I asked him if he wanted to come to Stade Toulousain but at first he didn't accept, because he was modest. 'I cannot play for a team in the First division of rugby,' he told me. But I told him, 'You have to come'. And so he came, although it was late by our standards. Normally, we would hope to find young players before they are twenty."

Rives joined a Stade Toulousain club which possessed a back row of rare pedigree; Michel Billière at No. 8, Jean-Claude Skrela and Jean Salut on the flanks, internationals each one. But Salut was on the point of retirement, and Rives was able to make virtually an instant impact in the first team. Villepreux says: "When he began at our club, he was a player who loved the ball; he wanted to run, not to ruck and maul; he wanted to play and have enjoyment". Villepreux talks warmly also of Rives' modesty. "He always thought he was not good enough to play at that level, even after he got into the team. It was only when he was in the French national team he really had more confidence." But even if Rives had a tendency to denigrate his own abilities, others at the Toulouse club were not deceived. Where on earth, they had wondered, shall we find another Jeannot Salut? For a club in which forceful, attacking play was the tradition, fast, mobile back row men were an essential ingredient. For teams playing adventurously it was a prerequisite to have back row men of pace. If possession of the ball were lost by the threequarters, it was imperative that the ball be recovered. Only loose forwards of the calibre of Skrela and Salut could virtually ensure that that happened.

Salut, the brave, potent flanker, would retire in 1975, and no-one at the club knew the answer until Rives arrived. Incredibly, even at such a tender age, he was almost the same man. Here was the new Salut; the King is dead, long live the King.

Rives took little time to make his mark. Already, he was a young player of great promise; as a junior international in 1970, for French Universities in 1973–4. He was to play five times for France 'B' – against Spain, Morocco, Wales (twice) and Scotland. His display for France 'B' against Wales 'B' at Toulouse, in October 1973, forced the selectors to take notice. The following season, again for the 'B' side, he shone unmistakably despite defeats by the Welsh and Scottish 'B' teams. It could not be long before Rives played at senior international level.

The player whose name was to become almost synonymous with Rives', Jean-Claude Skrela, well remembers the day Rives came plodding into Stade Toulousain's training ground, the new member embarking upon a career at the highest level.

Skrela says: "I was 24, Jean-Pierre was 21. I had met him already because I played with him in the French junior side and had seen him play with TOEC. I also played against him when he was with Beaumont because we were in the same league. But when he began to play at Toulouse, we got to know each other. He was already a very good player when he joined the club. The only thing was, he lacked training because, at that time, rugby was not his only interest. He played an enormous amount of tennis but after, he played so much rugby that he gave up tennis.

"He was already a very hard player on the field. Jean-Pierre was very strong and a strapping man physically, although he wasn't tall. When he came to Toulouse, he played more rugby and took it more seriously. Above all, though, he trained better.

"When he was young, and played in the juniors, he didn't train very much. But with Stade Toulousain, he worked on his game and developed his qualities as a player by training sessions. That was his greatest success because he understood he had to train every day. Initially, he played more in bursts. That's to say, he played on his power, his strength. He didn't have the stamina to play the full eighty minutes. But through training he developed this."

Interestingly, Skrela disputes the theory that Salut influenced Rives. "I don't think any other players influenced Jean-Pierre.

I believe his own personality made him like he was. Originally, he was a boy who was more an individual than part of a team. I don't think anyone influenced either his game or himself. Perhaps what did influence him most were the teams in which he played. He always followed, he was always able to adapt to the system of the side. But I don't think that is an influence. It's altogether normal. When a team decides to play in a certain way, all play like that.''

Skrela was already an established international, having made his debut in the 8–8 draw France secured against South Africa, in Durban on 19 June 1971. That result meant a drawn Test series, or a moral victory for France considering the venue. Skrela was one of the major 'finds' of that tour.

For the remainder of his career, following Rives' arrival at Stade Toulousain, Skrela was one half of a partnership; a piece of a picture, part of a union. Rives and Skrela of Stade Toulousain; the names, the club and the phrase became prominent not just on the lips of those who followed the game in France, but throughout Europe. The partnership was forged in those early games for the Toulouse club. It became honed to perfection in the national shirts of France when the two played together from 1975 and Rives' debut at Twickenham, through to Skrela's sudden, premature retirement, at the end of the 1978 season. It was a partnership of speed, of robust play; of attack and defence; of commitment to the tackle and support for the ball carrier. Attack, defence. The two men became inseparable on the rugby fields of France. In a very short space of time, they created one of the finest, if not *the* finest club flank forward partnership which French club rugby had known.

Film crews would arrive from London, specially flown out to capture the phenomenal pair on film. French journalists had a field day too. But the phrases of adulation which flowed did not come only from the media or the impressionable. Armand Vaquerin, the eminent Beziers prop forward and a veteran of nine international Championship seasons and even more French Championship final appearances with his club, said of the Toulouse flankers: ''They are the players I hated most to meet. When you faced them in a tackle, it was like hitting a steel post.''

Rives, at 5ft 10ins and 13 stone, was a stone lighter and three inches shorter than his partner. But if his height was a disadvantage at the tail of the line-out, the blond-haired player more than compensated with the ferocity of his tackling. Muscles like steel bulged in his arms and gripped opponents and the ball like a vice; Skrela, taller and the finer athlete of the two, was the tighter flanker yet still full of speed and penetration. Rives was the perfect foil; roaming off his flank, capable of mauling with the fiercest of men for the ball, or diving in to win it on the ground. Michel Palmié summed it up: "Jean-Claude Skrela might have had physical advantages over Jean-Pierre but I think Jean-Pierre had a way of playing, of self-sacrifice, a force of will to do things that Jean-Claude could not have done."

But they were never the same sort of player. Neither morally nor physically were they alike. Rives loved the city, the night clubs and the total involvement of a hectic life. Skrela preferred the country, living well outside of Toulouse and seeking a quiet, more placid existence. He was the introvert; Rives, in that same sense, the extrovert.

Nevertheless, a great respect and understanding developed between the two. They began to analyse their performances after club games, questioning each other on what they had done, what they had failed to do, and assessing strengths and weaknesses in their own play and their opponents' game.

But all the planning and discussion neither altered nor created the special understanding which the two possessed. As Skrela expressed it: "Things just happened because we thought along the same lines. We often found ourselves at the same place where the ball was. We just had this understanding, this kind of telepathy."

And, above all else, both men possessed the same Corinthian spirit, both were in love with the ideals of the Barbarians' approach to rugby. The game they favoured belonged to the players; the captain called the moves, long assiduous preparation was as foreign to them as skulduggery on the field. Rugby was played for the spirit, for the pleasure, for the spontaneity; it flourished in their minds.

Skrela's face bore the signs of a hard career in rugby, but would break into a smile at the memory. The scars, masked by the skill of surgeons who stitched loose skin together, reappeared as creases in the grin. The smile revealed a big gap in his upper row of teeth; on the bottom, there was a palpably new tooth, quite different in colour to the rest. Very tanned and bursting with good health and carrying not an ounce of fat, Skrela looked every inch the physical education teacher that he was. He has an almost boyish crewcut, but there is no doubting the strength of the man – broad arms flowing down to forearms of tremendous strength, a solid frame of 6ft 2ins. The fingers are stubby and chunky; far removed from those of the concert pianist or writer. Incongruously for so strong a man, his little blond moustache is trimmed so closely that it almost seems to struggle for life. The very big, blue eyes create an almost Germanic appearance.

"Why did it mean so much to us both to play for the Barbarians?" he wondered. "Very simply, I think that it is a spirit totally different from the French spirit. In the Barbarians we found again the game that we had practised at Toulouse. That's to say, the game with the responsibility for the players.

"It was the players who prepared for the match. There are no trainers and, with the Barbarians, it is the captain who decides everything with his players. We found there something that gave us great pleasure. It was always marvellous to find oneself with such great players, besides French players, and to share the life and ideas of foreign players."

Villepreux believes Rives and Skrela played their finest rugby at that time. "They were two players who complemented each other so well. I felt they were at their best together when they first played in the Toulouse team. Skrela was maybe stronger but together they were exceptional. Where one was, the other was beside him, always. It was incredible. There is a photo of them with Skrela first and Rives just behind, in our clubhouse. They were like twins on the field. It was, of course, two players but in reality only one, who had everything. Jean-Claude was more physical than Jean-Pierre. But Rives had more technique and more ability in the game, than Jean-Claude."

Rives said: "Maybe our partnership worked so well together because all the things Jean-Claude was not, I was. And all the things I was not, he was! He likes to live in the country; I like living in the city. He goes to bed early; I go to bed late. When we shared a room on trips, he would still go to bed early and I would come to bed much later.

"Always, I would undress without putting the light on. Each morning I was bruised from all the things I knocked into in the dark! And then, each morning he would wake up early . . . unlike me. We had very different lives. Jean-Claude was a perfect athlete, training all the time; fast, quick, strong. Good tackling, good strong running.''

Gradually, the pair became renowned on the grounds of the south of France. Skrela, known already, seemed enhanced with the new recruit alongside him in the Toulouse side. At Bagnères, where the icy waters from the Pyrenees form the Adour river and rush past the back of the rugby ground's main stand before sweeping through the town, their reputation was increased. Here, on a ground which combines rugby and canoeing – the equipment for riding the fast flowing water is stored beneath the stadium of the rugby ground – the two gave a typically exciting display.

It was the same story even at Beziers, where the dressing-rooms resemble jails, dark underground rooms hidden away from all natural light. Spartan, basic facilities; and, on the field, an even more intimidating welcome.

Home for Rives was altogether different. His parents' house, in a leafy suburb of Toulouse, has a welcome for all. Trees, bushes and shrubs fill the garden; just down the road, not far from Toulouse Airport, is a big open sportsground, ringed with magnificent trees.

Nowadays, as a concession to security, a large Dobermann roams the grounds of the house. The visitor touches the doorbell at the front gate and there is instantly a blur of colour, too fast to create a firm definition in the mind. The first sensation is of something flinging itself at the metal gates, akin perhaps to Rives arriving at a maul. Differentiating between the degree of physical pain suffered at either encounter would be difficult.

As a reflex reaction, you jerk back your body; as a secondary thought, you think of running. Or, at the least, getting someone or something between yourself and the trouble. But Jo, Jean-Pierre's father, quietens the brute, returning it to its pen. So you walk past the sliding glass doors into the hall, under bedroom balconies on to which roses clamber. Inside, in a big, sprawling sitting-room, a leather sofa faces an open fireplace; an old oak beam across the top and brick frontage, built up. A cosy corner on cold winter nights. The marble staircase, leading to the upstairs bedrooms, is open on one side. It is not English in style or design but nor is it classically French.

Each week after the game, almost invariably, Rives would return to the house, carrying some wound incurred on behalf of Stade

Toulousain. Jean-Pierre Bastiat, then the mainstay of the Dax forward unit, remembers: "My first impression of Jean-Pierre was that he would not finish his career when he did, because I thought he would be badly injured long before. It seemed inevitable he would break something important before then. Every match he played, whether a friendly or a Championship or an international, when I saw him I thought, if this is not the last, the next one will be. But finally he went on to become an old soldier.

"Off the field, he was rather quiet and unobtrusive in his behaviour, to begin with. On the field, however, he was the same Jean-Pierre Rives that everyone knew later on, that's to say he was a boy with extreme courage, a boy for whom rugby was his chief love; who was effectively, as we say, a kamikaze type and who, one by one in his matches, came to prove that, despite his limited size, Jean-Pierre Rives would be the number one in his position in France."

Bastiat also believes that Rives and Skrela created the finest flank forward partnership which the French international side has known. "They were the ideal partnership. They had an extraordinary advantage in that they played together every Sunday, week in, week out (Sunday, in France, being the principal club rugby day of the week). That is something which happens so rarely to two players who play practically in the same position. It certainly does not happen very often at that level. But given the abilities they had, the qualities they had, the temperaments they had and also playing every Sunday together, they could not have been better prepared for international matches. Between them, they had a marvellous understanding of rugby."

And so the call came, after initial uncertainty on the part of the selectorial team. Rives says: "Whenever I saw any selectors, they would say to me, 'How tall are you'. Always, I put three centimetres more on my height. I said 'I am big'. And always I added five kilogrammes to my weight. They said 'It doesn't seem so' – but I was not too worried. Jean Salut had told me it was the same with him. His reply had always been, 'I am like Jean Prat' (the Lourdes back row player who won fifty-one caps for France, as player and captain, from 1945 to 1955). So, after a little time, I said the same."

The selectors should have known what sort of an unpredictable, rare example of the species they were going to get from Rives' build-up to his first international for his country. Most players confess to nerves, paying unusually close attention to the small details which become superfluous with time. For the new cap, in normal cases, there is the obvious concern for the game, the desire to follow established trends, the early bed the night before the big game. For Jean-Pierre Rives, virtually none of those aspects applied.

Rives was to win his first cap against England at Twickenham, on 1 February 1975. It was his debut at the ground which Skrela calls "the temple of rugby", and before an audience of 70,000. Daunting for some, but not for Rives.

He says: "We trained on Friday morning, outside London, and then had lunch at our hotel. In the afternoon, I think it was usual for players to sit around, talk, play cards, or rest in their rooms. I expected to do that.

"But when we finished lunch, Claude Spanghero, our No. 8 who had already won seventeen caps, said, 'Come with me, Jean-Pierre'. So we went together to a meeting of the players, and the officials said, 'Who wants to go shopping?'

"For me, I didn't care about shopping – I thought I would rest in the hotel. But Claude whispered to me 'Say yes, say yes'. So I put up my hand and said 'I want to go shopping'. Claude said 'I want to go, too'. I think we were the only two.

"We went to London by taxi and went to Soho to a striptease all afternoon. We paid £1 and then after the curtain went down, another £1. We stayed all afternoon seeing big, fat girls. After some hours, we realised we had to go for dinner with the team – but we were late. When we returned, the officials said, 'Why have you been so long shopping?' And then they saw we had no parcels. 'You have been so long but you have bought nothing.'

"So I said to them 'Oh, everything is so expensive in England. I looked a lot but I could not afford to buy.' "

The team officials were equally unsuccessful in getting the pair off to bed early that night. Rives goes on: "After dinner, Claude Spanghero again said to me, 'Now we go off – come with me'.

"We sat up until three or four o'clock in the morning, playing poker. The other players went to bed at 10.30 – we were up for hours after." Once again Rives had shown his predilection for the contrary; the unconventional, non-conforming role. The trait was to remain constant throughout his career.

His captain that day, Claude Dourthe, the Dax centre-
threequarter, recalls: "Jean-Pierre was very shy, very polite, very
well brought up. He had an altogether English style, a gentleman;
very nice and very amenable. Three players made their debut for
France in that match – Rives, Alain Guilbert of Toulon, and the
Castres prop, Gerard Cholley. My policy was to integrate them as
quickly as possible because, of course, each man, each player, has
his own characteristics. I felt it was necessary to introduce them as
soon as possible and have them accepted by the others. One
doesn't want great differences between them.

"I knew Rives was a fine golfer, first-class bridge player and
good at tennis, too. So at dinner, because I was captain, I asked
him whether he played bridge . . . just to make conversation. He
replied 'Yes, of course'.

"So I, who had never played bridge in my life, discussed bridge
with him for an hour or more and he was so nice and polite, he
listened to me."

Dourthe also recalls the extraordinary tale of Cholley arriving for
the trip dressed like a man from the Paris Bourse. "Cholley was a
big, strapping man, thirty years old, who stood 6ft 3ins and
weighed 16½ stone. He turned up for our first team meeting
wearing a three-piece suit and carrying his little personal bag. It
looked rather odd to see a big prop dressed like that. The other
players saw him and said 'Who is this guy – a prop in a three-piece
suit with a handbag?' He even wore a shirt and tie; it shocked
some of the players."

The minute he stepped on to the international arena, however,
Cholley was to shatter any ideas about a fancy boy. Opposing
props would mutter darkly about the man and talk accusingly of
his physical presence which went beyond conventional rugby
challenges. But Rives was different. His pleasant manner meant
that he was rapidly accepted by his new colleagues. Roland
Bertranne, who had already won seventeen caps as a threequarter,
said: "We didn't know him very well. Just that he was blond, a bit
of a playboy. He had an exceptional personality. But he merged
into the side very well and showed very quickly what he could
do."

Dourthe told his new caps: "You are here because you have
earned it. But that doesn't change anything. On the contrary, for
players who are capable of playing at this level, the more you

become famous the better you become, the better you will express yourselves. A very good player in a very good team will do better and better. But a very good player in a reserve side is not going to change. So it is necessary for you to have confidence and then you will bring something into the group.''

Perhaps it was Dourthe's stirring talk – or possibly the extensive physical attributes of the ladies of London's Soho – which inspired Rives. But inspired the young man certainly was at Twickenham that day.

France had something to prove as a side. A fortnight earlier, the selectors had watched Wales trounce their team 25–10 in Paris, and decided to wield the knife. When they finished, eight different players had been called up into the team.

Wales had rubbed salt into French wounds when Graham Price, the Pontypool prop on his international debut, had outrun the entire French side to touch down for a try, after the ball had been booted more than half the length of the field. ''They'll never believe it in Pontypool,'' shouted the BBC commentator, Nigel Starmer-Smith. The French back row probably could not believe it either, but all three were missing from the side chosen for Twickenham, although Skrela, a replacement against Wales, remained.

Both the half-backs, Romeu and Fouroux, were replaced by Paries and Astre. Etchenique came in for Lux at centre; Cholley for Azarette, Guilbert for Senal, and Claude Spanghero returned, to the back row, in place of Bastiat.

Before leaving for England, Rives sought the advice of Salut. ''Stay yourself,'' he was told. ''And just one other thing. Follow Andy Ripley like he was part of you. Don't give up – go everywhere with Andy. Each time he takes the ball, tackle him.''

Rives remembers: ''I agreed to do that although I didn't really know why. I didn't even know who Ripley was. When I got on the field, I had to ask someone to point him out.''

Probably Rives was the only person among the 70,000 spectators and thirty players at Twickenham who did not know the England No. 8, for heaven knows, it was hard enough to miss him. The Rosslyn Park player stood 6ft 5ins, wore a white headband to hold his long, lank hair in some kind of order, and was frequently to be seen bursting away from set-piece play, thighs working like pistons, nostrils distended with determination.

Salut had told Rives, "If you stop Ripley, you will cause trouble for the English team". Rives, however, was by no means content to keep just one Englishman quiet. He tackled almost every player in a white shirt that day, together with Skrela, and succeeded in repulsing a spirited English recovery which, at one stage, threatened to snatch the match from under French noses. France had gained the early advantage, but England trimmed it, to two points, at 10–12, by half time. Again in the second half, an early spurt of points scoring took France to the verge of victory, before England, sustained by Rossborough's four penalty goals, chipped away at the advantage. But the French won, 27–20, scoring four tries against two; Rives' tackling had been astonishing and Claude Spanghero scored a crucial try. It must have been thanks to the women of Soho!

Afterwards Ripley congratulated the new cap from Toulouse. It was the start of a friendship of mutual respect. "Ripley is a fantastic man, a great person," Rives says. "He has a great spirit of rugby and was a great player. Unlike many people, he did not make the mistake of taking himself too seriously. You can be serious in the spirit but you should not allow the game to make you too serious. It is enjoyment; it is trying to improve yourself and your body and your mental attitude. It is not work, not a crisis."

Dourthe remembered: "I don't think Jean-Pierre was either nervous or worried before that match; rugby, for him, was only one of his interests. Like golf, or tennis.

"To be frank, I never thought he would become such a great player. I didn't know him very well because I only played one season (two matches) with him. In my opinion, he was not destined, at that time, for the career of captain or, for that matter, the career of superstar.

"I never thought he would become the captain he did because he was so reserved. He didn't want to assert himself. He was by no means an undisputed, natural leader in those days; it was later he emerged."

The England and Lancashire flank forward Tony Neary, winner of forty-three caps between 1971 and 1980, said of Rives: "He was always good with the ball in his hands; a great footballer. And, of course, always a good 'target' because of his distinctive looks. If you saw the blond hair and you were next to him, you were doing all right, because he was so fast and always close to the ball.

''Early in his career, when I played against him in his first match against us at Twickenham, I didn't particularly mark him out because the French selectors had a reputation for changing their players so often.

''Jean-Pierre's weakness was probably his height or lack of it. That went against him especially on tours to places like South Africa and New Zealand where they place great importance on the tail of the line-out. But he could launch an attack himself as stand-in fly half, centre, any position at all where he got to, in pursuit of the loose ball. He was one of the best because his game had such variety. And he was very solid and courageous. He always led from the front, a bit like the English captain, Bill Beaumont.''

Neary's abiding memory of the Frenchman? ''His energy and courage, I think. Also his ability to be out of the game for a month but then come straight back to the international arena. He must have had a tremendous personal pride and determination because most others find that extremely difficult to do.''

French elation at the Twickenham victory – only their second win on the ground in nineteen years – was soon dissipated. A narrow 10–9 win over Scotland in Paris hardly augured well for the difficult trip to Dublin, to meet Willie John McBride's side, and the outcome was a 25–6 defeat. Only seven of that side survived the short period from that match, on 1 March, to 21 June when the touring Frenchmen met South Africa, in the first of the two Tests, on their summer tour.

But for Rives, although he did not go on that tour because of his law studies, the future could only be bright. Like the launched rocket, his light was ascending. France had discovered, from a fog of mediocrity, a blond beacon to light the future path.

And what a path that would become.

1977: Grand Chelem

"Let me have men about me that are fat."
Julius Caesar, by
—— WILLIAM SHAKESPEARE ——
1569–1616

Rugby Union has never, at any rate until the World Cup scheduled for 1987, organised a World Championship. However, it is probably true that, during the period of twenty-five months from 19 October 1975 to 11 November 1977 – France's team was the strongest in the world.

During that period the French played 18 matches, winning 16 and losing only 2. The world's best teams were beaten; New Zealand, Australia (twice), a fine Welsh side in Paris, England, Ireland and Scotland (twice each), Argentina (three times), Romania, the United States of America and a French President's World XV. Wales in Cardiff, in a monumental struggle, and Romania, against a weakened French team, were the only sides to be victorious against them.

The seeds of that French success were sown in South Africa on the 1975 tour when, led jointly by Jacques Fouroux and Richard Astre, they lost both Tests to the Springboks, but found the basic components of a powerful forward machine which would demolish their opponents' panzer-style. The crowning glory for the side was the winning of the 1977 Grand Slam title, in Europe, for only the second time since France had joined the International Championship in 1909–10. Yet two experienced players believe that France's 1976 side was their finest, and possibly the best the country has ever produced: one was the man who led France to another Grand Slam five years later, Jean-Pierre Rives; the other, was Australia's uncompromising No. 8 from Queensland, Mark Loane.

"In 1976," Rives says, "we lost the deciding match for the Grand Slam in Cardiff to a magnificent Welsh team. The following season we beat them in Paris, so we won the Grand Slam. But it does not necessarily follow that 1977 was the better side. You must not judge teams only by the trophies they win. There were few changes between the sides but I still believe 1976 was the better. We did not win the Grand Slam but we won some very good games, and played extremely well for a lot of the time."

It is a view in which Mark Loane concurs. At the opening of 1976 France had already twice beaten a more than useful Argentine side; Porta, Travaglini, Sansot, *et al.* At Lyon, the tourists were crushed 29–6 (six French tries), and then, a week later in Paris, 36–21 with the Frenchmen scoring five tries against one. Only Porta's goalkicking gave the scoreline some semblance of respectability.

Romania had lost 36–12 at Bordeaux before the first of the Five Nations matches against Scotland at Murrayfield, which was a stern test for the Frenchmen. Scotland had built a run of ten successive home wins prior to the January match. The Scots should have increased their winning run, too, for they missed nine out of ten penalty kicks at goal, eight of them in the first half when they enjoyed a strong wind at their backs.

Chiefly through those Scottish errors in kicking, France took a 7–3 interval lead, a Romeu penalty preceding the sole try of the match, scored by the Montferrand wing, Dubertrand, after Gourdon, his opposite wing, had switched the point of attack with a neat cross kick. Romeu's two second-half penalties were too much for a Scottish side which could manage only a penalty goal from Renwick, and Morgan's dropped goal.

France had squeezed victory from a difficult encounter, with their forward unit looking formidable. Against the Irish in Paris, a month later, they looked even stronger up front, with Jean François Imbernon – 'the elastoplast man' as the Welsh dubbed him – replacing Haget at lock. Ireland had Mike Gibson at centre, but French power was decisive, producing a 26–3 victory, 20 points coming in the second half. Pecune, Cholley, Fouroux and Rives scored the tries, with Romeu and Bastiat each kicking a conversion and a penalty goal.

Wales, meanwhile, had beaten England 21–9 at Twickenham for their biggest winning margin on the ground in its sixty-six-year history. The irrepressible J. P. R. Williams became the first full-back ever to score two tries in an international, as Welsh quality and class, epitomised by men like Gareth Edwards, Phil Bennett, Gerald Davies and Mervyn Davies, proved decisive. Three weeks later, Wales overwhelmed Scotland 28–6 at Cardiff, and later that month, went to Dublin ruthlessly to crush Ireland by 34 points to 9. At half-time, it was 9–10 but Welsh flair again surfaced, like cream, to earn their thirteenth 'Triple Crown', thereby equalling England's record at beating the other 'home' countries. But by then the Welsh players' thoughts were already turning towards the meeting with the unbeaten French at Cardiff two weeks later. They were right to be cautious; it was to be one of the fiercest, most closely fought matches of the European Championship.

On a beautiful day which resembled early spring, France made a storming start. Fenwick lost the ball as he tried to wriggle from Bertranne's tackle, Romeu swept up the pass and raced away to put the flying Gourdon over for a try in the corner. Romeu converted with a majestic kick and France led 6–0 after five minutes. But Welsh resolve was not shaken. Bennett kicked two penalties, Martin, another, and J. J. Williams scored a try, before Romeu's penalty made it 13–9 at the interval.

The match was as neatly balanced as a piece of cotton sliding through the eye of a needle. Fenwick's penalty stretched the Welsh lead; Averous' try, from a clever kick ahead by Aguirre, kept France in contention at 16–13. Wales, in growing control, seemed certain to pull clear of the Frenchmen; but Rives remembers: "We maintained our work in every department of the play. Our forwards kept winning the ball and the backs used it intelligently. We felt we could yet win the match; we knew it would be very close and the Welsh would not be able to pull away. We would not let them."

When Fenwick kicked another penalty, with fourteen minutes remaining, the French task seemed huge. But quite suddenly, France dragged up hidden reserves of strength and determination, all but dissipating Welsh control. Sustained by the power of their forwards, the French pounded at the Welsh line almost incessantly throughout the final twelve minutes. Wales, it seemed, must break.

The decisive moment came on the right touchline. Gourdon,

short of space but not speed, took the ball from a thrust close to the line and dashed towards the Welsh goal line. As he prepared to launch himself in a dive to score, J. P. R. Williams, the magnificent Welsh full-back, appeared, like a tank, to shoulder-charge the French wing into touch, a yard short. Williams' whole body vibrated from the impact as he stood, rock like, by the corner flag. Gourdon crashed into touch, Williams clenched his fists with the tension, and Wales had survived France's final gambit.

France was beaten; the Grand Slam joined the Triple Crown in Welsh hands. Not until the two sides met again in Paris, eleven months later, would Europe see a closer, harder struggle. None of the other European countries could approach them for quality or strength.

France ended that season in style, scoring six tries in an exhibition style romp in Paris, against England, for a 30–9 victory. On a short tour that summer, the Frenchmen beat the USA by 33–14 in Chicago.

Of the eight matches played, Rives had appeared in every one, and his partnership with his club colleague Jean-Claude Skrela was now as respected throughout Europe as it was in France. Gareth Edwards rated it the finest flank forward partnership he ever encountered, beating, albeit marginally, the Springboks Piet Greyling and Jan Ellis of the late 1960s and early 1970s. Edwards said: "Rives and Skrela were different types of player although both had certain qualities. Skrela would knock people down and Rives would be in there to take it on. Sometimes, it was the other way round.

"It was a bit like Ian Rush and Kenny Dalglish, the Liverpool footballers. You couldn't say which was the better. One needed the other. But the Frenchmen were the best combination I played against. I like the back rows to be a unit, and to complement one another. It is no good just having the three best players in the world because that wouldn't necessarily work. In South Africa, for a special tour I was on once, we had a back row of Rives, Alan Sutherland and Ian Kirkpatrick. They were certainly the best flankers in the world at the time, Rives and Kirkpatrick, but the back row definitely wasn't the best unit, just because of that. It would not have been any good to France to have Skrela tackling everything in sight but no-one there to assist or take the ball on."

In 1975, Edwards had watched, fascinated, "this good-looking blond-haired player who looked more like a pop star than a rugby player. A lot of people thought early on it was more of a gimmick because he wasn't really good enough. But they soon changed that view. He was always first to the ball, and always brave. Only in his last year, when he started to get caught a little, was he showing signs of losing some speed.

"But in 1976 in the Grand Slam decider in Cardiff, we had a hell of a hard game against France. It was the heaviest pack I ever came across and probably one of the hardest matches I ever played. We put twenty minutes of real pressure on them but they rode it until half time. I thought, if we scored, we would be through them but we couldn't get that vital score.

"It was like two heavyweight boxers hitting each other. Neither could quite deliver the final blow. And even when we put them down on the floor by taking a good lead, we had to hang on late in the contest. It was an excellent French side but I felt it never really stayed together long enough to reach its true potential."

By the start of the following season, 1976–7, it was the turn of the Australians to discover the potency not only of the Rives-Skrela partnership, but of the French pack in general. Certainly, in the first Test of the short tour, Australia's unfancied side went close to producing a surprise, losing 18–15 at Bordeaux. Stubborn defence allied to Paul McLean's excellent goalkicking – he kicked all 15 points for his side with four penalties and a dropped goal – kept the scores close. But the Frenchmen scored three tries to nil, and a week later in Paris, with a stronger side which had six changes from the team in Bordeaux, they overwhelmed the Australians 34–6.

Loane played in both games, two of the twenty-eight caps he was to win between 1973 and 1982. He said years afterwards: "The French completely destroyed us in Paris. It was the most complete humiliation I ever suffered in my career. They had a superb pack and scored six tries that day. It was the best rugby side I ever played against; the best rugby side I have seen.

"They did the whole thing – they destroyed you in the scrums and line-outs by taking you on up front. After that, they let their light troops in to complete the job behind the scrum.

"With what they had in the tight six, Rives and Skrela were dynamite. Both those players would have been great performers even in a pack going backwards. But to have that kind of tight six with those two guys, so superbly mobile: brave, strong athletes tacked on to so formidable a tight six, it was murder; you could not slow them down.

"If you get superiority in the tight six, you can shackle breakaways. But not that day. They were not tiring in the scrums and line-outs so it became a nightmare for us. As a pair, Rives and Skrela would be very hard to beat. The South Africans always told me Skrela was the best player they had ever seen. But both men were extremely fine players and it is unfair to make comparisons."

Thirty minutes into the Paris international, the Australians had seemed to be going well, at 3–3. But the strain up front was already apparent. France was dominating possession, their loose forwards were invincible in partnership with the lively scrum half, Richard Astre, and the threequarters were in their best form. Six tries were scored, four of them within fifteen minutes in a frenetic second-half spell. Only Aguirre's wayward goalkicking – he converted just two tries and could manage no penalty – saved the tourists from a worse defeat. Harize, Averous, Bertranne, Aguirre, Rives and Cholley scored tries, Astre dropped a goal. McLean's two penalties for Australia were as ineffective as some of the Australians' tackles.

The 28-point victory margin was a record for France against any International Board country. It was, too, a splendid aperitif for the season ahead in Europe, even though, fourteen days later, the Frenchmen astonishingly lost 15–12 in Romania. Despite that minor setback, however, France had a side of audacious strength for the first of the Five Nations Championship matches. This was against the Grand Slam holders and defending Champions, Wales, in Paris.

In little more than a year since his debut on the international arena, Jean-Pierre Rives had made a marvellous impression. Jean Michel Aguirre, his colleague at Toulouse University years earlier, had also started to earn regular French caps, first as deputy for the injured Droitecourt at Cardiff in 1976, and then against England a fortnight later, and against Australia, in Paris. Thereafter, Aguirre's place was secure for the 1977 season.

Aguirre, however, had already noticed a change in the style of his colleague and friend. He said: "You could always see Jean-Pierre had a great talent for the game. He was a super player; always tackling, always very close to the ball. His defence was so good. His presence, too; he was present on the ground, every-where. He would catch the ball, give the ball, tackle; his was a very big presence on the game.

"But he changed his style of play when he became a French international.

"I do not know why; perhaps it was the different system of game he met. With Toulouse, he would combine brilliantly with Skrela in attack but for France, afterwards, he became less attacking. He was a different player for his country but what we have to say is whether he was efficient or not. Clearly, the answer was 'yes'."

The All Black hooker Andy Dalton, who was to face Rives in 1979 in the famous series in New Zealand, said: "The French style of forward play in the mid-1970s suited Jean-Pierre to a tee. His commitment was greater than just about any other player I could name. His play on the flank ensured reward for the tight forward effort."

Others, closer to home, believed Rives had already played his finest match for his country, even though his career was still in its infancy at international level. Michel Palmié, the strong Beziers lock forward, said: "I think the best game Jean-Pierre Rives played for France was against Wales in Cardiff in 1976. In the last quarter of an hour, the crowd in Cardiff did not sing at all because that day we lost by six points but could well have won. Five minutes from the end we had a five-metre scrum near the Welsh goal line. We pushed the scrum, we took the Welsh ball and Gourdon so nearly scored.

"I think that is the best memory of all the guys who saw Rives that day. We had a very good match and it was that day we realised our team had enormous potential. And when we saw Jean-Pierre Rives tackling J. P. R. Williams with such force, everyone was motivated.

"It was a defeat for France but a victory in a way because we returned to win the next year against Wales in Paris. But it was that match in Cardiff which had a deep effect. To be so close to winning in the last five minutes against such a good Welsh side, was fabulous. And that word would fit Rives' performance too. He was outstanding that day."

Already, his colleagues had noticed and respected the many facets of Rives. Jean-Pierre Bastiat, the No. 8 in the French sides of that era between Rives and Skrela, says: "For me, his best qualities were not of speed, endurance or anything like that. Jean-Pierre would take on one small man, one large, throw himself at ten, get up from under eight. He had a special ferocity in battle and always threw himself into the fray with whatever means he had. That I would say was what was exceptional about him.

"All people who play rugby at whatever level are brave, or they wouldn't play rugby. They would play badminton, or something. I think that courage is something else. But to be a kamikaze like Jean-Pierre was something different again. The only player who resembles him now is Philippe Dintrans. He's a similar boy. But Dintrans is not able to reveal himself outwardly, like Jean-Pierre Rives, because he is more restrained. Jean-Pierre was more often the first, more combative, picking up the ball more often."

Watching the young Rives enhance his growing reputation, like a politician making his name with the correct moves, was Jean Salut, who finally retired in 1975. Salut highlighted the evolution in Rives' game, from reckless youngster indulging his sporting fantasy to international rugby player, aware to a greater extent of the requirements of his colleagues and the side.

"Jean-Pierre was certainly more defensive than I was," said Salut. "I was more of an attacking player but he chose that medium because modern times demanded it. I think that if he had played in my era, he would have played like me, much more attacking.

"In a sense, we were not so different because we played in the same position, had the same level of game and the same 'British' style. But Jean-Pierre didn't copy my style of play."

The same 'British' style. Even at this initial stage in an international career which was to span another eight years, Rives, the Corinthian figure, had started to emerge. The open, honest sportsman; in love with the game, for the sake of its spirit, its friendship. His humour was already apparent, a fact confirmed by his escapade in London the day before his first cap. Now, the immense responsibilities which he would carry for the final six years of his career, were beginning to gain credence in his mind. He became aware of other matters pertaining to the game, even the political machinations from which French rugby is seldom divorced. The revolutionary had been born.

Years later he reflected wryly on the differences between the British and French tradition and spirit, and recounted a long-famous saying: "If you want to interest a Frenchman in a game, you tell him it's a war. But if you want to interest an Englishman in a war, you tell him it's a game.''

And another 'English' joke. ''In 1975, when I made my debut at Twickenham, it was windy. In 1983, for my last game there, it was windy, too. Just one question – between those dates, did the wind stop, or not?!!''

The match in Paris was confidently expected to be the decisive encounter of the International season. The clash of Trojan horses, the jarring of muscles and bone. Cardiff, a year earlier, had hinted at the less savoury elements of such encounters, when tension and expectation act as catalysts to violence.

Even the Welsh, hardly the choirboys of the international game, blanched at some of the treatment meted out, in the name of commitment and purpose. The Pontypool prop forward Graham Price, no stranger to the taste of blood and the locking of horns in combat, would talk, years later, of the giant French prop forward, Gerard Cholley, a former boxer, calling instinctively occasionally on old skills at the height of a battle.

Price knew about Cholley; he had left the field, at Cardiff in 1976, terrified by blindness which was to last twelve hours and more, after the Frenchman had poked fingers into the Welshman's eyes and scratched the corneas.

''At the first scrum,'' said Price of that match against France, ''Cholley tried a little bit of gouging. The first time was just an attempt. So I bit his thumb as hard as I could in a scrum. I could hear him squealing as I did it. I damn nearly took off the whole thumb.''

Cholley took a reprisal. ''In went his fingers at a maul,'' said Price, ''and I felt the nails scratching hard at the eyeballs. It was murderous. By his sheer physical size, Cholley could do such things and defy you to do anything back at him. That time, I could not do anything because I could not see anything. I did not go to the dinner that night because I was blinded. I had to be driven home and helped to bed.''

Eye-gouging was not the only trick. Players caught in rucks or mauls risked any method of assault. Squeezing of the testicles was a favourite trick, said Price, adding, ''There was too much adrenalin flowing at times. Trampling was another favourite method. I experienced that from a certain French player, apart from Cholley.''

Price's criticisms were made long after the match. But it was significant that, once Rives took over the captaincy of France in 1979, such incidents became altogether rarer. "Thanks to him," said Salut, choosing his words carefully, "French rugby has become more British. One thought that, before him, rugby was a game for hooligans in France. That people thought badly of the game. He gave an extraordinary image to French rugby – that was the best thing he did in all his career."

But in Paris, that February day of 1977, such thoughts about Jean-Pierre Rives were far from the players' minds. Cardiff, the previous winter, was more prominently in the thoughts of many, such as Price himself. The Welshman was again matched by a formidable French front row; Cholley, Paco and Paparemborde. "Paparemborde always struck me as a guy who would do his job properly. He was a good enough player not to have to intimidate opponents. I respected him and Alain Paco, the Beziers hooker. Cholley didn't have much technique but he caused me the most difficulty. For a tall man (and they don't usually make good props), he was so strong. Against Cholley I had to give everything in every single scrum to hold him."

France made four changes for the game from the side which had lost in Bucharest before Christmas. Imbernon and Palmié formed the engine-room department, Romeu and Fouroux returned at half-back. Shrewd veterans of Parc des Princes said that the French selectors had chosen their side with half a mind on the laundry bill – they were only going to get ten shirts dirty! The backs, they claimed, were there only to make up the numbers.

On the Welsh side Jeff Squire wore the No. 8 jersey, vacated so tragically the previous season when Mervyn Davies was carried from the field during a club match, the victim of a brain haemorrhage from which he was fortunate to recover. There were still some sterling performers although question marks probably hovered over a few ageing forwards. In the event, it was up front that France was stronger and, behind a pack which was always under strong pressure, Wales was unable to get the best out of Gareth Edwards while the wily Fouroux, berating his enormous forwards like a schoolmistress admonishing her naughty pupils, drove his men on.

At half-time the scores were level 3–3, but Wales were all but exhausted by repulsing the persistent attacks. The mighty French front five ground down their opponents; Rives and Skrela roamed everywhere in search of the loose ball, and the 6ft 6ins Bastiat dominated the back of the line-outs. There was no peace, not a moment of respite for the pressurized Welsh.

Soon after half time, Wales lost one potential match winner, Gerald Davies, through concussion. Surprisingly, Fenwick's second penalty of the match gave Wales a 6–3 advantage; yet the desperate fingers being applied to the dyke could not hold the breach. Skrela forced his way over for the first try, Harize dashed in for another. Romeu converted the first to add to his two penalty goals. Fenwick's late goal could give no reprieve to the gallant Welshmen and the French had won by 16 points to 9. But nor did they emerge unscathed from one of the hardest matches Europe had known. Paparemborde, his chubby oval face soaked in perspiration, was ill in the dressing-room afterwards and, even hours later, Skrela was so affected by fatigue that he had to leave the banquet early and go straight to bed.

At Twickenham, two weeks later, England posed a radically different proposition. The English had not the quality of the Welsh, but Twickenham had never been an easy venue for the French. This time the giant Bastiat met his match in the line-outs with the Moseley lock Nigel Horton, later to join Rives' club in France, in supreme form. Taking their cue from Horton, the English pack rallied bravely yet to little avail. The old English habit of creating and squandering scoring chances was to prove expensive in a tight match. France won 4–3 and Rives commented years later: "We were lucky to win at Twickenham. England were a good side but perhaps did not know it".

Even the French try owed much to fortune, for, as one of its creators, Jean Michel Aguirre, revealed later in his career: "It was not a try, it should not have been allowed. Fouroux passed to Averous on the blind side, after a ruck, but my pass on to Sangalli, who scored, was forward."

Aguirre was disinclined to say as much after the game itself because of the reception the French had received at Twickenham. He said: "The English people were very hostile. When we ran on to the ground at Twickenham there was much booing and also spitting at us. It was a very bad example for the English public to give. That was why I said nothing when I gave the pass – I remembered that reception we had been given."

Rives said little afterwards about the controversial reception. He was in no position to do so; Fouroux was the captain. But after he retired, Rives recalled the match and blamed the former Welsh No. 8, Mervyn Davies, for what happened.

"Davies wrote in an English newspaper about our team," said Rives. "He claimed we were dirty, were not playing good rugby; there was too much concentration on the forwards and our play was not good. He said we were highly physical. Bad allegations which the people in England read. It gave us a bad name, and unfairly so. All the players were really affected by it.

"It is difficult to win the Grand Slam; you need a very strong team to win it. We wanted to succeed very much in 1977 perhaps because of what people said. Hearing criticisms made like those of Davies made us work even harder. It was not pleasant to read such things from a former player. I was surprised perhaps but mostly disappointed that another player should say such things.

"Rugby is like cooking – you do not have just two certain ingredients. You need to add many things to have the best dish – spice, quality, spirit and a little 'je ne sais quoi'. Sometimes you must have a little more passing, a little more kicking – it is never all passing or all kicking. You have to enjoy yourself, too."

But if France was a shade fortunate to triumph at Twickenham, the 23–3 win over Scotland in Paris owed nothing to chance. Again, as in the earlier matches, Rives and Skrela led the French forays which caused much havoc in the opposing defence. France scored four tries, through Paco, Harize, Bertranne and Paparemborde. Romeu converted two and landed a penalty goal, against Irvine's penalty goal for Scotland. The Scots were soundly beaten but, as at Cardiff the previous year, the unsavoury aspect of the French forward play dominated most of the discussion after the game.

Cholley was once more involved, one paper talking of French 'brutality'. Early in the match, Cholley laid low the Scottish No. 8 MacDonald with a punch which caught the player flush on the jaw. On two further occasions, Cholley was in trouble with the Welsh official Meirion Joseph who claimed later he had not witnessed the first punch. Had he done so, Cholley could have been sent from the field.

The violence was overdone and unnecessary. Such actions justified the opinions, in some excitable quarters, that the French were steamrollering their way to a Grand Slam by foul play and illegal methods. Such was not the case, generally speaking; yet isolated and crude incidents did the French cause a disservice.

Such acts stained the good name of the noble game. Only one or two players were involved, yet others, perfectly innocent, found themselves tarred with the same brush. It was a pity that firmer action against the offenders was not taken by the French hierarchy.

Certainly, a Grand Slam is the summit of the European rugby achievement. It is a magnificent, ferocious journey through the might of British and French rugby to a peak of success; the scalps of all four challengers. It is a rare, monumental honour. Not for fifty-eight years has a nation won the famous 'Slam' and then repeated the achievement the following season.

The final match of the season was in Dublin. France travelled with a remarkable record to protect; they had still to concede a try. Jean-Pierre Bastiat highlighted the point: "We must have tackled very well to have that record".

Tackle, they certainly did, those two terriers on either flank. Rives and Skrela roamed like a pair of hyenas, snaffling off the loose bits and cutting down opponents. It was consistent, utterly ruthless, born of supreme fitness, speed and intelligence. The perfect foil, as we have seen, for a heavyweight forward pack which could take control in the tight. With two such players for the loose, France possessed just about the perfect pack of forwards.

Bastiat said: "In that side of 1977, each position was filled by players of prime importance. You could not find a better front row at that time anywhere in France, or even now, years later. Then we had a second row – the tractors – who were really the best in the Championship.

"In the third row, we had very distinct roles. That's to say that I, personally, at No. 8, effectively had the role of getting the ball, to be a supplier of the ball. Rives and Skrela who were at my side were the guard dogs of the flock; they systematically confined the scrum half, the half-backs, the centres, wings; they were there to break up whatever happened.

"I must say that Jean-Pierre gave an extraordinary performance because he took on his opponents in large quantities. He recovered an enormous number of balls which had gone loose on the ground and that enabled us to maintain the momentum of our attacks, through the forwards or the backs.

"Yet, at times, I agreed with those people who said Jean-Claude Skrela was the best flanker ever to play for France. In 1977–8, he was, I believe, better than Jean-Pierre Rives. But Jean-Claude had superior means: he was bigger, taller, faster, stronger. He had superior physical qualities. But Skrela, like me, had disadvantages because he didn't have blond hair like Jean-Pierre and on the television, we went much more unseen! No, Jean-Pierre's role was also of prime importance."

But men like Salut had spied the change in Rives, from his style as a young player at Toulouse. His game had altered. But how, and why?

Michel Palmié, later to become a valued friend of Rives, said: "In 1977, Jean-Pierre was not captain; he was a simple soldier. Each player had a well-defined role in that team. Rives and Skrela were the men to retrieve the ball. It was a covering role, but they didn't really like playing the forward game.

"Jean-Pierre was obliged to play in that way. I think he had other seasons which were more complete in a rugby sense for him personally, where he was obliged to set an example, to be captain and so to show on the field what he was going to do. In 1977 his was a well-defined role; it wasn't a complete role but it was the role he had to play in that team and he played it very well."

The captain of that side, Jacques Fouroux, was equally aware of Rives' contribution. "Jean-Pierre always performed beyond his maximum. He was a boy who always had the privilege of enjoying the admiration of his opponents as much as his teammates and that is very rare. You always have a few friends who like you very much and others who find faults in you. But Jean-Pierre earned respect from everyone because he was always over his maximum. He played very well all the time. When everyone else gave 15 out of 20, he gave 22 out of 20."

Rives' close colleague, Skrela, saw the change in his friend from early times in club rugby. Skrela said: "Jean-Pierre did change when he started playing for the national side, from an attacking player to a more defensive role. He adapted because he had to do so in whatever team he played. I, too, had to adapt, because I was more attacking than defensive and I had to change.

"I think the back rows of that time became more important in the play of teams. We became the players who hindered the opponents' play and so we had to transform ourselves into defenders. We tackled all the players who had the ball and it is that perhaps which caused the change in Jean-Pierre and for me in the game. It was because of that evolution that he changed from an attacking player to a more defensive one."

And Jo Maso, that lover of creative, open play, put the point succinctly. "The team of 1977 changed Jean-Pierre's style of play. He was obliged to play a much more defensive style and he was a prisoner of that. When he was a young boy, he was a very good attacking player; he knew nothing of defence, only attack. But in 1977 all the papers said what a wonderful tackler he was, but afterwards he was a prisoner of all that. I know he would have preferred to play another style."

That alteration in Rives' style, the willingness to allow himself to change as a player, is the only criticism Maso makes of his friend. "The only small reproach one could make about him is of being a prisoner of his defensive game. He was capable of playing an attacking game but he couldn't extricate himself from this defensive game. Who was to blame for that? Oh, I think it was the game of the team in general which caused it. It was the team of 1977 which practised this game of aggressive defence. The media, the journalists, saw him as a player like that and he was all the time obliged to defend, to tackle, to search for the wings in order to tackle them. He forgot a little the attacking game. But they wanted him to play like that and he played perfectly. He was capable but he was a prisoner in his head of the other game."

Such thoughts, of course, even in Rives' own mind, were buried as France prepared for the final leg of their attempt on the Grand Slam, against Ireland in Dublin. Nor did the Frenchmen travel overloaded with confidence.

It was ten years since they had won in Dublin. Furthermore, Ireland had lost all three matches in the Championship and, should they fall to the French, faced the ignominy of the Wooden Spoon. Irish pride, reasoned the French, was sufficiently spicy to ensure a hard match.

Such thoughts seemed highly pertinent when Ireland led 6–3 at half-time, penalties by Gibson and Quinn, against one by Romeu. Duggan led the Irish rearguard action with a selfless workrate and his usual disregard for personal safety.

Fergus Slattery, his back-row colleague, recalls: "The first time Rives played in Dublin, back in 1975, we beat France comprehensively, 25–6. Jean-Pierre went sideways that day, and the French team did, too.

"But in 1977, it was a lot different. He was outstanding for the French team; he was a very brave player, he tackled well and worked hard. He was very strong, too, and put players down on their backs.

"Skrela was regarded as the better player of the two at that time yet I always felt I could mess him around by hustling and jostling him and hitting him physically. In other words, you could knock him off his game and make him feel bad. But you wouldn't do that with Rives. On a losing side, Skrela would not be seen, but Rives, he was very different. You saw him all the time.

"It didn't matter how France did. From 1976 to 1979, Rives played very, very well in every match. It's the hardest thing in the world to play well as a back row forward if your pack is being beaten but Rives did that."

In the second half now in Dublin, Aguirre's penalty soon levelled the scores at 6–6. The stage was set for a finish suitable for a Grand Slam decider. The try which decided the match was certainly apt, a flowing seventy-five-yard move which started on the French 22. Averous and Sangalli combined to get Aguirre away down the heart of the field, in space which had seldom been apparent earlier. The full-back at last reached the cover but found, astonishingly, his hooker, Paco, up for the pass. Paco transferred quickly to Bastiat and the huge French No. 8, legs working like a cantering horse, raced twenty-five yards to score. Aguirre converted and added another penalty; and France had won only her second Grand Slam in history, by 15 points to 6.

Dublin is a city where people need little invitation to join celebrations, of whatever kind. So the French found their Irish rivals raising glasses with almost equal endeavour that long night. "In Dublin," said Slattery, "I saw Jean-Pierre plastered. It was different in Paris; he would stay in control, steadfast, demure. But away from France it could be different."

The closing of another European Five Nations Championship was by no means the end of France's programme for that year. Three months later, with only minor changes from the Grand Slam side, France was in Buenos Aires to beat Argentina, 26–3. Yet less than a week later, the Argentines produced one of the greatest comebacks the game has ever documented, by holding the French to an 18–18 draw in the second Test.

Yet even this far from Europe the grumblings about French play, the style used, the brutality too often displayed and general air of unpleasantness, rumbled on.

The chief criticism concerned France's dull, unadventurous approach. It was the quintessential ten-man rugby style; a strong pack of forwards dominating possession and feeding a powerful kicker, in this case Jean-Pierre Romeu, at fly half. Little else was seen of the French. In the first Test, Romeu booted France clear with four penalty goals and a dropped goal before 'the light troops', as Mark Loane had termed them, came in for some fringe action.

In the second international, it was even worse. The mood was sultry and unpleasant, the action frequently beyond the limits of natural aggression. The English referee, Roger Quittenton, found himself trying to tame an ugly scrap, and awarded 37 penalties in the process. It was a physical clash which soured the name of true rugby. The final score? A French newspaper got it right, the next day, by leading the report with the line 'Aguirre 18, Porta 18, Rugby 0'. Both kickers had landed six penalty goals apiece to level the match at the end. In a sense, justice had been done, for neither side deserved to win so ill-disciplined, bad-tempered a match. It was the first time that the French had failed to beat Argentina.

Typically, Jean-Pierre Rives was nominated the outstanding player of the tour; a fine example of a quality flank forward, with Skrela on that tour clearly second best by the standards of his younger colleague.

Rives, as was his habit, detached himself from the acrimonious goings-on. As the Irish flanker Slattery said: "He wouldn't get involved, he would stay out of trouble in matches. He was prepared to take plenty of stick, but you never saw Jean-Pierre in the middle of players throwing his fists around at opponents. It simply wasn't his way."

Why? Because it would have disgraced the name of the game he loved. The game, he said so often, was for spirit, for taking pleasure and giving pleasure to others. No romantic could associate himself with the darker side of the game, even if it existed. Rives' detachment from such incidents was to mark him down in the minds of officials as a cool, calming influence on often volatile French characters. Two years later, when it came to choosing a new captain of France, such qualities were rekindled in the minds of the French selectors.

Only once, in a long career spanning more than fifteen years, did Rives crack in anger. Even today, the memory is sharp, because of the rarity of the act which took place during a club match for Stade Toulousain at Avignon many years before; a match which matched the dull, dismal day. The game soon became as ill-tempered and bitter as so many French Championship clashes. Then Rives' colleague Skrela was flattened illegally by an opposing forward. A furious Rives completely lost his control. He buried a pounding fist into the face of Skrela's assailant and laid him out. Those players who saw it still bear testimony to the power and precision of the blow, flush on the jaw of the target.

But remorse swiftly followed. Rives apologised profusely in the dressing-room afterwards and still regrets his action. "It is not something of which I am proud. I cannot say it did not happen but I do not like to remember it," he said.

Outside the dressing-room a crowd of Avignon supporters saw Rives emerge to lift a small child into his arms, as he fielded questions from local journalists eager to dissect the whole affair.

The little boy, cradled in the player's arms, was drawn closer and Rives whispered in his ear, "Don't you ever play rugby like today, eh?" It was a moment of the real Rives, a glimpse of the true man.

A few years later, in another rare example of annoyance on his part, Rives had walked off the aircraft carrying Fouroux's victorious side home from Dublin, after that 1977 Grand Slam success. A supporter waiting at the airport shouted out: "Rives, you are the greatest".

The man of Toulouse half-turned, almost a sneer across his face, as he replied: "What are the others – rubbish?"

Before the end of that notable year, France met a team raised by their President from players around the world. The match, in Paris in October, was influenced by two factors – the French public's dislike of charity matches, particularly before Christmas, and a growing animosity towards a national side which had produced rugby based almost exclusively on the forward effort. A paltry 13,850 spectators saw the 'World XV', with players from New

Zealand, Australia, South Africa, Italy and every British nation, lose 29–18 to the French. Rives was one of five stars missing from the Grand Slam side.

The game provided a useful warm-up for the French, before their two-match international series with the visiting New Zealand All Blacks in November. The tourists, led by Graham Mourie, played the first Test in Toulouse, going into the match unbeaten after their first six provincial games.

Neither Rives nor Bastiat could play in either Test due to injury and perhaps both were better off out of it. Once more, the French method was drab, lacking in adventure, and a parody of their reputation for vibrant play.

Mourie, writing some years later in his autobiography *Graham Mourie Captain*, said: "The game was brutal, the French pack utilising the talents of prop Gerard Cholley, a former champion boxer, as much as they could, as well as the pugilistic talents of their two locks, Michel Palmié and Jean-François Imbernon, who would never have been let into a ring under Marquess of Queensberry rules. John West (the Irish referee), contrary to his later Test performances, seemed to be out of his depth and the French took advantage of this to attempt to intimidate us further."

Midway through the second half, another off-the-ball incident sent the rugged New Zealand prop Gary Knight stumbling from the field. Later still, Bryan (B. G.) Williams was carried off to hospital with a dislocated hip although his injury was a complete accident.

New Zealand somehow contrived to squander a 13–6 lead in the second half and go down to defeat by 18 points to 13. It was a thoroughly uncharacteristic decline by an All Blacks side which allowed the French to take victory in the first game of the series.

But All Blacks, like wounded bulls, have a habit of showing life when terminal illness has been diagnosed. One week later in Paris, the New Zealanders, raising their game splendidly, took on the French up front and showed far greater versatility and purpose behind the scrum. Their control of the match was seldom threatened and they finished comfortable 15–3 winners.

During the match, there was the quite extraordinary sight of French supporters cheering the All Blacks when they scored the only try of the game in the second half. A week earlier, in

Toulouse, sections of the crowd had demanded the sacking of the man generally credited with the introduction of the contentious forward style, Jacques Fouroux.

Clearly, the honeymoon was over. Less than eight months after France had won the Grand Slam, indeed in the same year, French supporters were seeking the head of Fouroux, the little general, le petit Napoleon, the 5ft 5ins man from Auch. Could it have happened anywhere but France?

Albert Ferrasse, the President of the Federation Française de Rugby (FFR), had listened impassively to the ironic cheers for the New Zealanders and jeers for his own men. Already, his hand was moving towards the axe. Fouroux stayed for one more match, the game against Romania, in Clermont-Ferrand on 10 December 1977. As Jean-Pierre Rives jokingly said afterwards: "We gave Jacques a real send off – we beat Romania by a very big score, 9–6. We won through a last-minute penalty goal by Romeu, his third of the match. But Jacques had spoken with real feeling before the start of that game – it was a special occasion for all the players who had been with him through that remarkable year. Jacques Fouroux had led us to the Grand Slam. We remembered that and what he had done for all of us."

Fouroux had made his debut in 1972; he won twenty-eight caps through to the end of 1977. But in the year of his greatest triumph, at the age of thirty, he was hastily jettisoned by the alarmed French selectors. Never again would Fouroux play for France although his influence was to be considerable for the foreseeable future, as coach and selector.

Two of the All Blacks involved in the series with France that year, Bryan Williams and Andy Haden, recalled their thoughts of Rives and of specific incidents. Williams said: "Jean-Pierre played a big part in French fortunes but you have to remember he came into a pretty good side anyway in the 1970s. He had a good grounding but he carried it on brilliantly when he was made skipper. As a winger, I counted myself lucky I did not usually come into direct contact with Rives in the course of a game.

"By himself, Jean-Pierre changed the pattern of rugby in the 1970s with his speed and mobility as a lightweight loose forward. Once he was on the ball, he could dictate exactly what the team was going to do next.

"He was a player with tremendous courage; how often did we

see blood pouring down the side of his face? But he was also a great sportsman. He wasn't just a rough and tumble man but an intelligent, articulate person. Rives and Mourie were very similar in terms of style and tempo.

"You would often see Graham or Jean-Pierre smile when one had beaten the other to a loose ball. They both had a tremendous capacity to pat each other on the back and that is great for the game."

Haden, that giant of a man from New Zealand's North Island who has enraged officials the world over but charmed so many friends and followers of the game, recalls a story from Toulouse, after France's win in the first Test of the 1977 series.

Haden said: "Jean-Pierre took Stu Wilson and myself to a 'do' after the game. He was the life and soul of the party, what with his piano playing and everything. He kept commiserating with us and saying we had some good young players but there was no side that could hold France at that time because they had such a formidable team. But a week later we thrashed the French in Paris and Jean-Pierre came up to me and said 'It's not possible, it's just not possible'.

"But the whole situation was reversed two years later when we beat them at Christchurch and I consoled Rives by telling him the French hadn't played badly but we had played exceptionally well. However, when they hammered us at Eden Park seven days later, Rives gave me a big smile when I said to him: 'It's not possible, Jean-Pierre; it's just not possible'."

Haden too saw the close links between the Frenchman and Graham Mourie. "He played the same game as Mourie. Above and beyond his physique and aggressive effectiveness, he was a great thinker . . . a real mental giant of the game. And he certainly added a new dimension to loose forward play."

So 1977 at last drew its curtain on the game in France: a Grand Slam, a shared series with the All Blacks, a series win in Argentina; another win for Beziers, by 12 points to 4 over Perpignan, in the final of the French Championship. Stade Toulousain, for all the contribution of Rives and Skrela, failed even to reach the quarter-final stages, losing 17–16 to RRC Nice.

The omens were hardly auspicious for those who sought an end to the all-conquering forward play. France, herself the Five Nations Champions; Beziers, king of French club rugby; both had achieved their successes through concentration on rugged forward play and a big kicking half-back, a style totally alien to French rugby men. A colossal explosion of anger was about to take place.

"To keep that special spirit"

*"Oh East is East and West is West
and never the twain shall meet."*
——RUDYARD KIPLING——
1865–1936

Toulouse stands as a major crossing point for travellers and rugbymen alike in the heart of the Haute Garonne. A drive of scarcely more than one hour and a half can take one to the first beaches of the Mediterranean; less, to the ancient city of Carcassonne – which dates in part from the third century – and through the vineyards of the Corbières region which produce traditionally robust red wines that possess an earthy, full bouquet. At the eastern extremity of the snaking motorway that links the Mediterranean and the Bay of Biscay, stands Narbonne. But inland, the city of paramount importance in the region is Toulouse itself, a city of grand Renaissance architecture, with the exquisite St Simon church as a focal point of historical and religious interest: a city of cathedrals, basilicas and museums; and of wide, open spaces and elegant squares. On summer evenings, violinists play, pavement cafés offer seats, from which one can surmise the principal activities of the Toulousains. It is a place of pleasing ambiance and excellent restaurants.

On a rugby map of the south of France clubs, Toulouse is a border town which divides the clubs of the Mediterranean – like Beziers, Perpignan, Nice and Toulon – from others dotted along the fringes of the Pyrenean foothills – Pau, Lourdes, Bagnères and Bayonne.

Dax and Biarritz in the west fall firmly within the latter group; others, like Agen, Montferrand, Angoulême, Brive and Grenoble, divide into categories between the two. More still, like Mont-de-Marsan, close to Dax in the beautiful Landes region of the west, ally themselves decisively with the open, attacking rugby philosophy.

The regions are important, for they significantly marked the dividing lines between the two styles of the game in France in 1977. The game found itself partitioned by the success of Fouroux's side in clinching the Grand Slam.

In one camp, there was celebration at the first 'Grand Chelem' since Christian Carrière's side had succeeded in 1968. But the hum of satisfaction was far outweighed by heavy storm-clouds of criticism, rolling up at the manner of its achievement. Old romantics of the south-west, rugby folk weaned on the exploits of figures like the Boniface brothers, Christian Darrouy and Jean Gachassin, condemned it as an abortion of the game, a cheap promiscuous method of attaining success without regard for style. And style, chic, elegance, has always formed an integral part of French life; from the courtier, to the fashion designer, to sportsmen and sportswomen.

Such people bemoaned the dominance of Beziers, with its predilection for powerful, intimidating forwards capable of starving opponents of the ball and largely negating the sparkling runners in an opposing back division. Raoul Barrière, coach to the Beziers club, ignored the rumpus with Churchillian disdain.

Inveterate defenders of the true faith, the free, enterprising approach to the game, talked of success at any price. But what a price! From the opposite camp came cogent arguments justifying the project as a necessary adaptation to modern trends. 'Oh East is East and West is West and never the twain shall meet' wrote Kipling. His words could almost have been devised to encapsulate the rift in French rugby circles!

It is some measure of the divisions the furore created that, even today, one can still detect the faint rumblings in the French game. In 1985, for example, Beziers' ageing players pitted once again their simplistic, ruthless style against the more adventurous approach of the Stade Toulousain club.

Beziers' sheer physical aspect was the supreme factor. How would Toulouse cope? With what rapier could they repel the crude thrusts of their rivals? Seldom was violence far from the surface. The laws against physical intimidation were stretched to the limit.

Beziers' law is the law of the jungle. Opponents caught illegally in Beziers' territory expect instant physical retribution. Very simple, perfectly straightforward. And for years it worked.

To succeed against so ferocious an approach it is essential to eliminate every mistake. Each error is potentially a score for such ruthless professional opponents. Little tricks have been honed to perfection over the seasons. Among the forwards, the twisting of the scrum prior to insertion of the ball, creates a delay which will later take its toll on the lighter pack. Beziers' forwards, renowned for years as the hardest unit in the French game, have dominated so many rivals in the final stages of matches; earlier dodges such as the scrum wheel or collapse have frequently contributed handsomely. The sound of horns at the game is akin to the serenade of a bullfight. 'Beziers est au rugby ce que Pigalle est à Paris' claims one banner. Away in the distance, as at so many of the picturesque grounds of the south, towers an elegant, imposing range of mountains; in this case the Pyrenees.

By 1985, however, Beziers' power was on the wane. Toulouse, accepting their opportunities with aplomb, confounded the defending Champions 21–0, on their way to seizing Beziers' crown.

But back in 1977 no such chinks were yet visible in the Beziers' armour. The clubs debated at length yet indecisively the Beziers' style; the failings and attractions of the south-western clubs. It was an argument without resolution or outcome, for the two sides were too firmly entrenched to bridge the gap. Both scorned the other's attitudes. And as Beziers continued to rule the French domestic kingdom one had to concede, whatever one's political colour, the inexorable efficiency of the Beziers system.

Every member of France's Grand Slam winning team of 1977 pondered the merits of the rival claims. But Jean-Pierre Rives was unequivocal in his condemnation of the style. "The joy and pleasure, the fun had gone out of the French game. By that time, I had played more than twenty times for France in full internationals and I think we had lost only five matches. A fine record, and yet not very much to be proud of. In France, the move had been made from just playing to winning rugby, but we had lost the excitement along the way. The fun had gone out of our game, and it was the same in international rugby.

"I like the rugby played by men like Jo Maso – that was real French rugby at its best. Open, attacking play with running and time for handling. But a wing forward's life became nothing but hard work afterwards; work with the forwards. Helping the bigger pack to dominate and so win a game. It was not the way I liked to play the game.

"It had been more enjoyable a few years earlier. Then, the game was played with only two things in mind – pleasure for the spectators and pleasure for the players. But I do not think either the players or the spectators really enjoyed what was by then being presented."

Rives was speaking with sadness in his voice at that time: "Our club Championship showed the way for the French international side. Always the strong, hard teams who always have the biggest pack – like Beziers, Perpignan, Nice, Romans and others – do the best. Beziers has been the most successful side in French rugby for years but they are the poorest side to watch."

As a young man still cherishing images, embracing the fine style of the old French game, Rives found it impossible to contemplate so ignoble a method, a brutal, inglorious approach to a game hitherto of beauty and flair. He was, though, not alone; the New Zealand forward Andy Haden was another player to question that damaging trend within the French game.

Haden and Rives were strong men. They were not weaklings bemoaning the physical excesses which had crept into the game. Yet Haden complained: "When I left France I was very disillusioned because of the amount of violence. Some skills were being compromised because of violence. The French had a great pack but it was above all violent, an intimidating pack. Their level of skill was very low. Rugby needs a good window and the game, especially at international level, is a shop window."

Rives' thoughts at the time were crisp, articulate and positive; but perhaps it is possible to detect his shifting status, closer to the political machinations of the game's hierarchy, in his assessment of that turbulent period years later after his career had ended.

In 1985, he reflected: "France was very divided at that time. There was a big controversy about the game, the style, the forwards. It was open rugby or forward rugby. My feelings now? Open rugby is the best way to score. The best way to play is to win but having said that, I fought a lot for a certain spirit and a certain play. To win is good but, for me, attacking, open rugby is the best way to win. Controversy is not the solution but people did not realise that. To criticise is not the answer; we had to talk and be positive and say 'We are playing and winning. But how?'

"The feeling was great at that time and the style of the French team today is good, maybe because of what we went through in those difficult times. Perhaps France needed to see that other side to force a return to this traditional play which I love. Maybe it was an evolutionary period.

"It was great for me to be involved in the Grand Slam. You can always play better rugby; you can always improve and you must always improve yourself. You do that by playing with spirit and improving your spirit. Many people fought for what we have today and they were right; we could play better. Now, it is much improved.

"But, of course, we must always remember we have to play with a smile in our hearts, all enthusiasm, positive. That is my philosophy of rugby. The game is for the spirit, to improve yourself, to express yourself. To take pleasure from the game; playing the game you love with those you love. It is the idea of improving yourself, playing to enjoy but also learning to love. The game and the people."

Rives expands the point, with compassion and definition. "For me, rugby is a good background because, today in society, you have to share with people. We need communication and, for me, rugby communicates. It is about sharing emotion. You become less afraid of physical contact and you find your mind is opened through contacts and the travelling and meeting people. There is a very good correspondence between life and rugby today; a good balance. The social side of the game in France is the same. OK, there is more pastis than beer but otherwise, it is similar. The singing, the people meeting together after games. But I think that is changing, for a lot of the boys are not drinking so much.

"It has changed a lot in the last ten years; then you were playing by yourself and you felt you had to fight by yourself. Coaches said to you, 'You have to do this and you have to do that', and you did it because of simple belief in authority. But now that is changing; you have to explain to people. They will train harder than before if things are explained but not just for the sake of authority alone. Rather, for a certain idea. It is more interesting because it shows more responsibility for individuals.

"The power of people around the players in the past was too

much. Even today, it still is in certain aspects. All the people in the club, the committee, all the people around – their influence is too strong. Why? Because you have to make sports people responsible, that is a very important thing. I speak about France – maybe it is less in Britain.

''Take any sport. It is between 11 or 13 or 15 players on the field, on opposing sides. At the time those players are involved in the game, they are becoming men. But all the time they are training and the involvement is becoming heavier and heavier. They train three times a week, they play each week, sometimes they play in summer on tour; players in work have to take their holidays when they go on tour. Family life is affected a lot and all this is difficult; very difficult to find a good balance.

''In France, the clubs almost think for the players. They say 'You have to train' and 'You cannot take holidays'. Now, players are playing all over Christmas – even in a professional sport like soccer, the players have their holidays and know when they can take them. For me, it is too much. The way this is all imposed on players is not right. It is not the true objective of sport.

''The real objective of sport is to take some small boys and give them enjoyment, first of all, and make them into men. That is my best definition. Sport allows boys to become men quicker and yet for men to stay a little like children and to enjoy their life, and to have enthusiasm. Today, the enthusiasm is dying. You are the age of your own enthusiasm. But it should not be so because it doesn't matter what age you are as long as you have enthusiasm. In painting, sculpture and such things, men of sixty are only ten in their minds. They are so enthusiastic, there is such curiosity – all the time, they say 'It is lovely, enjoyment'. There is no criticism, nothing like that.

''So, to come back to all the people around rugby, I know they are not paid and they give a lot of time. They say 'We are responsible, we want this and that'. But I don't agree with that; we need to make the sportsmen more responsible, make them more important. Especially if you are becoming a little star of your village, of your town, of your country these people become involved. They say 'Oh, I make your arrangements for this and for that'. It is a social promotion, it is great rugby, but we have to make the players more responsible. Because when the big circus stops at about thirty, so many do not know anything. They are like ten years of age in their minds because these people around the clubs have done too much thinking for them.

"All the management around the clubs and players is too serious. There is too much of this 'Oh, we are in charge', kind of approach. The players should have more say. There needs to be a different spirit from these people; helping, giving, but not taking. It is not a matter of too many of them – you could have double, as long as they had the right spirit.

"Perhaps too many take advantage of the system. They have a very nice jacket with a nice club crest. If they give to the club it is great, but not when it is only authority they can offer.

"My professional job is with Pernod but Pernod gives more consideration to their employees than some people in rugby give to the players at their particular club. Some people think they are the kings at clubs. These people exist through the sport and by the sport and this is a crime. If the sport were to stop, they would be naked. What you need is one passion and a thousand enthusiastic people.

"It is a similar position with coaches. Who could teach playing rugby to Jean Salut or Jo Maso? You can speak about a certain spirit to make players feel they are all together, to help them seek enjoyment together and to make them want to win together; to play with each other and share things together. That is fine – but who could teach anyone to say, we must play this way? All they should do is to try and create those things.

"Something I fight against – and I have made some enemies – is the influence of the physical education teacher in our game. Because they are professionals, they are living through the sport and are making rugby professional, like them. It is not a good thing. If you become professional, you start to create a situation where players have to say 'OK, you are a professional, you say this and as I am a professional, OK, I must do it'. Where is the enjoyment in that for the player?

"I am free and I fight all my life to be free. The freedom of any rugby player, any person, is very, very expensive. I am amateur in my spirit because I think my spirit cannot be bought. It would be too big a price. And, besides, I am not ready to sell. The amateur spirit is, for me, the greatest attraction in life, whatever you are doing.

"Music is very special to me. I was once in a taxi with a musical conductor and he kept whistling the same three notes all the time. After ten minutes I said, 'Why do you keep whistling that? It does not sound good'. But he said, 'When I whistle those notes, I hear an orchestra and it makes me happy'.

''It is the same for me. When I play the piano, no matter how badly, it is my music and I dream about the orchestra playing with me. When I played rugby, I dreamed of being Jean Salut. That is very important. You have to try and do – to succeed is not as important as trying. Besides, you always succeed if you are happy with yourself. I play badly but it makes me happy. What is to succeed? To be recognised or not? No. To try is the most important thing and to be happy trying. To be happy, to be at peace with yourself, to have enjoyment . . . Some people in rugby clubs take things too seriously . . . it is a game, never forget that.

''Rugby is strong, it is a fine sport. But it is only by recognising the problems, the failings, that it will continue to be in good health. People talked about the World Cup and said they were worried about money. But for me, money or not money is not the question. We must try to make some more really interesting competitions like the World Cup, the Five Nations Championship tournament, etc. Why not a European Championship with other countries like Italy, Romania, USSR, Spain involved? Perhaps rugby should be played in the Olympic Games; it is, after all, an amateur game.

''But I am certain of one thing – the season should be shorter. It is too long everywhere in Europe. The players are playing too much – even if they were professionals, it would be too much. Tours are OK and we in France are lucky for we only make short tours. I believe a maximum of four weeks is best. Certainly, on tour is the best time to play because you are in a professional squad system thinking only of rugby. But only for a short time. Besides, French people are really bad tourists. I would not like to have played on a British Lions tour of 11 or 13 weeks. It is much too much. Too much because of the time away and too much because the economic system is difficult – wives and families need more time from their husbands and fathers. It is not good to be away so long.

''But there should be a place for a world-wide World Cup. Rugby needs a world audience. All the countries of the world should play in the rugby World Cup. Maybe there should be a qualifying competition. I would have loved to have played in a World Cup. Certainly, big companies will want to get involved with sponsorship but for me that is not a danger. It is not a choice – we have to do this. The game can remain amateur if we choose a special sort of help. It should not be a problem, as I have said.

"The present French international side has shaken off the problems and controversies of the past. At the international level, which is the most difficult of all, the game has become more exciting to watch. But it is not the same game as in the past, you cannot make comparisons and talk about judging present-day players and games with those of past times. That is because the game has altered. I remember when there were often 100 kicks to touch in a match. I remember when teams also played good rugby and it was no thanks to the rules! It is too easy to say, ten years ago we had better rugby than now. We must be careful not to make this mistake.

"With regard to the 1977 Grand Slam team, some people said 'OK, you won but you gained your success with a certain style and you didn't play very good rugby. It was just the forwards all the time'.

"But when I think about the wonderful time I spent in the French team and all the great people I played with, I have special thoughts from that period. Maybe the rugby was not the best, maybe we should have played another style. But of one thing I am certain – all the players who were together in that side have a special feeling about that year. We were very close together. And I will say now, it would have been an honour for me to play under Raoul Barrier for Beziers because that forward power was one part of the rugby I like. But remember, only one part!

"Beziers could have done much more in their play. Maybe it was boring for people to watch but it was also very difficult to play against. It would have been even more difficult if Beziers had used their threequarters with all the possession they achieved. That would have been formidable."

The debate raged on, creating a dilemma for many players who had taken part in the international team's success. Jean Michel Aguirre, full-back, explained: "Jean-Pierre Rives was right to feel disillusioned with the rugby the French team played that year. After every game, we tried to explain the things the French team did not do; for Toulouse, Skrela and Rives had been magnificent with their attacks from the back row. But with France that year, it was only tackling and defence for them.

"So I feel for Jean-Pierre, it was a problem at the end of the season. It was a problem for me, too, but in the particular style of play used by the French team I had a particular job to do and that was good. But I know I did not touch the ball enough in attack. The coach, 'Toto' Desclaux, and the captain, Jacques Fouroux, wanted to play the way of the hard forwards. Certainly, we had a team where the forwards were very good, very strong and it was good to have them. But in the backs, we were not so bad as people said. However, the forwards were the strongest France had ever known.

"The players in the team accepted playing with this group – by being there, we accepted it. But there were players, just a few of us like Rives, Skrela and myself, who said nothing and played all together for the sake of the team. Why? Because it is important to go on to the field determined to win.

"But I would have liked to see France run with the ball; that is much better. People in half of France said it was not enough to win the Grand Slam that way; we were not accepted by half the country and certainly not by the media, the journalists. But the other people said 'You have won the Grand Slam' – there can be no criticism. True, we won a Grand Slam title and that is not known very often. So that was one positive point.

"But I do not think it was enough.

"Yet for most of the players involved, it was sufficient just to win the Grand Slam. Perhaps for me also, at the time, I do not know. Even to this day, I am uncertain as to what I truly feel. There was the special memory, a title for history, for the future. Can one ignore that? I do not know."

What Aguirre did know was that a real crisis had emerged within the French game. It was split, 50–50. You were either "for" or "against". No in-betweens, no don't knows. He continues: "The best French team was Beziers and their style was the style of the forwards. In 1977, Beziers had been Champions five times in the last six years, so that most of French rugby tried to do what Beziers had done. The French team simply followed the example of Beziers. But that meant there were two rugbys; the rugby of the south-west and the rugby of the Mediterranean. Two different conceptions. Later, the 1981 French Cup final was the meeting of those two conceptions; the small club of the south-west (Bagnères) attacking and trying to run the ball to score tries, against the team of the Mediterranean, Beziers, with the hard play and accent on the forwards. Beziers won.

"But in 1979, Bagnères' style succeeded – they beat Beziers in a quarter-final and reached the final, only to lose to Narbonne, another club of the south-east. It was a very bad final, a very badly behaved crowd. Very bad. I don't wish to be reminded of that match – I prefer to forget it."

Pierre Villepreux then said: "In France, to win is not enough; it is important for the public that French teams play and win in the right manner. Also, it is very important for the media. But 1977 was the Grand Slam of only eight men plus one scrum half and one fly half . . . that was all. It was not the idea we had of French rugby. So France became polarised and, although to a smaller extent, it is still true today. There is a clear distinction between the teams in one area which favour the strong game of the forwards, and other clubs which try to run the ball with flair and movement.

"When I took over as coach at Stade Toulouse in 1982, my first job was to give liberty to the players; to run and to play. I told them, 'Don't be afraid to play'. This is a problem of world rugby, not just France. But the Australians showed what we can do with the ball in the hand when they toured the British Isles in 1984."

For Jo Maso, the idol of creative threequarters young and old, it might seem inevitable that he should criticise the style. But even Maso reveals the indecision, the uncertainty which the debate created when he said: "It is difficult to criticise a team which wins. And perhaps if I had played in that team, I would have said in the end, 'Well we won, and that's best'. But it is true it was not the ideal game for the image of rugby in general.

"Jean-Pierre was, of course, conscious of this and I am sure he would have much preferred to play a game involving the backs, a lot more. But at the same time, he was an intelligent boy, he knew very well the strong point of the team was the forwards and Jacques Fouroux, who was captain, took the decision to play a strong forward game. Despite his disagreement with the approach, he did his maximum so that the team would succeed. Jean-Pierre always did that, whatever the style.

"The problem of the French team is that, although normally the best players are selected, the game depends on the quality of the spirit of those who compose the team. I think the present French team plays good rugby thanks to the quality of players like Codorniou, Blanco, Lescarboura, Sella. They have the qualities to play the game and it is *they* who make the game. One must never forget people like coaches and trainers who are involved in the life of the group in general; but on the field itself, the game belongs to the players. And if the quality of the players is great, that is when one sees great teams.

"At that time, in 1977, I would not run down players like Roland Bertranne or François Sangalli, the two centres in that Grand Slam side; Sangalli was at my club, Narbonne. But they did not have strong enough personalities to pass on to another game. The problem was the personalities of the players who made the game.

"Of course, after 1977 the style of the game changed a little because the players realised they had won the Grand Slam but everyone – the public, the media and many clubs – gave the clear impression that they would have preferred them to lose the Grand Slam but play another style of game. And as Jacques Fouroux and Jean-Pierre Rives were not stupid, they realised it was necessary to do something else and so they tried to make a more interesting game. By doing that, they won the hearts of people; they won the enthusiasm of the public. And that is positive."

Thus we can see how individual events and general trends combined to dismay Rives, the brave adventurer. In 1977, it was the rugby of his national team which so disillusioned him; a trend which was to continue at specific points, during later years too. In addition, the growing power of club officials was clearly to his distaste in the closing years of his playing career.

But every coin has a reverse side, each dark day a glimmer of light and hope. And, typically, Rives experienced the direct opposite of those rugby feelings and styles when he was chosen for the British Barbarians team to play the 1977 British Lions, just six months after France's controversial Grand Slam success.

The match, played at Twickenham in September of that year, was to mark the Silver Jubilee of Queen Elizabeth II, and raise funds for the Jubilee Appeal. Unimportantly the Lions, after enduring every misery imaginable in New Zealand that summer, won the match 23–14. What was of importance, indeed the essence of the occasion, was the spirit which Barbarian rugby has fostered since the club's inception. Rives, as a modern-day philanthropist, revelled in the occasion and the comradeship inherent in the affair. It was a meeting of Rives' British colleagues and friends; and to share the occasion with him, he travelled from the south of France with two honoured colleagues, the remainder of France's Grand Slam back row . . . Jean-Claude Skrela and Jean-Pierre Bastiat. At scrum half for the Barbarians was Rives' great friend, Gareth Edwards. At full-back, another splendid old adversary, J. P. R. Williams.

Bastiat remembered the day, years afterwards, and probed its meaning for Rives. "It was a special memory for every one of us Frenchmen," he said. "To be invited to play in your Queen's Silver Jubilee match, meant a special honour for us. At least, that was how we took it. Jean-Pierre loved it; it was the sense of occasion, the match of great spirit which he enjoyed very much. It was a marvellous moment for all of us."

Rives said: "It meant a lot of things to me, to play for the Barbarians. This game was very, very special. A special spirit. For me, it was like having passed the church every day, and this one time I went inside. The church of rugby. It was a great honour; an event of great spirit."

From this match would emerge the germ of an idea to launch an equivalent club in France, to be known in years to come as the French Barbarians. Rives, inevitably, was the guiding hand behind its creation; the romantic who fell deeply and hopelessly in love with the spirit and cause of the Barbarian approach to rugby football. The club was founded in August 1979.

He said in later years: "The idea for the French Barbarians came from friendship. We played in that match for the 1977 Silver Jubilee but also at that time, the players in the French Grand Slam team of that year said they wanted some team to carry on such great spirit. To show the rest of French rugby this example of that special spirit.

"It seemed a wonderful prospect to create the French Barbarians, a club which reflected friendship and spirit, the finest parts of our game. So we spoke with our President, Albert Ferrasse, and Vice-President, Guy Basquet, and we had great help from the English Barbarians. They said we had to be very careful to look after the spirit; to keep that special spirit. I am very pleased that a Barbarian rugby club now exists in France because it is something for the future. Now the spirit is improving . . . I wanted us to lift up the spirit.

"Today, France and England are closer; the mentality is different particularly in sports, and maybe it has changed because of sport. The French have a lot to learn from the British people – we should listen a lot. We can learn all about sports spirit from the British. And about tradition, too.

"I do not accept what some people say, that England is buried in the past. Tradition is really very important. To define a group. And you need to be defined as a group to fight for an idea. If you destroy the characteristics of your people, of your group, you have no more identification. And if you have lost that, then you are by yourself. And a man alone, by himself, dies because he has no identity, no spirit.

"In this world of terrorism and people being killed, sport and rugby in particular can show people a better way of life. One man who speaks very loud makes more noise than one million. When politics and religion married to produce terrorism, a very bad child was created. We must show that is not the only child now in the world and perhaps teach that child the error of its ways; why it is wrong. Only by friendship, by warmth, humanity and love can we do that. Any sport which shows that feeling has to have an important part to play in the future.

"Rugby must cross all barriers; it must pass above them. Like in Ireland. They play together for only a few hours in a winter rugby season but they do and that crosses barriers. Even those few, brief hours are important; they are a light for others to follow to a better future. Rugby, in that example and many others, has shown it can build bridges, create harmony in a divided world. I believe so strongly in that role for rugby in the future. To show the world, to show to politicians and people who believing killing is the only method, that that is wrong. Friendship and good relations are the way forward; if rugby can show that to the world, it will have succeeded in its most severe task.

"I firmly believe sport is the best way to make people closer. That is why I still visit South Africa and why I believe we should play rugby with them. Maybe we can show them the way of friendship and respect for every human being. This is why I was angry when our tour of South Africa was called off. On previous visits when I was there, I met many French people. They were building a nuclear power station or selling arms to that country. I am not stupid and I want to be treated as an adult. Those people are allowed to take their work there; why, as a sportsman, am I not also allowed that right?

"I get so sad about things I read in newspapers today. But more than that, I fear that sport is in the middle of the problems in the world. Our rugby tour to South Africa was called off; and remember, further back in 1972, how sport was caught up with terrorism at the Munich Olympic Games. I feel not depressed but humiliated by things like that. Really, really humiliated. Because my freedom, as a sportsman, as a human being choosing to do what I want, has gone."

A year after his appearance at Twickenham for the Barbarians against the British Lions, Rives, his popularity and reputation by now considerably enhanced throughout Europe, was invited back by the Ba-baas, for their meeting with the 1978 New Zealand tourists. It was the final match of the All Blacks tour in Britain, and produced a close, 18–16 victory for the New Zealanders, this time at Cardiff's National Stadium.

Skrela was there too; but a damaged knee probably denied the affable Bastiat the No. 8 shirt this time. Rives and Skrela seemed rapidly to be becoming synonymous with the Barbarians for the pair had also been invited to tour with the club on its traditional Easter tour to South Wales in 1977. The Frenchmen, both new Barbarians for that tour, each appeared in two matches: Rives against Cardiff and Swansea.

But against Swansea, Rives was forced to depart after only twenty-eight minutes of the first half, due to a rib injury. However, he brushed aside suggestions that he ought to go to hospital for an X-ray, replying with some vehemence: "I do not want to miss the fun after the match".

When the tour was over, Rives summed it up thus: "For four days, I play rugby with some of the best players in Great Britain. I sing and I laugh and I drink some beer. C'est magnifique. The Ba-baas are magic. For me and Jean-Claude it is a wonderful honour. The memories will last until the day we die."

It had made compulsive viewing, like watching a brilliant sunset dancing with great colour and spectacle across the sky, seeing Rives in the celebrated black and white shirt of the Barbarians; an alluring, irresistible sight, augmented by Skrela's presence on the opposing flank. One flanker of exceptional speed and quality is not unusual; discovering two, in the same club, the same national team, is all but unique.

Rives' love for the Barbarian approach was to last throughout his career. Yet by a tragic quirk of coincidence, it was while playing for the French Barbarians in their historic, first match on English soil that he received the injury which ended his career. With such vile humour does lady luck smile wickedly upon us all.

But by then, Rives had built a career which earned him instant acclaim the world over. From 1977, when he divulged the great qualities which would keep him at the summit of the world game for another seven physically exhausting years, Rives was to charm, enthrall and excite rugby spectators on grounds of almost every continent where the game was known.

Captain of the Second Grand Slam

"Foremost captain of his time,
Rich in saving common sense;
And, as the greatest only are,
In his simplicity sublime,
O good grey head which all men knew!"
— ALFRED, LORD TENNYSON —
1809–1892

A combination of the most extraordinary, unlikely events confounded French hopes of building an impregnable castle in European rugby in the wake of their 1977 Grand Slam success. No-one, not even Jean-Pierre Rives, could have foreseen the eruption of indignation at the compromising of traditional Gallic values. It shook all who had participated in the success; what more, they asked, bewildered, could we do? After all, we won the Grand Slam for only the second time in French history.

But such soul-searching was only the beginning of a period of great uncertainty interlaced with splendid peaks and dismal troughs. Unimagined outside events came together to break up a French pack which could, in harness with greater invention and flair behind the scrum, have created very nearly the perfect rugby team. It is a wonder to all non-Frenchmen – and a few Frenchmen too – that astute men like coach 'Toto' Desclaux and Jacques Fouroux failed to realise the enormous potential of a side which could amalgamate great forward strength and power with a dashing spirit intent on utilising traditionally speedy, elusive French threequarters. With two flankers of the quality of Rives and Skrela to roam at will, supporting threequarters on the move, a heady cocktail would have been created even for lovers of the real

French game, steeped in the exploits of great players of the past.

Fouroux had retired by the close of 1977, but Jean-Pierre Bastiat, his chosen successor, was fated to fall victim to a crippling knee injury which ended not only his chances of a sustained spell as leader of his country, but, more importantly, his international career. After four matches, France was searching for another new captain. It was almost exactly eleven months to the day after Fouroux had retired that that search reached a climax.

But, by then, much more had gone wrong. Playing in a club match against the Racing Club, Beziers' fierce lock forward, Michel Palmié, had been caught up in an incident which was to bring to a premature end also his own highly promising international career. Palmié, twenty-six in March 1978, was only entering the period generally acknowledged to be the peak for a good lock. But in that club match he had allegedly gouged the eyes of Armand Clerc, the Paris hooker, blinding him in one eye. Palmié was fined FF80,000 and had to pay the costs. His appeal was turned down. Palmié was in the dock in more ways than one, his career on the line and with his own reputation damaged his international career destroyed. He had now a thoroughly unsavoury reputation. Rives, his colleague in the Grand Slam side the previous year, made a stringent defence of his friend's manner, in later years. But it had no effect. Palmié, because of the uproar the incident caused, was never to play again for his country once the appeal had been heard. France lost a major cornerstone of its invincible pack.

The lock had won twenty-three caps in just three years; a host of others would certainly have followed. Palmié's loss was still felt by France fully seven years later as her national side struggled to discover locks of similar strength and power.

Worse was to come for France. Jean-Claude Skrela completed the 1978 Five Nations season and then announced: "I quit". The Toulouse flanker had gathered forty-eight caps in only seven years from his debut in 1971. In a flash, France had lost three crucial players from a pack which had battered Europe into submission. Perhaps never again would France field as powerful a front unit.

Rives carried on. He hid the scars left by Skrela's departure, but he missed his friend, the man with whom he had grown up on the international rugby field. Only after his own retirement from the game did Rives reveal fully his feelings on Skrela's early retirement.

"He retired too early; much too early. He could still have been playing when I retired after the 1984 international season. Maybe he could have had five more seasons at least in the French team. It seemed a cuckoo decision to me, when he retired. He always trained more than anyone; he was fitter than any other player. Even today, when he trains Stade Toulousain, he says 'Follow me' but no-one can follow Skrela all the way. He is still probably the fittest.

"When he retired, France lost a great player. And for me, when he retired, I retired a little bit too. A part of me stopped, the day Jean-Claude finished. I respected his decision and, after all, that was life. But nothing afterwards was ever quite the same for me."

Two-thirds of France's magnificent Grand Slam back row had gone; and there was, too, major disruption in the engine-room. Jean François Imbernon, that lumbering 6ft 5ins lock from Perpignan, was to become a frequent sufferer of major injuries over the course of the next few years. A broken leg badly interrupted his career, forcing France to find not one but two new locks, with Palmié also absent. It was a breaking-up of the powerful 1977 side which took four years to conceal.

Aptly, Jean-Pierre Rives led his country for the first time, in the city of his birth, Toulouse. The honour fell to him on 11 November 1978, for the match against the Soviet Union. Only a scattering of support saw Rives' debut as leader, 6492 spectators for a match which France won 29–7. It was scarcely an auspicious start.

Nor was Rives' second match in charge an undisputed success. Romania were beaten, in Bucharest, but by the slender margin of 9–6. Was Rives truly the man for the task, some wondered? And exactly how had he been given the job? In fact, much soul-searching and discussion had gone on in selectorial circles before Rives was chosen.

Claude Dourthe, his first captain for France, had followed the tortuous path towards Rives, as Bastiat's successor, from his committee involvements which followed the end of his playing days.

Dourthe said: "It was the 'After Bastiat' players who created the reign of Rives. By that I mean, Jacques Fouroux, Jean-Pierre Bastiat and the players of that era who were left. Cholley was finished, Paparemborde was strong but silent. But they admitted Rives easily because he set an example.

91

"Jean-Pierre Rives was not like the others. Both Fouroux and Bastiat were obvious choices; it was their era. But one can be a captain without being a leader. And you can be a leader without being a captain. But Jean-Pierre Rives was neither captain nor leader through and through. He became first one and then the other by setting an example and by what he showed. And he also had a lot more personality than those other players who were left.

"But Jean Desclaux, who was trainer of the French team at that time, did not think of Jean-Pierre as a captain. Other selectors told Desclaux 'You must give Rives the job. The other players rely on him more and more and he will become a good captain'. And it was from that time Jean-Pierre took over. To become a good captain, you must set an example. If you want to set an example, however, you find it is often necessary to make sacrifices. And the sacrifice is defence. To save the ball. And Rives was the strongest at searching out the ball as quickly as possible. He had so much courage, so much force in getting the ball out. And this became his strong point because he is very intelligent also and, from the point of view of collective defence, he led everybody to defend. That is very important. But Jean-Pierre was capable of being defensive *and* attacking."

Dourthe confessed that Rives' qualities of leadership, which became increasingly apparent once he assumed the post, surprised him. "Although I knew him as a player, I didn't think at that time he would become the captain he did because, early on in his career, he was so reserved that he didn't want to assert himself. He was by no means an undisputed, natural leader. Indeed, he was a little anonymous among the others in the early part of his career.

"But to an increasing extent he showed the qualities of leadership. He sacrificed himself often and was admired by others and elected leader. But I don't think he tapped on the table in order to become captain. It was others who elected him leader."

Jo Maso would, long after Rives' retirement from the game, select the years from 1978 to 1980 as the finest seasons the flanker probably enjoyed. "I think he had two or three seasons in that period which were great for him. He was always present for the big occasions, he never disappointed.

"When he assumed the captaincy, he got better and better. He differed from other captains. He was not a player who knew how to shout or blow up players. And what you noticed was that, from the beginning of his captaincy to the end, he made enormous progress because he won so much respect. At the beginning he had difficulties and he used to say to me, 'Oh, it's so difficult being captain', because it wasn't his mentality.''

Rives was, most certainly, radically different in his style of leadership to both Bastiat and Fouroux. The sight of the tiny Fouroux, bossing and bullying his giant forwards to greater exertions, still evokes a smile. Bastiat, a tall man, always led from the front.

The Rives mannerisms were different. There were the little strides on to the field at the start of internationals; Rives leading his men out by dallying at their sides, encouraging, talking, like a shepherd fussing over his flock.

Could he shout at his men, could he bully them? ''He was,'' said Roland Bertranne, that most experienced of players, ''a captain who could talk a lot. He was very good at communicating. Before the game, during it and afterwards. He had lots of personality. Before the match he would go and see the important players. He liked to surround himself with several players in whom he had faith. He took great delight in that; he was always open to discussion. He loved to talk.

''He would tell his players they should play for pleasure mostly. And for a good game. Rather than for France. He also said you must be enthusiastic. He could shout at players before a match – he was certainly capable of motivating a team when he needed to. Everyone followed him because of his enthusiasm. He loved rugby above all, he always gave his all. He was always first to the ball, he was faultless. For a captain, that is essential but also he was very communicative, another vital requirement.''

Jean Michel Aguirre remembered Rives' captaincy in the formative years. ''He always believed in the intelligence of each player. He could be very quiet in what he said to his teams but his words gave great confidence to his players. He would say in the dressing-room, 'You can play for your family or your friends or your country, if you want. But mainly you should play for your pleasure'. Yet, at times, he seemed uncertain, to be seeking something, but I did not know what. Perhaps one of his characteristics was not to speak too much yet sometimes not enough. But that was in his early days as captain.''

Jacques Fouroux provides a definitive version of events which led to Rives' takeover. He said: "At the time Jean-Pierre was being considered, there was a possibility Paparemborde and also Bertranne (for he was the record holder for caps) would get the job. They were the only two who had a chance. But Jean-Pierre was chosen because, first of all, he was an absolutely marvellous player who made a mark on his generation as a rugby player. And also because he had a very communicative game, that is to say, he was a player who led by example and as he played, the others automatically followed him. He was always at the front. And so it wasn't so much a choice of technique but a choice for his way of playing.

"It is true the first time Jean-Pierre was chosen as captain, everyone expressed reservations because he was not a boy who was impassioned by the tactics, by the technique or by the game itself. He was impassioned by the fact of participation, that's all. For him, the game started at three o'clock and finished at half past four. In general, a captain has to live before, during and after – all the time for rugby. And when he was picked everyone had doubts. They thought he was not capable of being captain.

"But then, by his manner of playing, he suddenly gathered the total approval of everyone – players, directors, spectators – purely because he was an example to all. Besides, in French rugby, the captaincy has to be learned. Overall, it is not something one has; you have to learn how to do it. There are several forms of captain. Jean-Pierre was one sort. When I was captain, I had a different style but Jean-Pierre imposed his own style on the captaincy."

Rives, himself, could hardly believe the news that he had been chosen for a job which demanded playing ability, knowledge of different languages, and skill in dealing with the political mavericks of French rugby. No ordinary task.

"I simply never thought about the captaincy and I didn't even want the job," he reveals. "My reputation was the opposite of a captain. It never occurred to me that they would even consider me as a possible captain. When I was nominated, I was very surprised; in fact, it surprised everyone. No-one could believe it.

"I felt I was captain by default. I considered I only got the job because I was experienced, and anyway, if Jean-Pierre Bastiat had not injured his knee so seriously, I would not have been thought of. But once I was given the job, I tried to remember the lessons I had learned from Jacques Fouroux. Because I consider he was the best captain I ever knew. He was a great motivator and he understood his players well."

Rives' debut as captain of France in a European Five Nations match, in the season 1978–9, proved inconclusive. France drew 9–9 with Ireland in Dublin, a dropped point which was to cost them a share of the Championship by the end of the campaign. But, for all his uncertainty as to his own suitability for the role, Rives was already stamping his own, highly individual mark on the job. The French national team was moving away from the 1977 era of rumbling forwards. The arrival of Jerome Gallion as an international scrum half had significantly contributed to the expanding game which France now sought to play. The Toulon half back, a nuggety quick player with a penetrating, flat and fast service, released his threequarters, especially with the adventurous Alain Caussade, such a success in New Zealand that summer, outside him at fly half. This time, too, France had introduced wings with the intent of using them. Players like Costes, Bilbao, Gourdon and Noves proved more than a match for their rivals in the British and Irish sides. At last, under Rives' urging, a spirit of enterprise was returning to French rugby.

Rives said at the time: "When I began playing international rugby, France won with a massive pack of forwards, backed by kickers. We rolled up the field like a tank and we were very successful. But it is important that the national team should reflect the instinctive style of the country's players. It is more fun, too.

"France could field four or five international teams with not very much difference between them. Wales could probably field two and England, Scotland and Ireland, one each. In one way that is France's strength but in another way it is our weakness because if you don't have a choice of players you don't worry about whether you have picked your best team.

"Look at our situation in France. We have seven or eight wings who are all genuine international class players – Gourdon, Averous, Bustaffa, Costes, Bilbao, Noves, Harize. There are others, too, but which is the best? Who can play?

"The result is that if one man is picked and maybe he doesn't play too well, it is too easy to replace him and that diminishes team spirit. Look what happened in New Zealand this summer. We had many injuries and illnesses while we were there. For much of the time, we didn't have two fit locks. We had troubles at loose head where Colomine is perhaps a bit too young at the moment, we didn't have quite the right balance in the back row, and although he has a great talent, Serge Blanco didn't have a good tour at full-back, either. Remember, too, that none of our top three centres were available for the tour and neither were some of our best forwards.

"And yet we won the last Test and shared the series with the All Blacks. We enjoyed the game and we found some more good players."

Wales, contrary to expectation, won the title despite the retirement of players like Gareth Edwards, Phil Bennett, Gerald Davies and Terry Cobnor. What happened? Why Wales jolly well went out and picked up a couple of half backs from Cardiff High Street, named Terry Holmes and Gareth Davies.

France's title it would have been in Rives' first year had his old friend Aguirre not missed four relatively straightforward penalty attempts which enabled England to squeeze out a 7–6 victory. No matter, the trend had been reversed, the brighter dawn reached. No longer was French rugby regarded as dull and dreary. Once more, the threequarters were being given the ball, and thrilling, heartening play it was too.

Michel Palmié, discarded forever by the national selectors, believed Rives had already compromised his own performances by his duties as captain.

"When you are captain, you have so many things to think about," he said. "In respect of his individual game, of course, Jean-Pierre had to sacrifice his own game just at that time. It was the threequarters, when he was captain, who were especially good in that season. Perhaps he sacrificed his game to the collective benefit of the game of the threequarters because they were then stronger than the forward pack.

"In 1977, just as a player, Jean-Pierre had experienced a very good season. But after that, when he was captain, he was obliged to be the natural leader – which he did in an excellent fashion – to the detriment of his personal game. That is, his own game did suffer." But Rives made the sacrifice without question, paying scant regard to his own feelings or desires. "When you become leader, you play for the team in every way. It is a different attitude, a different approach. Everything you attempt is for the team; there can be no room for your own ambitions. It is for your side, for the players. That you must remember.''

The tour of New Zealand, in June–July 1979, had offered Rives greater scope to bed down his individual style of leadership, chiefly to young recruits who formed the core of the touring party. In that respect, the captain's task was simplified; there were few survivors from the Fouroux Grand Slam era, against whom to make comparisons and judge Rives in an ill light. The new period had begun.

Rives' clarion call was unmistakable; play for the spirit, for the pleasure, never for the result alone. Thus, the ruthless efficiency which had made itself manifestly apparent in 1977, was discarded in favour of greater liberalisation in manner. Remarkably, the erratic and often disappointing results, which followed in the next two seasons of international rugby, were notable in that their reception was devoid of the caustic comments hitherto accepted as the norm in French circles. It was a measure of the potency of Rives' argument that French élan and flair should return, that supporter and media alike should accept, with barely a murmur of disapproval, the logic of the argument. Besides, Rives' quiet charm would smooth most ruffled feathers.

Nevertheless, even Rives was hard put to it to quell the dismay in France at the results from the 1980 season, especially the lessons inherent in the outcome of the Five Nations Championship. England won the Grand Slam with a fearsome pack of forwards which had far too much might and muscle, plus experience and technique, for every other country. The French had been crushed by a more powerful Welsh pack in Cardiff, 18–9; had again been beaten, through the strength of England's scrummage, in Paris a fortnight later, by 17–13 and then had squandered a 14–4 lead over Scotland at Murrayfield. The feeling from that match came through as loud and clear as bugles on Bastille Day morning in the Champs d'Elysées; namely, the old French pack would never have allowed opponents back into the game from that promising position.

When permitted, the French ran the ball with dazzling speed, like furious bees revenging the death of their queen. Only a slim 19–18 victory over Ireland provided an escape tunnel of sorts but fresh thinking was required to combine the merits of Rives' approach and the practicalities of the old forward strength.

There had been a resort to bad old French habits; twenty-five players had been selected that season. Rives, judged as a player, did his best but he lacked the freedom to roam, through the inability of his tight forwards to establish supremacy. Thus, Rives' strength as a creator was dissipated, his value as a defensive lynchpin diluted. France conceded ten tries, something which would have been unheard of in the aftermath of the Grand Slam season, when not one was scored against them. Some compromise was required.

Before that, Rives, a sedulous devotee of the cause of his club Stade Toulousain, had the pleasure of playing in the final of the French Club Championship – against Beziers. Finals are fine, as long as Beziers do not stand in your path to the plank of wood, or 'Le Bouclier de Brennus' as France's huge Championship shield is known. History did not bode favourably for Les Toulousains; they had not been Champions since 1947 while Beziers had dominated the French domestic game since 1971. But curiously it seemed that Beziers would win two years in succession, but never three times. The results were to follow the same pattern right through to 1985:

1971	Beziers	1979	Narbonne
1972	Beziers	1980	Beziers
1973	Tarbes	1981	Beziers
1974	Beziers	1982	Agen
1975	Beziers	1983	Beziers
1976	Agen	1984	Beziers
1977	Beziers	1985	Stade Toulousain
1978	Beziers		

Paris, and a French Championship final. A unique event, a festive celebration of the climax to the long French Championship season. It all begins in early autumn, almost before the last of the summer travellers has departed for home from the south of France resorts. In Toulon and Beziers, Toulouse and Bagnères and Bayonne close to St Jean de Luz in the west, the training squads are in action by August, ready for embarkation on the journey which can end in faraway Paris, at the end of May.

Clubs are paired off into several groups, featuring all the leading sides. They play each other, home and away, through the major part of the winter until the top sides in each group go into a knock-out for the final stages of the Championship. These matches start with the round known as the 'Barrages', usually in mid-April. Sixteen teams play each other but the strongest seeded sides are given a bye through to the next round, where they await the winners of the first knock-out stage.

In 1985, Toulouse, Beziers, Agen, Montferrand, Lourdes, Biarritz, Nice and Toulon awaited opponents in the 'Huitièmes', the round of the last sixteen. This stage is played on a two-leg basis, home and away. The winners are determined by the side with the greater number of points from the two matches, when they are put together. For example, Stade Toulousain beat Bayonne 10–3 and then 15–9 for a 25–12 aggregate win. Toulon were too strong for Aurillac, winning 21–6 and 32–15 for a crushing 53–21 success.

So on into the quarter-finals at the start of May, with every match from this point played on neutral territory. Due to the great distances across the South of France, teams and supporters find themselves making long journeys, with certain towns strategically placed on the map at major crossing points for the travelling fans.

In 1985 Toulouse met the holders, Beziers, at Perpignan while another match between local rivals, Nice and Toulon, was held at the nearest large centre, Marseille. The round produced four semi-finalists, Toulouse, Montferrand (by 13 points to 12 over Agen), Lourdes 13–9 winners against Biarritz, the club of Serge Blanco; and Toulon, who won a fiercely contested 'derby', 15–6.

Club Championship matches provide prime television viewing time so the organisers traditionally elect one match to be played on a Saturday, for live transmission on television. Of the two semi-finals, both again at neutral venues, Toulouse met Montferrand at Bordeaux on 19 May, the Toulousains getting through 17–6. The journey back to Toulouse, a two-hour drive south-east along the 'Autoroute des Deux Mers', was a happy jaunt for thousands of excited Toulouse fans – car horns blaring, flags streaming from open windows, the club's colours draped all over the vehicles. At motorway lay-bys, groups of supporters congregated to start the celebrations. And in Toulouse that night, happy fans wandered through the streets or drove around the squares and wide boulevards, their car horns tooting into the small hours, flags waving from the windows of the vehicles.

The next day, Toulouse again found itself the focal point of attraction, this time from the invading supporters of Lourdes and Toulon, the other semi-finalists.

The match, at the old Toulouse Olympic stadium, was a dour struggle in the warm sunshine, Toulon managing a 6–3 victory, which was all but dashed from their grasp when Lourdes squandered a 4–1 overlap advantage with a rare threequarter movement inside the Toulon 22, minutes from time.

The fans left quietly . . . that is, the Lourdes followers. Toulon supporters drove off to the accompanying sound of klaxons and horns which filled the city streets on the hitherto quiet Sunday afternoon. The joy, the great pleasure is the apparent ability of the supporters to accept their fate, whether it be glory or disaster they encounter. Fights rarely occur; one can see the supporters walking away, side by side, usually discussing the match. One of the pleasures of the game in this part of the world is the strong affiliation to clubs and teams because of the unique links through the villages. But the intensity is healthy, seldom straying into wild behaviour.

In Paris, the invasion from the south begins early on Saturday morning. Championship finals used to alternate between three venues in the south; Toulouse, Bordeaux and Lyon. This was more convenient for the supporters but not as financially productive for the FFR. Thus, the Parc des Princes in Paris became a regular venue, with fans forced either to stay at home and watch the match live on television, or make the long, tiring, expensive journey to the capital.

In 1985, I met many supporters from the Toulouse and Toulon areas who were bemoaning the inconvenience of a final in Paris on a Saturday night. The match, which kicks off at 20.30 hours, means that few supporters attempt the long drive south during the night, thus involving them in a costly overnight stay in Paris. It means a great many followers simply cannot go to the match; a pity, for the ordinary fan is the lifeblood of the game in the south all through the winter. To deny him a day out at the final, should his club progress so far, puts the great prize of the season beyond the scope of many ordinary supporters.

Those who go, however, more than make up for the missing ones left at home. Bands play, supporters flood the Champs d'Elysées for much of the day, horns are heard in the city from first light.

Class barriers, happily, are non-existent: the farmer taking his wine with town hall clerk, the peasant worker eating beside fellow supporters of radically different sections of society. There is a coming together, a spirit which many sports nowadays seem unable to capture, still less foster.

Local bands from several towns in the south-east and south-west compete for the title of best band which earns them the right to play at the final. The band, of course, plays throughout the match, but is sparked like a flame to gunpowder by a score or a particularly exciting piece of play. The members of the band are also varied in background: young with old, the local baker beside le patron from the local café and behind the village butcher. They have, almost invariably, come a long long way; up the autoroutes either through Bordeaux towards Paris or up the 'Autoroute de Sud' through Dijon, home of the French kings centuries ago, and on past the Royal Palace of Fontainebleau to Paris.

In 1980, Stade Toulousain had possessed some notable players behind the scrum: Gabernet, the international full-back; Harize, holder of eight caps on the right wing; Noves, another international, on the left wing; Martinez, later to become an international, at scrum half. They had, too, Rives and Skrela on the sides of the scrums; but did they have the power, the strength, the technique and the aggression to take on Beziers in the front five? Surely, it was in this department that the game would be decided.

Beziers, on the other hand, had its internationals, two a penny, among the forwards, although Cantoni, at full-back, was already an international (he had been a thrilling right wing in his halcyon days) and, later, Fabre was to earn senior international honours.

The forwards were impressive: Vaquerin, Paco, Martin in the front row; Palmié and Esteve, at lock – each one internationals many times over. In the back row, Cordier, Buonomo and Lacans – Cordier, the only non-international in the pack.

Michel Palmié recalls the atmosphere prior to the start at Parc des Princes, the pregnant moments before the explosion of energy. "My greatest memory of this match is when we were lined up facing each other, before the start. Spontaneously, Jean-Pierre and myself looked at each other and embraced. Then we played."

It was the meeting of old friends, lifelong companions. Nothing, not even a French final, could come between the friendship, the spirit. Rives felt emotion at that moment; Palmié understood completely the feelings of his friend. The combat which was to follow might make a mockery of such niceties in the minds of some. But not to those involved, those, like Michel Palmié, who knew Rives as a man, as a friend.

"It was a hard match but not especially so," recalls the Beziers man. "It was the strong points of one side, against the weaker points of the other. Of course, Jean-Pierre was very disappointed to lose the match because he is a winner. He is like me – when you lose a game, you are never happy. Always disappointed. Especially for the Championship of France. But because of his intelligence he realised that in life there are many things more important than affairs of rugby. You feel bad at the time but it's only a game. Jean-Pierre is a very philosophical sort. Even in defeat you have moments when you analyse certain situations and can find some truth. Something good comes out of it."

Skrela, not Rives, was captain of Toulouse. And he was quickly concerned as Beziers took a 10–0 lead, their forwards creating the position for two tries, one converted. But two penalties by Gerald Martinez gave Stade Toulousain great hope. Instantly, like a battery re-charged, they came again at Beziers, moving the ball at speed whenever they secured possession and running from great distances close to the Beziers line. It was nearly decisive.

"Beziers had exceptional players with great spirit together," said Rives. "They were a very strong team. People criticised them but that is easy to do. First, you have to beat them. The best way to criticise a team is to beat them. But we could not criticise them very often!

"However, in that final, I remember we almost scored in the final minute. Gabernet was given the ball by Harize with the line close by. If he had caught it, he would have scored a try. But he was like us all – very tired after a long, hard match. And he dropped the ball. So Beziers won, but they deserved that match.

"We lost and that meant Beziers were better than us. I was happy for Beziers because they merited the Championship again. Nine times out of ten, I knew they would beat us at that time because they were such a good side. But I thought maybe this would be the one time . . . you must be positive in your attitude. But it was not to be.

"People want change all the time, they don't like one side to dominate. Maybe that is why Beziers made people a little bored and so attracted criticism. I am not defending Beziers but I have no reason to be too critical of them.

"I do not think there will ever be another club like Beziers; so strong, so successful. It will be very difficult for any club to enjoy ten years like that. It is like the English football side, Liverpool. Who will equal their record in recent years, never mind improve it? Beziers had extraordinary results with remarkable players. Vaquerin, for example, was one of the best prop forwards we ever had in France. Patou (Paparemborde) is the same kind of man – exceptional men, and extraordinary rugby players.

"I cannot remember beating Beziers in a major club match, in the later stages of the Championship. Possibly, in a group match early in the season. But not when it was vital to win, in the qualifying stages for the final. That was when Beziers were at their best. They were supreme because they took on every side and were feared and respected by all, throughout France. That was a notable achievement."

Beziers' men like Esteve and Palmié earned reputations as untamed men, merciless in the execution of their business upon the field. But Palmié's involvement in legal actions was, according to Rives, totally unfair.

"I want to say a little more of the truth about Michel Palmié," says Rives. "He was a great player and a great man. But he was a victim of what happened. Yet even as a victim, he was an example in the way he behaved. He never said what he really felt; he did not become involved in bitter words. I had a lot of admiration for Michel as a player but also as a man, after what happened.

"People said bad things about him which were not true. A reputation was created which he did not deserve."

Rives, the defender of his friends, the defender of the faith and creed of sportsmanship, friendship and the proper spirit. But it was not always like that, according to some adversaries who knew Rives quite well. Fergus Slattery, who played fourteen years in the Irish international team from 1970 to 1984, remembers that France–Ireland match in Paris in 1980; a game which, he claims, showed the differing aspects to Rives' character.

French motivation was high; that was to be anticipated, with a whitewash facing them. Slattery was no stranger to Paris and its own special atmosphere. "Matches there tend to be very physical and quite violent. It is generally expected that is the way things go on over there. In Paris, they will kick you all over the place. On the field, Jean-Pierre would say 'This is not the game' – but two minutes earlier, his colleague had kicked someone.

"In that match, Ollie Campbell was kicked in the head by Vaquerin. I said to Rives, 'Keep that goon under control, will you?' Then, minutes later, Vaquerin kicked me and got up on my leg and did a pirouette on the leg. I knew who it was. Within two more minutes, John O'Driscoll had to leave the field with a head injury. And we'd only had twenty-two minutes of the first half.

"All the time Rives was saying 'I do not know who it is; this is not the game I like to see'. But he did nothing about it. Through that I felt to some extent he was a bit hollow. He had tremendous respect for the players who played for him in the French side. Perhaps he couldn't see any faults in them."

Slattery called his rival "a good-mannered player", adding "he wasn't a nasty player. He wouldn't go hunting for assailants whatever they had done to him."

But Slattery recalled another incident, in later years, when he felt Rives should have shown greater strength of control towards his own men. "In 1984, when we played in Paris again, the atmosphere was about the same as usual. I tackled Blanco after the ball had gone up in the air and he had caught it. We came down with a crash and I was on top of him. Nothing illegal in that but Blanco likes to lay on the ground and complain he has been hurt. He lay there and kept on moaning.

"Dintrans came up to me in a nasty way and asked what the hell I'd done to Blanco. I grabbed Dintrans by the shirt and threw him on the ground. I was mad at his approach and from Blanco's moaning from a perfectly fair challenge. Dintrans had a go at me and kicked me on the ground. So I returned the kick, to his bum. I told him to shut up. Rives came up and started joining in the yackety-yack going on. That was typical of the French; they always loved to have a disgruntled chat about it. I was so mad I nearly gave Rives one, too."

Back in 1980, Serge Blanco, coffee coloured from his birth in Caracas, the capital of Venezuela, was a star about to emerge in French rugby (he had returned to France at the age of two). He forged his reputation as a dashing, exciting back with the Biarritz club. In late October 1980 he set out for South Africa on the brief, four-match tour which the French arranged at short notice. They played Natal, Western Province, an Invitation XV and, finally,

South Africa, in a Test match in Pretoria. Three wins going into the Test was comforting, but insufficient. The Springboks won 37–15, with five tries against one. Rives was brave but he could not do everything.

Back home in Toulouse, his parents rose early in the morning for the telecast live from the Republic. Rives piled into one ruck and felt Springbok boots opening up his scalp. His mother recalled: ''He went off for about ten minutes and came back with so many bandages and so much blood I could not bear to watch any more. It was horrible.''

Nor was it a simple cut which healed without difficulty. An infection set in so that, by the time Rives landed in Toulouse from the flight home, he had a gross swelling on the side of his head. His family doctor demanded immediate entry into hospital for an operation.

Rives, throughout his career and still today, has hated hospitals. The man who showed not a trace of fear at tackling giant forwards and lying on the ball on rock-hard Australian and South African grounds with the boots piling into his body like nails into a coffin, visibly shakes at the prospect of hospital visits. It was the same this time. Rives had received ten stitches in the wound just to the right and above his eyebrow. He returned to the fray, was tackled and got knocked out cold for sixty seconds. Yet all that pain paled into insignificance beside the prospect of a fleeting visit to Toulouse hospital.

So, as the patient refused to go to the hospital, the hospital had to go to the patient. ''The doctor did it in our kitchen at home,'' said Rives. ''I don't like hospitals – I don't need hospitals. I got maybe 250 stitches in my career, some even from training accidents. One time, I cut my nose badly on some stones on a training ground and they stitched me in the training room, so that I would not have to visit hospital. I had ten stitches in my nose that time.''

And so Rives had his operation, close to the kitchen sink, on a special bench laid out for him, with surgeons drawing out the infection and re-inserting stitches, just across from the family's living room! His mother said: ''Jean-Pierre had great faith in his local doctor. But he has always been so reticent about going into hospitals. It is one of his whims.''

By 1981, Jacques Fouroux had replaced Michel Celaya, the grand old Biarritz international of the 1950s, as French coach. And his strong personality led to a compromise of ideals with Rives over the thorny question of strong forward play. 1980 had shown France that it was essential to have might up front. England, after all, had won the Grand Slam for the first time that previous season, since 1957. But with the creativity and speed of players like Woodward and Carleton behind the scrum, the English had proved it could be done in a style which encompassed the two aspects of play, however different they might appear. Thus Rives stuck firmly to his belief that, even if Fouroux did want some strong forwards back in the French side, it should not mean a total desertion of the threequarters. There ought to be room for both.

Somehow the two men worked out a system which gave France the Grand Slam in a season when even the most optimistic of Frenchmen would hardly have dared forecast such riches. There is no doubt that Rives had been forced to give ground; the previous season's disasters ensured as much. And after all, there were players available, players like the massive Imbernon and Daniel Revallier, a 6ft 2ins and 17-stone lock from the Graulhet club whom the French described as 'a force of nature' and who was known colloquially as Sam (whether this was a term of endearment or shortened 'Surface to air' missile, as someone suggested, was not known). But Rives and Fouroux did a grafting job, as was essential. John Reason, writing in the *Sunday Telegraph* at the conclusion of the season, called 1981 'the year of the donkey'. It was not hard to see what he meant.

France also introduced a grafting flanker to play beside Rives, the late Pierre Lacans, from the Beziers club. He was no slip of a lad, either, at 6ft 2ins, and 14st. 3lbs. And in the front row, they called up the renowned Basque scrummage, Pierre Dospital, to provide a solid, experienced front three with Dintrans and Paparemborde. Add the enormous contribution Jean-Luc Joinel was making at this time from No. 8, and one can see the return of the forward might which had served France and Fouroux so well back in 1977.

France overran Scotland in their first match at Parc des Princes, 16–9, after leading 16–3 at half time. It was not the sort of rugby to recall the great old days of Maso, Lux, and Trillo but there was some flair in the creation of tries for Blanco and Bertranne, the latter wisely retained by Fouroux even though he was by now well past thirty-one and nowhere near the fastest or daintiest of centres. But, next to him, France had found a boy of rare genius, a tiny 5ft 7ins player from Narbonne who had the knack of instinctively doing the right thing whatever the limitations of time or space, in releasing his wings with some room to move and judging his passes with a flair which is not learned, but given by birth. Didier Codorniou was a gem of a player.

The youthful inexperience of the French side was a source of wonder. Laporte and Berbizier, the half-backs brought together like strangers in a crowded pub, and Revallier were making their international debuts. At the start of 'the New Year grind' – as some term the hunt for the Five Nations Championship, coming as it does between January and March and often in the foulest weather – Blanco had one cap, Pardo, one. Dospital was a senior statesman in the French club game but still had only one cap, the same as Lacans. Carpentier and Gabernet possessed two apiece, Mesny just three. By such tender standards, Codorniou and Dintrans were positively senior citizens, with six caps each. One man stood out; Bertranne started the season with forty-six.

The next match was in Dublin against the side expected to win the Championship that season. French optimism, rarely strong in the Irish capital, seemed to vanish like an eerie figure on a misty Irish peat bog, as a flu virus struck the French camp before the start. Blanco and Codorniou, the two players who personified spirit and individualism in the side, were both ruled out, so Caussade, a stand-off, played right wing for Blanco and Mesny took Codorniou's place at centre. Laporte, Revallier's colleague from Graulhet, was a new cap.

Mesny was elusive, quick and difficult to predict; qualities which should have given him far more than the fourteen caps he earned up to 1985. But in Dublin, the replacement was replaced by Lafarge of Montferrand, after 27 minutes of the second half. No matter, French inspiration was considerable, supplied by the captain who worked relentlessly to steer the ship through difficult waters. That he succeeded was a measure of the man. France won 19–13, despite conceding the lead until ten minutes from the end.

7 March, at Parc des Princes, was 'high noon' for the French, with Wales visiting Paris. The two nations had dominated

European rugby since 1975; Wales, of course, had tasted a glorious era and as such it was ending, but Welsh resolve was far from conquered; and recent meetings between the two countries had stoked up some measure of resentment.

In 1980 at Cardiff, a Welsh player definitely appeared to be pressing a self-destruct button, when he kicked Rives in the head, in brutal style. The sour taste of 'a little bit of afters', as the players called it, was wafting across the Parc long before the two sides, like armies of ancient times, lined up for the fray.

John Reason, never a correspondent to pull punches, wrote in the *Sunday Telegraph* the following day: "France made sure of at least a share of the Championship when they overhauled Wales in a furious onslaught at the finish of the match which, at one stage in the first half, looked as if it might start the third world war. France were always the more inventive side but it made that disgraceful match between England and Wales at Twickenham last year look like a tea party. Quite apart from the punching and the butting, there was more aluminium flying around than in an aircraft factory. The referee gave two public warnings."

Jim Hill, writing on the Monday morning after in the *Daily Express*, hardly bothered with the niceties of the game:

"Rugby's image took another battering from a series of ugly, bad-tempered and often violent Parc des Princes punch-ups," he wrote. "The English referee Alan Welsby seemed powerless to control the mayhem."

Rives tried to cool tempers but admitted, after Welsby's second warning, that he asked his forwards to stop behaving like children. "All the time, I tried to stop the trouble," he said. "It was not a good game but there was no ill-feeling after Cardiff on my part. There were just a lot of threatening gestures but no kicking." A mild summary of an inglorious affair.

Clive Rees, recalled to the Welsh side after a three-year absence from international rugby, remembered: "I think both France and Wales realised they had the beating of the other home countries. And so it was one or the other at that time – Wales or France. Hence, the rivalry. When the two countries met, that match was always the one to win.

"I loved playing in Paris; it is such an enclosed ground that the noise volume generated reverberates all around. The fire crackers take you by surprise, the boos, the band playing; it's quite a tough task playing there. Wales tend to get their own back in Cardiff so the French regard Paris as their chance to get *their* own back. You always try the softening up process, but neither set of forwards gives up.

"At that time, the French didn't make much attempt to move the ball. I remember the bloke I was marking hardly ever got the ball in attack and I don't think I touched it, in an orthodox movement, very much. It was a forward battle, being slugged out."

Wales, who had the better of the main part of the game, led 15–9 with under twenty minutes of the match remaining. But Rees highlighted a point of crucial importance concerning Jean-Pierre Rives and his influence on French teams of his era: "He got the best out of all his players – he had the ability to extract every ounce of effort and class from his forwards particularly," said Rees. "And, perhaps best of all, the French didn't panic so much under Rives. They kept the pressure on even if the scores did not come immediately. And they maintained it until they did break through.

"French sides used to panic if things didn't go right for them straightaway. You always felt, if your side withstood a bit of pressure, the towel would be thrown in and that would be the end of the French. But not when Rives was in charge."

It was the 'British' attitude of France's captain once again in evidence, in which Rives showed himself to be totally different from the traditional Gallic figure which was excitable, temperamental, unpredictable and hardly likely to stick to the task. So much which was classically French changed once Rives took over as captain of the national side.

Injuries, France's difficulty the entire season, again cropped up against Wales. Bertranne, much the most experienced international on the field, departed seventeen minutes after half-time, Mesny taking his place.

But Rives now inspired his side, urging, cajoling, pushing, inciting, impelling his men to sterner efforts. Such exhortations had their reward. Gabernet scored from a scrummage close to the Welsh line and the full-back then punished Welsh indiscretions by kicking two penalty goals. France had squeezed to a 19–15 victory and now only the English, at Twickenham, stood between France and a Grand Slam.

For three matches, France had lost the services of five players either before or during the games. Nonetheless the French had forged a side of increasing team spirit and commitment. Now England, victors over Scotland and Ireland but defeated in Cardiff as seems to be the norm, had to be taken at Twickenham.

Twickenham: Rives' favourite ground. "It is simply not the same playing at grounds like Eden Park or the Sydney Cricket Ground. There is not the same mood, the same atmosphere; it is different at those grounds to the ones in Europe. I like Twickenham so much because of the tradition of the place. It has an aura, a feeling which is unique in the world. Those stands seem to climb into the sky, they are so high. It is like the Barbarians club; my favourite spirit and my favourite place. For me, it is a special spirit and a special feeling. It is what rugby should be about; tradition, the sense of history. It is a symbol, an expression. Like a perfume, a fine reminder."

Beside Rives, as France prepared for her Grand Slam bid in London, was his old friend, Robert Paparemborde. A crucial man in the French pack, 'Patou' was respected and admired by most foes for his sloping shoulders, great bull neck and powerful scrummaging. Fran Cotton, probably England's finest prop of the last decade and more, paid tribute to the Frenchman in his autobiography *Fran*: "He was the most difficult tight head that I played against not only because of his strength and technique but also his sloping shoulders which seemed to go down to his waist. This made it very difficult to scrummage against him as there was very little to push against and only in England's Grand Slam year (1980) did I feel that I got the better of him." 'Patou', of course, had come this way before, in 1977, with Rives, Bertranne and Imbernon. Like Rives, he would remember the story of the little can which Jacques Fouroux found, and which the Frenchmen involved still believe, to this day, helped to bring them two Grand Slam victories at Twickenham.

"In 1977, before that match at Twickenham," Rives explained, "we stayed at a hotel beside Heathrow Airport. On the Saturday morning before the match, we crossed the road to go for a walk and found a small square of ground. There we found a can, an ordinary discarded can, and we kicked it around for a while. I remember Jacques (Fouroux) picked up the can and said, 'This can will bring us luck'. So we put it in our bag and went to Twickenham. We won at Twickenham that year, and we won the Grand Slam, but were

With Claude Spanghero in London on the afternoon before his first international in
February 1975. His unorthodox preparation, sitting up until 3 am playing poker,
succeeded. France beat England, and Rives played superbly.

'Follow Andy Ripley everywhere – keep tackling him' Rives was told by Jean Salut,
his mentor, before the match, at Twickenham.
Credit: Presse Sport

Always at each other's shoulder, for club and country. Playing against Ireland, Jean-Claud Skrela and Rives follow the U-boat philosophy: hunt in pairs.
Credit: Miroir du Rugby

Rives is seized by his great Irish protagonist, Fergus Slattery, as he tries to attack Irish fly half, Tony Ward.
Credit: Robert Legros/L'Équipe

ABOVE: Look out, here's the new Jean Claude Killy.

RIGHT: Trouble all behind him; how about a five iron to the green?
Credit: Pierre Hussenot

LEFT: Rives the cricketer? His Australian fans can't keep a straight face.

BELOW: The cox hangs on for dear life as Rives and Skrela dice with a watery grave.

The hunchback of Notre Dame. Sydney, July 1981, in the second test against Australia with a shoulder he had dislocated four times just 14 days earlier. Australia's Mark Loane, a doctor, said of his decision to play, 'It was bravery to the point of insanity.'
Credit: Patrick Riviere

Rives has always had a taste for gateaux, but wearing one on the top of his head seems curious.

Against Scotland:

Rives celebrates a try over Scottish centre David Johnston.
Credit: Alain Lafay

Before the controversial 1984 Grand Slam decider against the Scots. Scrum half Jerome Gallion, on Rives' left, shows the tension. Rives said later, 'I enjoyed the game – until the first whistle. With that referee (Welshman Winston Jones) only one side could win and it was not France'.

The agony and the ecstasy:

Dintrans, in tears, is comforted by Rives. Joinel *(right)* is in despair. Is it only a game?
Credit: Presse-Sports

Victory over the Welsh. It was sweeter than most because of the intense, often unhealthy rivalry between the two teams.
Credit: Michel Pansu/France-Soir

Playing pleasures and problems:

Rives, playing against New Zealand, evades the lunge of his great friend Graham Mourie. Rives enjoyed a New Zealand tour most of all, and in Mourie saw a player who mirrored his own views on the game.

Irish referee David Burnett stops the warring Richard Moriarty of Wales *(left)* and Daniel Revallier of France *(far right)* as Rives listens in. Rives seldom enjoyed matches against Wales, and all players found them ferociously hard.

Credit: Presse-Sports

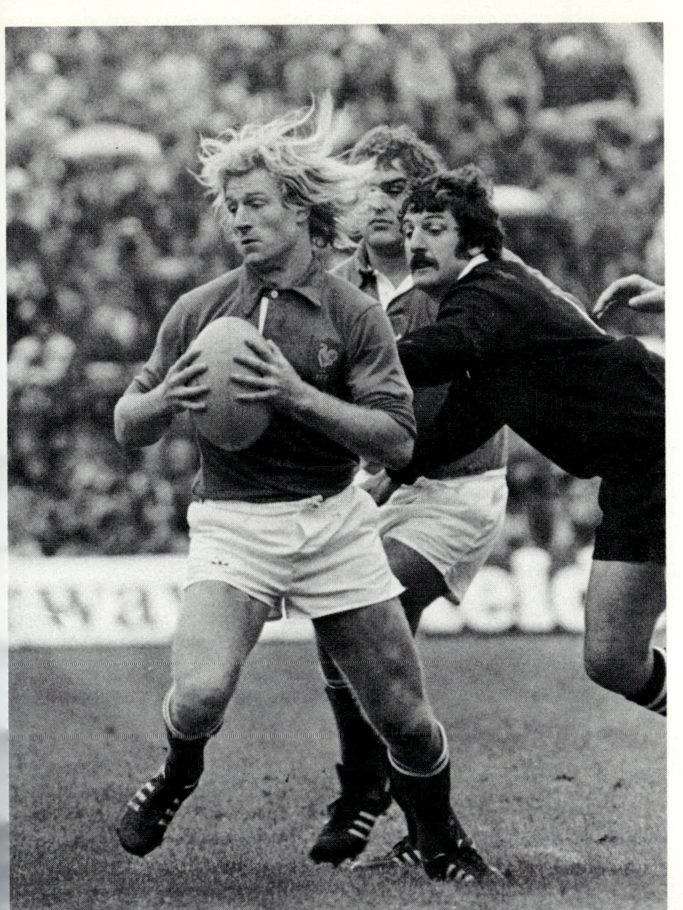

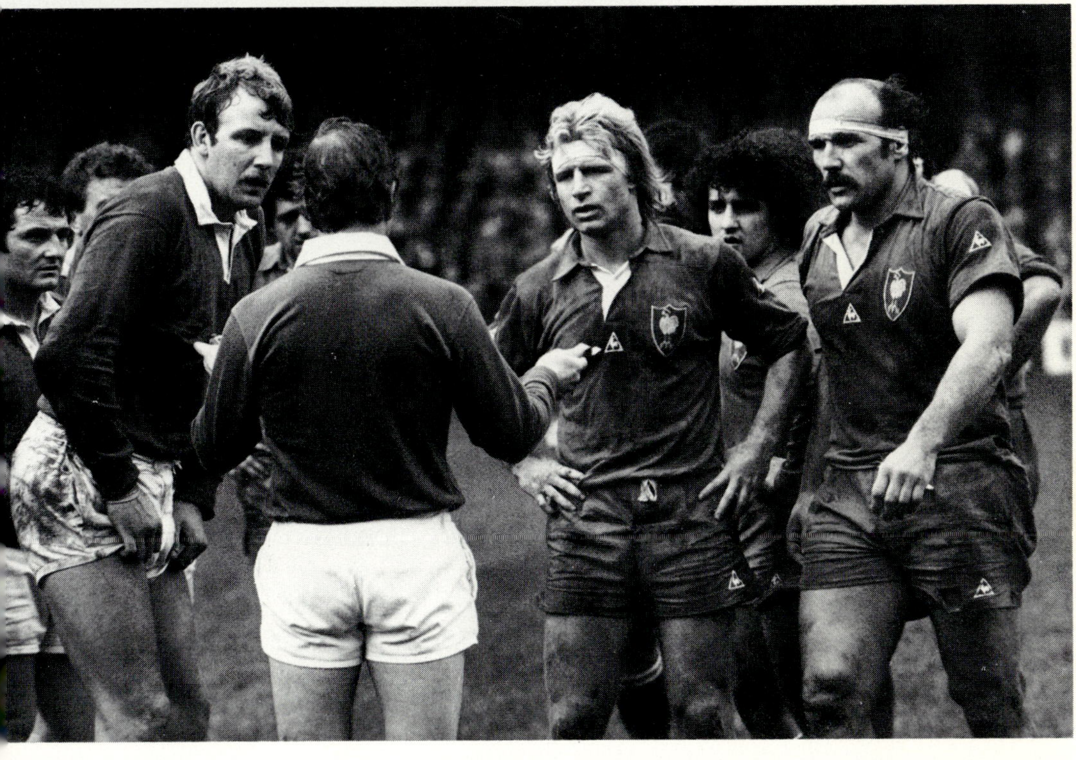

Rives watches as the brilliant New Zealand scrum half, Dave Loveridge, gets the ball away for the President's XV against Wales at Cardiff, April 1981. Perhaps the distant look in Rives' eyes was understandable: he had just led the French to the Grand Slam title in Europe.
Credit: Mike Brett

OPPOSITE: The magnificent Parc des Princes stadium, Paris, as Rives leads out the French team beside Dospital, the prop forward.
Credit: Henri Szwarc

Rives with the man who succeeded him as French captain, Philippe Dintrans.

'Lift your spirit, expose yourself to art' as demonstrated by Rives' great friend, Albert Feraud.

Solace from the crowds – the company of his friends from the world of art, Albert *(left)* and Gaston.

Jean-Pierre with friends, who produce a quarterly satirical magazine, *Les Quatres Saisons*, in Paris.

Referring to Jean-Pierre's famed capacity for bloodying his jersey, a do-it-yourself 'couture pattern' which appeared in the magazine.

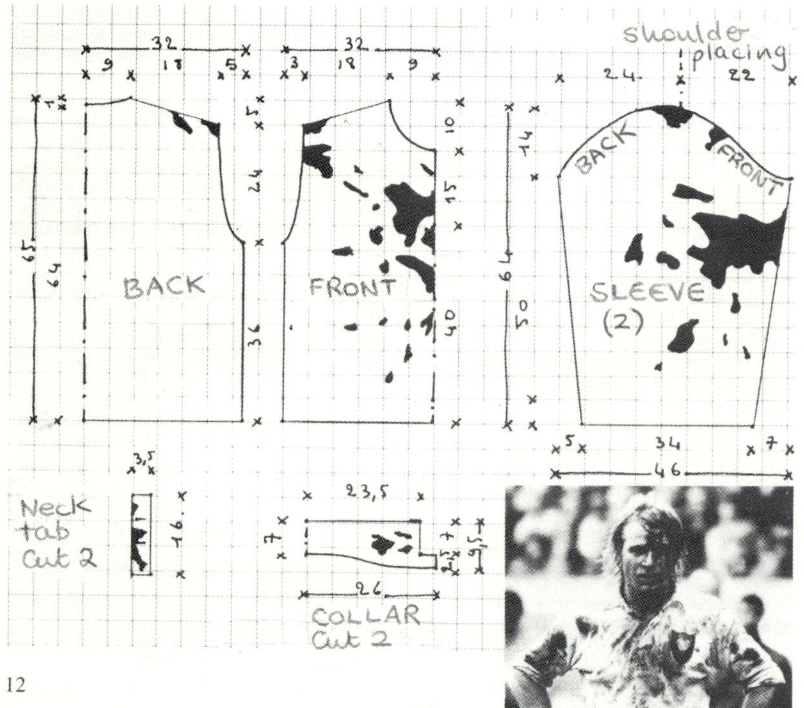

very fortunate to beat England. We could have lost that match very easily.

"In 1981, Fouroux was trainer and we stayed at the same hotel. We went to the same piece of ground for a walk before the match and Jacques said to me, 'Do you remember that can from here'. I replied, 'Yes, I remember it well – it brought us luck'.

"Jacques said, 'Now we must find another can like that one'. We found one and Jacques said, 'We have found another can. Again, I feel it will bring us good fortune'."

France certainly prospered through fortune that March day in 1981. The loss of Neary, Uttley and Cotton palpably weakened England's scrummage, a factor the French were swift to comprehend. Without the rigid control and authority up front which their magnificent forwards had achieved the previous season, England lacked a base to release talented runners and movers of the ball like Davies, Woodward, Carleton and Slemen. Yet England's four penalty goals almost matched France's goal, try and two dropped goals. The try which was decisive should never have been allowed.

Pardo, the French left wing, put in a kick ahead which Rose, the England full-back, gathered and cleared into touch. The ball sailed high into the crowd and Rose turned away, assuming a stoppage prior to the line-out. A stoppage there was, but the briefest imaginable. Rives, spotting the absence of England cover, called to Berbizier to make a quick throw-in. The scrum-half took a ball from a young ball boy, certainly not the original one which Rose had cleared, threw in to Rives and the captain put in Lacans, his fellow flanker, for a crucial try.

The ruling was clear; a quick throw-in would be permitted if the *same* ball was used, and if no-one apart from the players had touched it. That, clearly, was not the case. England, in truth, should have castigated themselves for some dozy, shoddy defence. The Scottish referee, Alan Hosie, had equal reason to castigate himself, for the simple fact of not forcing the players to keep to the rules. Perhaps that lucky can had done its work too!

Rives' reflections on the incident are tinged with the black humour which he has frequently made his trademark. "The big problem was after the match when they said 'You were not allowed to play with that ball'. They told me it should have been a different one.

"I replied, 'Oh, I don't know the rules very well. A different ball? I don't know . . . I am sure it was oval-shaped. And it was a rugby ball, I remember. Not a whisky bottle or a Pernod bottle!'

"They said to me, 'But the other ball went high into the stand'.

"I replied, 'Did you make a mark on it before it was kicked?' "

Whatever the legal implications of the decision, the try stood. And France got another, through an impudent piece of ball smuggling by her captain, before the end. A French movement was halted close to the halfway line, a mass of bodies, still standing, mauling the ball. Suddenly, from the pack of perhaps fifteen forwards, a blond beacon emerged, like a schoolboy attempting to smuggle sweets from a corner shop, clutching the ball to his chest. Rives tore on, those short legs furiously pumping into overdrive, before releasing to Berbizier. Down the line it went, England's defence as exposed as a startled hare before, with a little piece of his brand of magic, Didier Codorniou created the try. Codorniou, sensing the cover arriving, took a pass and, with Pardo looping around outside him, twisted his body beautifully to throw momentary yet vital indecision into the minds of the defenders. Pardo strolled arrogantly over, touching down for the score. A beautiful piece of open rugby. France were on their way home to a 16–12 victory, and another Grand Slam, their second in five years.

Rives confessed his views on open rugby had prevailed; to a degree. "The French team had changed its style by then from 1977. We changed; we fought hard to change to open rugby. At least that is what people said. In fact, there were no battles. We talked among ourselves and we agreed to play a more open game. There was no fight between us. Both sides had a point to make and there was compromise. Neither side won or lost, it was a coming together of ideals, a meeting of views halfway. And from that accord came success and greater, deeper friendship. It is the way rugby should always be."

Whatever the assessment of the critics, who termed the 1981 Grand Slam another success for the forward effort, Rives found solace in his own satisfaction at the accruing of victories in Europe to combine for a Grand Slam. "Firstly, it is difficult to play any of the European countries. Sides like Romania have improved considerably and are just as difficult. I do not live my life believing this day will be worse than the previous one, or that match is certain to be harder than the last one. You cannot do that.

"It is hard to play these teams; harder still to win. And when you beat every team in the Five Nations Championship to win a Grand Slam, it is a rare honour which should not be devalued. Some people tried to do that; I disagreed. It is good to win any game.

"In Europe, the matches abroad – whether it is in Ireland, Wales, Scotland or England – are traditionally difficult. In an away match, you always have a handicap, wherever it may be. In Romania, it is the same. Some players have psychological handicaps about playing abroad. And every ground has its own characteristics. That is the charm of the Five Nations Championship, that at each ground you find a different reason for motivating yourself. There is no ground in the Five Nations which it is easier to win at than another. You have no means of knowing which match will be easy or difficult. In the career of a player there will be grounds where you win often and other places where you never win. But for another player, the grounds will be different. It is very subjective.

"For example, I waited all my career to beat Wales in Cardiff. I did that on my last visit, but only once. The truth is, to play anywhere but in France, is always very difficult."

By the close of the 1981 season the new coach, Jacques Fouroux, was able to assess Rives' captaincy style. He said: "Jean-Pierre knew spontaneously that he wanted to be different from me as captain. I think I had my own style, a certain manner of command. But after, there was a little osmosis between the two. Without making it sound too pretentious, I think that when Jean-Pierre was captain with myself as trainer, I found much of myself in the attitudes of Jean-Pierre. Not as a player but at captaincy level. In his manner of life. I believe he may have taken inspiration from when we were together."

Claude Dourthe, back home in Dax, was no different from every ordinary Frenchman in raising a glass in toast to Rives' Grand Slam success. And of his captaincy Dourthe said: "He was a very, very good captain. Of course, I didn't know him myself as a captain but from what I heard – from his friends, from his teammates – he was an excellent captain. He was a good captain from the point of view of preparation, of intelligence in the game, on the field and off the field. He was always very attentive, very close to the players. He was interested in everyone. Admirable qualities for a leader. I don't think there was a player in that French team who didn't think a lot of him."

Dourthe reasoned that maybe Rives was too nice at times, especially to journalists! Certainly French captains bear a heavy burden in that field; theirs is a cluttered horizon of microphones, recorders, cameras, notebooks, pens. Assessment, in part; dissemination, in truth. But Rives' ability there matched his skill on the field. The more that was required of him, the greater his acceptance level. It astonished bystanders. Long after the Paris internationals, for example, one could seek out the captain of France, still crouched uneasily, uncomfortably, in a corner of the huge bath. The other players had washed, changed and all but gone, the water was cooled and dirtied. All the while he was conducting the last of the interviews, accompanied, invariably, by the gentle plop-plop of blood trickling down his face from a cut, into the grey water. Old friends would come by, for a wet handshake, a word of greeting in congratulatory or commiseratory tones, depending upon the outcome of the game. Rives, his humour alive or his brow crestfallen, would acknowledge each one, courteously, warmly. It was a moving sight amid the linament, bandages, blood-soaked shirts and lumps of mud which lay strewn across the dressing-room floor like relics from a battlefield.

Those who played under him as leader differed in their assessment of the effect the captaincy had upon his own game. Palmié expressed reservations, Bertranne disagreed. "I do not believe Jean-Pierre suffered by being captain; on the contrary, I think it motivated him. He had to prove himself more. I think he liked being captain."

Skrela believes it was a logical advancement, the kind experienced by most men. But he said firmly: "I don't believe Jean-Pierre changed. He advanced, developed. Rugby advances, men advance. There was the price of responsibility when he became captain as well as player. And when you have responsibilities like that, it is sometimes difficult to do what you would have done simply as a player because you have to take results into account. You would have to take upon yourself the direction of the game, all that. Jean-Pierre certainly developed in many ways but he didn't change basically."

Jerome Gallion, the dentist from Toulon, is not only one of the finest scrum halves of recent times, he has also proved himself an articulate, friendly man and an astute thinker on the game; as cool in his diagnosis of matches and individuals as of his patients. He says of Rives: "In any team, you must have an engine, a motor at the heart and it is necessary that someone is in front, to intervene, to stimulate his players. And a brave captain, even if he does not decide the match, knows he can depend upon the players in key positions. But on the level of physical engagement in any match, Jean-Pierre was always an example to us. Sometimes I asked him if he had not put an engine inside his shirt. Because he was always so close to the ball and always at the centre of proceedings and that is very important for a side: to know that, whatever may happen, he would be there at the heart of everything.

"1979 was a peak for Jean-Pierre, both as a captain and player. It is true that afterwards he had injuries which, given the role he had in the team and given his manner of playing in which he took a lot of knocks and exposed himself a lot, was normal. And I think too much was asked of him. He was asked to play matches when he was only partially recovered from certain injuries, notably to his shoulder but also other parts of his body. He was too imposed upon in the game. But he became indispensable to the team because of his spirit."

The details of France's Grand Slam under Rives that year have been sufficiently documented. What has not been asserted with sufficient clarity was Rives' monumental part in leading his side to the unexpected success. Fouroux admitted surprise, in later years, that the new side could become Grand Slam champions so rapidly. Rives, too, had similar thoughts: "Normally it takes two or three years to build a successful side. In 1977 we won the Grand Slam but many of those players had been brought together in South Africa, in 1975. They had two years coming together. In 1981, it was a new team and therefore a considerable achievement for them."

Quite possibly. But for the captain, it was an even greater achievement, probably the finest of his career. He would certainly lead better French teams than the 1981 vintage, yet none with such success. Admittedly, the standards of the British and Irish teams had tumbled; but there was every bit as much chance of the Irish or Welsh beating their moderate rivals. That they failed so to do where Rives handsomely triumphed is a mark of his quality as a leader. He was, at that time, by far the most inspirational captain in rugby. There may have been better technicians in charge of certain teams, but none had the qualities of the Frenchman: the quintessential qualities which would drive on tired, physically exhausted men to a last effort, in support of their leader.

Rives was no staff-room general. He was almost invariably first to the breach, shoring up the defences before the others arrived. Among the boots, he lay trapped, encircled by huge bodies, clinging to the ball, refusing to sacrifice possession as the antidote to his own physical suffering.

Clive Rees, the Welsh and British Lions wing, summed him up eloquently and succinctly, from one match: "Jean-Pierre went off briefly, but returned swathed in bandages. There was blood everywhere. He was leading the French as if he was on the barricades during the Revolution."

Captains won matches, of that, there could be scant dispute, following the example of the Englishman, Beaumont, in guiding England to a rare Grand Slam in 1980. For years, England had possessed players of sufficient quality, yet their value had been reduced by inconsistent selectorial policy. Amid the disruption, England possessed no man of sufficient inspiration to take the flock and weld them into a unit, disregarding the foibles of their masters. Beaumont did it; Rives followed, a year later. Yet his was the greater achievement. Beaumont had led an experienced, excellent side to success. In players like Cotton, Wheeler, Neary, Uttley, Blakeway, Carleton, Woodward and himself, England possessed men of world class. Rives had no such riches to deploy.

The French captain had to assuage public reaction at the mixing of playing styles, ensuring that there was not complete surrender to the views of those who favoured a return to the forward-orientated style. That completed, Rives had to mould together a bunch of raw recruits, some unproven at international level. He did it by inspiration, drive, sheer example. His discipline was strong, his leadership firm. His players knew their role, understood their duty to follow the captain. He fought inexorably, as a player, to achieve domination or, at worst, parity, in his own department of play; he inspired others by example. Players found themselves spurred, encouraged. A word of comfort for one, a sharp response for another. Rives knew his men, understood their strengths and failings and resolved to weld the differing elements into one successful machine. In doing so, he remained very far from the incult characters one has known in certain sports. For that his men had all the greater respect for their captain.

Many of his players had clear limitations, others were unproven. To create a Grand Slam team from such a base was the finest achievement of Jean-Pierre Rives' career. He would enjoy purple patches, fine victories all over the world. The triumph in Auckland was memorable, the rugby his team played for the greater part of the 1984 season, a lingering reminder of quality, lasting like the taste of fine wine upon the palate. But in 1981, no such factors applied. Only Rives' ambition, determination and inspiration lifted France to such heights. He was the Pied Piper figure, who drew others to him as moths to the light.

As a performer, he was at his peak; twenty-eight, worldly, experienced, yet still committed, always courageous, and retaining his remarkable speed. Now, too, his knowledge of the game had been enhanced by overseas experience, especially in New Zealand. In 1981, Jean-Pierre Rives reached the zenith of his career. Renowned throughout France, revered for his bravery and talent, respected the world over, a son of France who had brought glory, humanity, charm and a restoration of old ideals to his role.

A week in the life of . . .

*"O Lord! Thou knowest how busy I must be this day;
if I forget thee, do not thou forget me."*
SIR PHILIP WARWICK's
prayer before the battle of Edgehill
1642

Through his success on the sports field and his charismatic approach and appearance, Rives became the first sportsman to find himself public property in France, but also to an extent throughout the world. He was the first of a new species; the sportsman from an amateur world, successfully straddling the line dividing sporting excellence and society fame; known alike to sports follower, theatre-goer and opera enthusiast. To young and old.

Of course, there have been rugby men of immense achievement through the years, particularly in the smaller nations, where the game enjoys a greater intensity. But today, in France – and more even than Gareth Edwards, Barry John, Willie John McBride or Billy Beaumont in their countries – Jean-Pierre Rives is as recognisable as leading politicians or the stars of stage and screen. His achievement has been to vault clean out of the sporting pool into other echelons of society. In part, the twentieth century, and its demands for bright, shining human packages of star material, is responsible. We package up our greatest sportsmen, gaze adoringly at sleek, fit frames and revere them from near and far. Theirs is an unreal existence. Placed high on a pedestal, they remain there until the arrows of the jealous or the envious bring them down, or they simply become over-exposed.

Yet Rives shows no signs of being toppled. His life is a whirl of society engagements, overseas travel, official functions, promotional work. At every meeting, in each arena, he is unmistakable; accepted instantly, respected enormously and feted by all. But his life is as private as that of a goldfish in its bowl.

Rives finds sanctuary of a sort in an apartment hidden away in a quiet Paris back street. Yet his commitments, both official, through his public relations work for the Pernod drinks company, and private, are extensive. The metal shutters outside his broad 'picture' windows seem more than a security measure; they epitomise his shutting out of the world, for his time is both precious and remote. From here to there, he lives in a frenzied rush which exhausts everyone else. Airports are as normal to him as a bus stop to ordinary people; he arrives, he departs with scarcely a sign of emotion or awareness.

The clock is his enemy; his engagement diary, a burden. Friends, clients, acquaintances are shuffled together, like so many cards, with Rives selecting particular ones at intervals to spend brief moments in their company. And then he is off once more to the next venue, another meeting, perhaps in Tokyo or Toulouse, Paris or Dublin. Quiet moments of reflection seem as foreign to Rives as our modern world to the Nepalese.

Paris is a suitable setting for such restless activity. The chaos, pace and disorganisation somehow personify the twentieth-century manner of the man's life. Yet Rives does not so much accept it as embrace it. "My life is very tiring but I like it," he says. "It isn't too much. It is not enough for me because I would like to do so many more things. Especially spending more time with my friends. But maybe that will be possible later.

"Someone said to me once 'Don't look backwards, life is not about looking behind you. It is in front of you, in the future. The past is finished; it is the next thing you do which matters.' That is so true. I live life for every day. I use every minute of the day. Maybe I am afraid to miss a lot so I try to do everything although one never can. So it's a big problem. I don't get tired of all the travelling . . . I am very enthusiastic, I enjoy it. I have to move, always. Why not? It is me. It is the way I am.

"When I look at my diary some weeks ahead, it is all blank, just a very few things. But then I put things in it, one after another, and it's a huge traffic jam. Maybe I should have a bigger diary!"

A big traffic jam, yes, right from early in the morning, as Rives leaves his home on the eastern side of the city to walk slowly across a major road to the local patisserie, looking for all the world like a

Paris artist, wearing floppy old worn-out shoes, a scruffy top, and old trousers. Strictly functional, seldom elegant, unless it is a day for work or formal occasions.

The walk to the patisserie is a rare glimpse of routine in Rives' life. No wonder; the apple and chocolate-filled croissants, as well as fresh brioche, are a tasty start to any morning, a fresh aperitif for the day. Here good, strong black coffee is an institution; the coffee, not always hot, is consumed with a religious intensity. Rarely does Rives eat or drink alone. Many people call, on the telephone, at the door. The sound of the doorbell clashes with the ring of the phone.

Around eight o'clock they arrive, from Paris, from all over France, some from overseas: friends, acquaintances, business contacts, virtual strangers. At the door there is the man to install new lights above a recently acquired painting. Stepladders are produced, discussion works out the best position. Then Rives, leading from the front again, clambers up the steps and wrenches with some venom at a light which has to be moved.

A while later a post boy brings photographs by special delivery. And then Maurice Arnal, his close friend from Clermont-Ferrand, dark haired and chubby, is there, lifting enormous paintings off the wall, to re-arrange part of the flat. Rives' conversation becomes distracted, erratic; like a child who has yet to learn the art of concentration, he talks absentmindedly to one person, animatedly to another. Soon we are all helping to hoist huge canvas frames on to hooks near the top of a wall, a feat which involves some measure of balancing on small, plastic chairs. A perilous business.

Then another friend arrives to see about some pictures to be framed. And Rives says, 'I shall be back in five minutes'. He needs some glass for a picture. Off he goes, disappearing around the corner down some back street.

And still the calls come in. For hours, often days, the voices speak from the dark, alone, remote, their only contact a taped message on the answer-phone. There are frequently as many as thirty or forty calls a day to his flat. Many more will come to his Pernod office.

"Jean-Pierre Rives," said Jean-Pierre Bastiat, Rives' predecessor as captain of France, "is known everywhere in France. From one end of the country to the other. If you asked 100 people in the street, 99 would know him. I cannot recall any other sportsman of whom that would be true.

"I still talk to him on the telephone – sometimes. But trying to catch Jean-Pierre on the phone is like trying to shoot a swallow with an arrow. You don't get much luck!"

They all wait for the man; from the famous, in their own fields, to friends and complete strangers. "It is not difficult to find the time to talk with Jean-Pierre," said Maurice Arnal, with his warm smile and infectious laugh. "It is impossible."

Yet Rives, just by his conversations on the phone, reveals, probably unknowingly, another side to his character. Portable telephone in hand, he paces the floor of his roomy, modern apartment offering advice and counsel to those in rather less fortunate positions in life. "I get calls from people who have problems," he explains. "Maybe I have met them once and have said, if I can help them, to telephone me. There are sometimes four or five calls a morning like this; and often, I will talk on the phone for half an hour."

Rives is reticent about this 'agony uncle' role. He says simply: "It is great to be able to communicate when you are in trouble". Yet it is hard to conceive most famous people offering their personal telephone number to complete strangers, merely to provide some comfort to those in distress. Often, the strangers break down into tears on the telephone to Rives. He talks to calm them, tries to offer advice and comfort, and is prepared to listen and discuss particular problems.

"One woman telephoned and asked me what she could do. Her son had no work – I guess that is a big problem all over Europe, now."

Not surprisingly, his friends and business colleagues have only slowly come to understand the many qualities which comprise Rives, the man.

"When you travel with him," said Daniel Hémard, President of the Pernod company, "you realise there are no problems. You do not queue anywhere; people take care of your luggage or your car. Always, you have tickets for what you require or where you must go. I wish," he added, reclining in a plush leather chair, "I only wish I had the same power. Nobody knows who I am but everyone knows Jean-Pierre."

Hémard is himself something out of the ordinary. A neat, immaculately dressed man in perfectly creased trousers, Gucci shoes, silk tie and smart French summer lightweight jacket, he arrives for work at the company's offices, clad in motorbike gear. He prefers his Yamaha 750 bike for personal transport to any company car; he plays tennis, trains regularly and breathes fitness, far removed from the caricature business executive of dark, crumpled suit, stomach line bulging and hardening arteries.

Hémard understands Rives; an excellent start for business with the man. And he needs to. Prepare a day for a meeting with Rives and you might wait another sixty hours for it to become actuality. "I must make a little business here; only two minutes," he will say.

The going rate for Rives' two minutes is usually around half an hour; five minutes is worth forty. Rives grins, shrugs wryly at the joke. "I never sit in alone with nothing to do and no-one to meet. The only time I am really quiet is on an aeroplane. I read on a plane and in bed. Even ten minutes or half an hour – that's a quiet time. I prefer to go out; I love people. I am very happy with a lot of people, a lot of friends around me. I just want to share; and if I can share through this book, that is great.

"I enjoy life every day and every minute. If I can share an expression of feeling, I am happy, that is sufficient. Maybe I am still looking for my real self, I do not know. Certainly, the image that rugby players have is not the correct image. It is not fair on them.

"I do so much because I like it; everything I do, I enjoy."

Rives' job with Pernod is officially described as 'Chargés l'Exterieur'. But he says: "Everywhere I go, I have a role in public relations. I represent the Pernod company wherever I go. I must make contacts in all sorts of fields." The job, Rives will tell you, suits him admirably. "I like what I do and I share with people I like. That is ideal for me."

And then a joke. They come frequently, lacing the conversation like tonic complementing gin. "Really, I don't know if I am working for Pernod or Air France."

Yet the role suits him; he is the butterfly figure, flitting erratically from plant to plant, arena to arena. Bright, colourful, majestic; yet ephemeral, attractive but flimsy. The vagaries of his make-up defy a layman's logic. Profligate in his generosity to close friends; at other times, apathetic. A frustrating character, yet as much an emissary for harmony and peace; a contradiction in most terms.

At his flat, cases of wine, bottles of the finest brandy, arrive, and are consigned to the cupboard by the non-drinker. All are offered to his closest friends, with disarming candour. His home is yours; you have the run of it, with access to everything he owns. Nothing is too much trouble, he is a giver, not a taker.

Personal gifts lie idle for months, perhaps years. Or they are given to others. On a huge glass table are the remnants of the day's breakfast; coffee cups with only a final mouthful remaining. Yet he will drink it, without a second thought, when he returns in the evening. Spoons lie close to cups, like dead soldiers beside their tanks. Perhaps, too, a few remaining pieces of croissant; destined, like the coffee, to be finished later in the day.

Rives rarely eats a set meal, preferring to pick abstractedly at food left from previous meals. He has a careful concern for his figure since his retirement from the game; his way of life allows little time for visits to the gymnasium. Thus his meals become snatched intervals of minor importance. One favourite, however, often specially requested at restaurants, is grilled tomatoes with garlic. A little water to drink, never alcohol; occasionally a sweet. No more. Yet his generosity knows no bounds. Dine with him and you are brought the finest wine on the list. True, some topic of conversation will distract Rives from the business of actually pouring the wine; but there it is, ready. However excellent the vintage, he has no interest.

Menus mean nothing to him. If the establishment has omitted his requirement for a particular night, it is obtained, without demur.

Such traits, exclusive to the man, are apparent time and again through his crowded, busy life. Yet there is one tiny oasis of calm close to Rives' life. His ground floor flat leads on to a small garden; a profusion of plants and shrubs. Azaleas, rhododendrons and acers provide a splash of colour; rich, green leaves from bushes such as laurel, camellia and fuchsia; ivy climbs up the walls against carefully positioned green trellis supports. Thin bamboo trees spear upwards in search of the light from above, for the garden is completely enclosed on all four sides.

At night the whole area is floodlit, offering a peace and charm seldom available in Rives' life, a tiny strip of sanity, all but choked by the city and its frenetic life, where tiny sparrows flutter down, to peck away contentedly at the lumps of brioche and croissant discarded from the kitchen window. The area has been assiduously cultivated by Rives; it is a hint of the other side of the man, yet one which gains scant exposure.

Our week starts here, Paris on a Bank Holiday Monday. It seems that even the driving is subdued, the venom diluted. People are not dashing everywhere at the usual pace. Everyone has caught the mood.

Past four o'clock and the streets close to the Roland Garros tennis arena are jammed. No matter, we negotiate the tourists and trippers and the merely curious and find an unlikely resting place.

Up the steps to the hospitality tents, five of us, bounding off towards hours of distraction. Led by Rives, the Pied Piper figure, the opener of doors, the man who negates the value of passes of any description. If challenged by an officious gateman you utter the magic words, 'Avec Monsieur Rives'. It is analogous to receiving life membership!

We follow, weaving through the obstacles and hurdles of tents and celebrities. Held up here, swallowing champagne there. Like the alcoholic driven by an inner urging, we visit each drinking house in our path; peeping in, we quaff drinks or food with the distracted air of the bored or sated. In a world where millions seek nourishment to remain alive, it is an absurdity to the point of obscenity.

Eventually, we cross the main concourse of Roland Garros, bound for 'Le Coq Sportif' . . . and another little reception. Publicity men await, drinks at the end of outstretched arms. More? Very well, if you insist. And then, a buffet reception upstairs. Rives, surrounded by bodies like a hive encircled by swarming bees, somehow maintains progress. We have long since abandoned the pursuit, grateful for the conversation of some old friends discovered loitering nearby.

Our arrival time was 4.30 pm; by now, the sun is slipping away to the west like the last of the party goers. Dark clouds, on a blue background in the sky; streaks of light, from the dying sun's rays. A picture of beauty, missed by most. For the pretty lights are on, and the evening's champagne bottles are already opening.

'Champagne, sir?' 'Ugh, non, merci.'

Another tent. 'Who are you and what are you doing in this tent — it's private' is the gist of the translation. Wearily, another sigh . . . 'I am with Monsieur Rives'. The Spanish inquisition becomes the Treaty of Rome; handshakes and another offer: 'A glass of champagne?'

'Well actually, no, all I wanted was a seat to watch the circus go by.'

'Pardon, sir.'

Rien, rien.

And so it continues. The sun has long since pulled the sheets over its head, even the smart set has moved off to the first of the night's clubs. Still we talk, always there is a last personality. Now, it is Pierre Barthès, coach of the great French hope, Yannick Noah, and his wife, Caroline. Nice people – but after six hours of it . . .

So at last we leave, around 10.30 pm. A six-hour slog through a vineyard of champagne, a sea of prawns, a field of strawberries. What can the morning bring?

Pernod's new swank headquarters at Creteil, on the western side of Paris, is no more than a twenty-five-minute drive through the morning traffic from Rives' east side flat. The building, a cube shape with an orangey, bronze coloured reflecting glass, is incongruous amid the dreary, predictable blocks of tower flats in this part of suburban Paris.

Miss France 1985 (or her twin sister) sits forlornly, like the passenger who missed the last train, in the midst of a vast entrance hall, a solid copper distilling vat almost dwarfed in one corner. A glittering smile; did she flick a switch below the desk, or is it a permanent fixture?

The third floor is a vast, wall-to-wall front-to-back conglomeration of departments. Public relations, future planning, overseas export . . . all jumbled together, separated only by flimsy screens, with a plethora of desks.

To a man, or woman, each occupant disregards current business, to greet Rives. A shrug, a shy grin; a raised eyebrow, a movement of the lips. The greetings are doled out pleasantly like cough medicine for the invalid child.

The desk is unpretentious; almost spartan. Behind, on a few drawers, stand some trophies. On the screen are pinned half a dozen pictures: Rives as a rugbyman, Rives at company receptions, a few others of colleagues.

There is the collar and tie, but the shirt is short-sleeved. The jacket is draped around the back of the chair; and yet, for all that, the image is incongruous. Rives the rugby man, Rives the piano player, Rives the recluse, padding around his flat, away from scrutinising eyes . . . they all have a modicum of credibility. But Rives the office worker?

Danielle, his secretary, arrives, bearing messages with the apprehension of an envoy for King Charles I recounting Cromwell's latest success. Poor Danielle; who would fill her thin, slight shoes? Cast into the role of pursuing her elusive quarry around Paris and the world with the telephone her sole support, she bears her burden with equanimity. Lesser beings would reject the scenario as an impossibility, yet cheerfully she negotiates a conservative course between Rives' unreliability and the demands of clients. Working for the stars of this world is a thankless task.

In the Pernod dining-room democratic socialism has arrived to stay. Canteen would be too crude a word; after all, one can order a good steak there, medium to rare. And the big white chief might sit at your table. French socialism is flourishing.

As we take our meals and sit down, Rives disappears into the kitchens to meet the chef in person. After all, grilled tomatoes are not on the menu today. No matter; the necessary is procured. Laughter, handshakes, waves from the kitchen staff; nothing is too much trouble for Jean-Pierre Rives.

Afterwards we clear up; no trays to be left untidily on the tables. All are neatly stacked away on trolleys, before we leave. And then, back to work.

A few calls, prompted by Danielle; 'Monsieur, il est Jean-Pierre Rives.'

'Oui.'

A little talk, an arrangement, perhaps, to meet. A series of calls. And then, a while after four o'clock, we embark upon a protracted journey to the airport.

Charles de Gaulle International, the most recent addition to Paris' list of airports, has been scorned for its futuristic architectural design and questioned as to its need in the face of other competitors. But on one aspect it cannot be faulted; its position.

English tourists ought to know it well. It sprawls on both sides of the main motorway linking the French capital to the channel ferry ports. To the south it is but a short dash into the heart of the city. The airport runways cross the motorway, creating a peculiar sensation as your car slips underneath a 747-Jumbo jet rolling out for take-off.

Finding the place ought to be no problem. Yet here we are, piloting the car through sleepy country villages, up sharp inclines and past rural landscape scenes which belong more to Corot, not to a modern airport.

Our inquiries meet with blank stares from the locals; no signs, no compass even, to plot our path. Charles de Gaulle airport, it appears, has disappeared off the face of the map, this particular Friday afternoon. The rain is as helpful as the locals.

Jean-Pierre Rives sits in the front seat, dozing off to sleep. Katherine, our erstwhile guide, leans forward from the back, her brow creased in a frown. I press a large boot to the accelerator; Rives awakes with a compliment. "You are a good Paris driver – fast, wild. But more, more; we are late."

An understatement. Air France's flight, non-stop to Geneva, is scheduled for a 6.15 pm take-off. The clock on yet another village church tower shows 5.50. 'I see somewhere the sign,' sighs Katherine, unconvincingly. 'Which airport are we trying to find?' I answer, equally unconvincingly. 'Oh, faster, faster,' says Rives, with a trace of disadain.

Katherine's short guided trip around the back roads has not paid off; the rush-hour traffic up the motorway might have been better. Frowns deepen as the clock moves on. At last, the motorway, and the tired office workers scatter in fear as a lawless English driver weaves through the scrum of vehicles, fantasising he is Jo Maso at Parc des Princes.

Gendarmes gaze with a mixture of awe and disbelief as we approach the Air France airport terminal at 60mph, a screech of tyres as we brake. Katherine disappears in a flutter of flowing white skirt and top, jumper slipping off her shoulders as she runs for the check-in counter. No use, a white jet is climbing into the sky, as we unload the baggage. Air France has taken its revenge on Rives, its tormentor.

'Bah, Air France,' says Rives. 'Breakfast in New York, lunch in Paris, dinner in Hong Kong . . . luggage in Tokyo.' No-one laughs. We head for Swissair's check-in for the next flight to Geneva.

Rives wears the expression of a man who has just been handed his third parking ticket in one day. 'I know he does not like this,'

Katherine confides to me. 'Forget it; it's good for him,' I smile back confidently. She looks sceptical.

Monsieur, meanwhile, has engaged Air France's contestant for the French beauty stakes, 1985, in a deep, intense conversation. 'But eet is not possible,' says Miss France as Rives parades his English. 'Sure, but why not?' he says. 'Pas de problème; see.' Hoisting up a bulky golf club bag on to his shoulders, the man defies every new IATA traffic regulation concerning the restriction of passenger hand baggage, by hauling the new, red bag through security screen after security screen. Katherine carries, half pulls it until I drag the wretched bag on board the Swissair jet. Just as easy as hauling sacks of gold out of Fort Knox.

And so we take off for Geneva. "I go tomorrow, so you come, too, yes" Rives had said at breakfast, the previous day. "For a little golf with Alain Prost and Jean Garailde, the Champion of France. A Pro-am tournament. Interesting I think."

He was as good as his word. Interesting it already was. And no sooner has the Swissair jet swooped in, on a cloudy wet evening, than our driver collects us, and promptly attempts a re-run of our Paris journey at the Swiss end. Of course, we are late. Toujours le même problème. Presently, we pull up at a quiet restaurant in the hills above the city and hurry inside. Alain Prost lifts eyebrows, the colour of John Player Special racing cars, in greeting. A profusion of apologies from Rives. Katherine talks animatedly in a corner; I ruminate on an intriguing evening. We all are tired, yet Rives transforms the scene. A quiet dinner party for six becomes a spirited table of jokes and conversation. The women, their ear lobes sagging under the weight of jewels, listen attentively to the newcomer; Prost manages only the intermittent retort.

Rives is the soul of the party. Jokes, anecdotes, stories; one precedes another. The finest river trout is rejected; a sumptuous steak receives equally scant consideration. Room, and time, only for a sweet as the hour moves past midnight.

"A demain." We retire. Or, at least, some of us do. Rives' unpacking amounts to burrowing into a bag and emerging with a bar of soap for a wash. And then, off to the hotel's gambling rooms, for a hand or two. I decline gracefully and ring London: one link with sanity.

"Well, are you a millionaire? Do we buy a Rolls-Royce in Paris when we get back?'' I enquire, as the grey light of morning, comes drearily through the windows. It is dark, very wet and the scenery is shrouded in mist.

Rives, sadly forced to abandon the life of a millionaire at least until the next time, is up and out by 8.30. By 9.15, he is studying a golf ball on a driving range flanked by mountains, with a gorgeous rolling valley disappearing away into the mist. Practice for half an hour; and the golf balls take some fearful punishment, particularly from a sweet, no. 4 iron.

With a spit of gravel at the tyres, Prost arrives; his sleek, black Mercedes is suitably the pick of the car park. He has dark, mournful eyes which screw into a mischievous little smile; the look of a small boy, more so when he stands up. Between two medium-sized women, he is dwarfed. The dark, curly hair tumbles down towards elongated eyebrows which seem to twitch, as though controlled by some invisible string. The voice is nasal and comes from the depths. I trust his driving is more consistent on the race track; this day, at least, on the beautiful Divonne course, it is a little wayward.

Rives, by contrast, is solid, secure and impressive. He strikes the ball well, with a studious whack. Invariably, it climbs high above the soaked fairways and we trudge off in pursuit with Katherine, in more functional cords and casual shirt, performing her new duties as caddy with commendable cheerfulness. As a reward for her diligence, the sun warms the afternoon players so that we finish beneath a backdrop of mountain peaks and green forests of pine, upon the slopes. Even a cuckoo makes a timely entrance; a commercial plant?

Garailde, an elegant golfer and graceful man, is a fine host. After lunch, we leave for the airport in his Mercedes, while Prost drives across the border to his home, twenty kilometres inside Switzerland. Before he goes, he tries to answer my query on Rives' popularity.

''It is all to do with his great character,'' he says. ''Jean-Pierre has enormous charisma; he is popular everywhere. And he is a person of simplicity, too. He can talk with all people, whoever they are. No-one feels uncomfortable in his company. Perhaps that is his great charm, his easy-going manner, the fact that he is so approachable.''

Significantly, as we left the eighteenth green, a little cluster of youngsters scurried after Rives. Prost, a motor-racing driver by some distance the finest exponent of the art in his country, attracted only a single claimant for his signature.

The businessmen on the early evening flight to Paris, sidle up to Rives like a seductress closing on her victim at some party. We are sitting in the wrong seat but . . . wait a minute . . . there is no problem. They are re-arranging themselves across the aisle, to accommodate us. As he says: "Pas de problème."

The bravest among them starts a stilted conversation. Katherine and I sigh wearily, and leave him to it. The man's stamina bewilders us. The merely inquisitive simply turn and stare, as though at the second coming. 'He does only have one nose, doesn't he?' I enquire.

Approximately sixteen hours later, we are sitting in a sponsored tent, beside the Roland Garros tennis centre, sipping champagne, served by 'le Patron' of this particular hospitality unit. It is 'Patron' Paparemborde, Rives' former playing colleague. Champagne, champagne and yet more champagne! Of course, it is a solo session; Rives is off and away, "a little talk with Pat Cash". And, a while later, "a little business with the father of Pat Cash". Between the two engagements, there are probably more than twenty brief meetings with friends, long-lost acquaintances, celebrities, tennis personalities and the like.

Pretty women, pretty awful women, approach. 'And you're with Jean-Pierre Rives.'

Mid-afternoon, and our hero sits under the shade of an umbrella in another hospitality tent, engrossed in a live 'Radio Monte Carlo' broadcast. The subject? Who knows? Outside, Ivan Lendl is struggling against a Swede; and Virginia Wade is smacking her thigh in anger as though scolding a child.

Up here, in hospitality row, the beautiful people still flock around like sheep. Daniel Hechter, Lacoste, Lois, RTL; a clutter of business companies. We lunch at 'Le Coq Sportif', downstairs; a simple snack of Coquille St Jacques, langoustines, caviar, rocquefort, and a worthy Chablis, followed by strawberries.

And now, at around four o'clock, Rives talks on, meets still more new associates; and promises again, 'just another five minutes'. Paparemborde, with that sad, drooping moustache and sagging eyes, pours two decent beers and joins me. Across the other side of the tent, a couple of teenage American girls, all shining white teeth, blond hair and mouths moistened by the gum rolling around inside like some afternoon thunderstorm, giggle.

'Patou' is as refreshing as the Mistral blowing in the summer; a man of rugby; simple, without pretensions.

I never did make it back to the flat with Rives. The metro proved more reliable. But then, I should have known. "Je suis désolé," he said. I concurred. Who else could make an appointment for three in the afternoon, and finally meet up at midnight?

A few hours free. Time, then, to drive south out of Paris, to a little old village on the outskirts, which is the home and workplace of Rives' great friend Albert Feraud. Feraud, a slight balding man with eyelids which droop mournfully, is a sculptor of the contemporary style. His creations, in stainless steel, are sometimes eight feet tall; others are stylised masks.

In his workshop, he cooks, eats, lives his art, bending the steel into a multitude of shapes, some blunt, others sharp; here, a neat curve, there an expansive bend. Rives loves the man, and his work.

"For me, if I could be one small part of such a man, I would be happy," he says. Feraud is a kind, deeply caring man, who cultivates the interest of his friend by example and long conversations. 'Lift up your spirit,' Rives will tell you; Albert, through his work, illustrates the spirit and freedom of life.

Rives has an example of Feraud's work in his apartment; a vast, stark piece of steel, over six feet tall, on a round, steel base. Pieces protrude at all angles; it resembles no other sculpture.

Rives says: "It is not done for meaning; it is not something to look at and say this means something. This work is done in spirit, for pleasure. You assess it by whether you like it. If it pleases you, OK, then it is for you."

Nowhere, ironically, is Rives happier than away from the crowds – from strangers, prying eyes and the attention of others – working with Feraud in his huge garage. It has a long glass skylight in the roof, a little flight of steps to a second level on one side of the building, where a long table can accommodate his friends.

Here we sit, with an artist friend and his wife, a producer preparing a film on the artist and Albert. The conversation encompasses art, life, the world, modern tastes. Albert, cradling a glass of wine in his thick, firm hands, talks with intensity, his voice trailing off almost into despair at some disagreement. 'Non, non . . .' It is a lilting voice, full of emotion and feeling.

Downstairs, as we eat cheese, bread and meat with our wine, Rives hunts out a saucepan, knocks in a couple of eggs for scrambling and adds his favourite tomatoes. Happily, he stirs the concoction, oblivious to the conversation continuing above. Eventually, it is ready; he delves into the pan with a large wooden spoon. He will eat until the pan is empty; a rare sight.

And so an hour passes, and two. And we find a new rugby ball, the finest leather, without a mark. It is sacrificed in the pursuit of art, in the most unusual manner. Rives opens, with a clatter, the big metal front gate and disappears off down the road. Ten minutes later he returns, bearing a bag full of paint spray cans.

The reason for his purchase soon becomes apparent. His artist friend has taken a thick, black pen to the rugby ball and is sketching shapes and patterns right across the leather. Soon, his work with the pen is over; the paint spray cans, of varying colours, are needed.

With a wristy flourish, he flicks the little white button at the top of the can, producing a jet of colour on to the ball. Then, another; some red, a squirt of black, a longer burst of yellow, a dash of blue. The ball takes on a totally new appearance; the colours and shapes vivid and startling. It is a new concept, yet fascinating and effective.

Rives talks with him, suggesting, discussing. Lost in his interest; a world away from sport, or from the trappings of show business. A simple, unpretentious man in humble surroundings. Happily integrated with his friends, the subject, his great love, modern art. Is it the real Rives? The Rives few have seen? Or just another facet of the man?

Perhaps only Rives knows, if at all. He says: ''For me, it is one of the greatest pleasures of my life, being able to spend time with Albert. But I do not spend enough time; never enough. If you think you spend enough time doing anything, that means you don't like it very much. I could spend all the time with them. I enjoy being with my friends there; I am so very happy with them.

''For me, art is another expression, another way to express yourself. Some people said to me, 'Do you miss playing?' But the answer is clear. To play rugby is to give an expression of yourself; to create something, to do things. It is a great way to express yourself.

"My new team is Albert Feraud; that is very important for me. That is now the way I express myself. And in my job, too. So I have no real regrets about not playing. Although sometimes, especially on winter Saturday afternoons between 3 and 4.30, I have something inside me which wants to be on a rugby field again. Yes, I had ten great years at international level but in my heart I could have played for a century."

Maurice Arnal says of his friend: "He has nothing of the image of a rugby player about him. He is more like an artist. But in rugby he was as generous to the other players as he is now in his life.

"We have known each other for ten years. Jean-Pierre still doesn't like to command. But he always fell on the ball to protect others; he preferred to be stepped on by the other team than let smaller players in his own side do it. That is an illustration of his generosity and he was the only one like that. That is why he was a god and why he is so popular today.

"He is as generous to his friends; he takes good care of them. He is a warm man. Jean-Pierre is not a man to order people to do things. I do not believe he did that in rugby. But he became a great captain because of the way he played. Others wanted to follow him. He is a very good friend and a person you respect. That is enough. In rugby or in life."

Rives will swear by the values of an early night and proclaim: "I must sleep early tonight. So many late nights." And then, at around 2.30 in the morning, you reach home, another evening of great conversation, time with his friends, work with Albert. Full of good intentions but a man who finds it hard to subscribe to any time-table, real or imaginary.

If it is Friday, it must be Japan. Not only United States Presidents crack that joke; bright and early Rives is up, throwing selected shirts into a case, for a journey to the other side of the world. No time to wash the old coffee mugs; scarcely an opportunity to refill them.

Into a taxi, and off, away to the airport. For five days Rives will accompany his President to a Pernod company congress.

"Last year, the company met in Greece, next year it will be

Vienna," says Rives. "Representatives meet from all the stores; all the managers. We have two work sessions a day; morning and afternoon. Discussing the markets, evolution of the product. To investigate problems between factories and commercial outlets. How to develop over the years, markets in separate countries."

Japan, says Daniel Hémard, is an important market. And Rives' name is known to a great many people. Rugby is the second biggest growth sport in the land, a fact confirmed by the astonishing interest the game and its players create, wherever they go.

For one friendly club match, which Oxford University plays each autumn against a select side under the name of Major R. V. Stanley's XV, a Japanese company, Kobi Steel, flew a player over to England especially to appear in the invitation side. Kobi Steel also paid a six-figure sum to fly in a six-man film unit to record the match, the play of the solitary Japanese player, and to make a film of his visit to Oxford and other parts of England.

Japanese national sides have yet to beat, consistently, the strongest sides in the world. The size of the Japanese players, despite their speed, is a major problem in the forward area. But for a company anxious to develop its markets in Japan, Pernod possesses a worthy representative in Jean-Pierre Rives. Perhaps surprisingly, the top-selling destination for Pernod's products, outside France, is England. Other countries, like Ireland, South Africa, Argentina and parts of Europe, have their importance.

Japan is a land of great contrasts. Peaceful, glorious scenery with tranquil gardens of great beauty. Beside them, or at least close by in so crowded a country, are vast sprawls of concrete, factories and skyscraper buildings, spreading to the horizon.

Rives will spend almost a week there. But at last, the long flight back to France is made. A break, but not for long. No sooner has the 747 touched down at Charles de Gaulle airport than Rives is thinking of his next flight; a short one-hour hop down over central France, to Toulouse and 'a little business' in the city of his birth.

The 'Bistro des Arts' is a new venture; Rives is the owner of the vast, 1950s-style-decor restaurant, in an old part of the city. His parents run it for him, happy to leave the overall direction to their son. Day-to-day management is their role; a not inconsiderable function, considering the place is open until two o'clock almost every night.

The restaurant resembles a large dance hall, decked out in pink with rounded pillars. In one corner, there is a raised platform, a small area of seating. Wooden floorboards, no carpets, a couple of small, squat heaters, a juke box, stark black chairs in a simple café style. Everywhere in the room, the ceiling apart, is pink washed. Little cubicles line one side, with Art Nouveau lamps over each, and black vinyl seats. Seven huge pillars provide support: three pink washed, four in white but all with ornate plaster work at the top.

Around the walls there are any number of 1950s cinema posters. James Dean, Marilyn Monroe, Rock Hudson, Jayne Mansfield, Kenneth More, Humphrey Bogart, Clark Gable, even Steve McQueen. Vivien Leigh and Leslie Howard, hair all tousled and dramatic, stand beneath the giant words 'Gone with the Wind'.

Jayne Mansfield, hair the colour of corn, is dressed up in a fetching little leather holster, advertising 'La Blonde and Le Sheriff'. In the entire restaurant, there is only one visible connection with Rives and rugby, a small, 15in. × 24in. painting of him with the ball. It is a print reproduction, taken from a painting.

But Rives sees no value in his face or name; he does not covet attention. True, the wily character that he can sometimes be uses the reputation craftily. But never by blatant advertising.

The restaurant owner paying flying visits to Toulouse, the artist happily at work in a garage full of rusting steel; the Pernod representative, casually chatting to clients and acquaintances in any part of the world; the simple man sitting at home, telephone clasped to his ear, attempting to raise the spirits of those he hardly knows; these are some of the faces of a man of many parts. But no two weeks are identical in Rives' life; nothing is the same, or constant. By the very nature of the man, his is an unpredictable, unusual, turbulent lifestyle. Drawing parallels or extracting firm conclusions from such a pattern is all but impossible.

Apartheid and professionalism

*"South Africa, renowned both far and wide,
for politics, and little else beside."*
——— ROY CAMPBELL ———
1901–1957

*"They had been corrupted by money,
and he had been corrupted by sentiment.
Sentiment was the more dangerous
because you couldn't name its price."*
——— GRAHAM GREENE ———
1904–

The lift cage on its rickety old steel chain plummeted down, with a clatter and a shudder which froze its occupants into a state of fear, their eyes blinded by the sudden blackness. No time was given for adaptation.

For those of my fellow travellers accustomed to this means of reaching their workplace each day, it was not much out of the ordinary. At the bottom of the shaft, the cage door opened with a clank and the lift spewed out its human cargo into an underground world. Yet even here, hundreds of feet below Johannesburg in its fabulously rich gold fields, apartheid is alive and flourishing.

'What you done with this min's lamp, boy?'

A sheepish black youth retreats before the snarled question of the boss man.

'Ah, ah forgot it, boss.'

'You forgot, uh. You shit. You hear me, boy. You shit.'

South Africa is one of the world's loveliest countries, yet it is a place where humans are graded and packed, and where white turns against black and even his fellow white.

The world over, sportsmen argue and debate the most effective path to tread the South African tightrope. Boycott or maintain links. We will play sport with you, or we will not. Even great friends disagree. Jean-Pierre Rives, as he pushed an errant lock of blond hair into place, sighed wearily and said: "I do not know what will become of South Africa. All I can say is I will fight all the time for freedom in sport, even in Russia."

Rives stands firmly and squarely in the lobby which proclaims the value of sporting links with the apartheid managers. Conversely, his friend the New Zealander, Graham Mourie, flatly refused to take part in the Test series against the Springbok rugby team in New Zealand in 1982, when the name of the game was dragged through the dustbins of world politics. It was a series which tore apart the 'land of the long white cloud' as the Maoris call it. Father was pitted against son; wife against husband. Every ideal associated with rugby football was sent flying through a barricade of broken glass, tacks on pitches, barricades in streets, riot helmets, and aircraft dropping flour bombs.

But while Mourie walks away from South African connections, Rives remains a staunch associate, not of apartheid, but preserving the links, keeping alive contact: "I don't believe you can fight for liberty by putting that liberty in jail. For me, it is forbidden to forbid. I go everywhere as a sportsman because, for me, sport is universal.

"The only part of life in South Africa where people are the same, where they wear the same jersey and come under the same rules, is on a rugby field. It's the only place almost you can go for the same rules whether you are black or white."

So Rives continues to visit the Republic, in contrast even to his own French Federation of Rugby which cancelled its scheduled tour there in the early 1980s. Rives insists that that was a wrong decision: "I never let politicians have any influence upon my own destiny. So I regret that the French side did not fulfil their tour a couple of years ago. The Government refused permission, so we did not go. But that was the reason why I went by myself in 1985 – and now I am at peace with myself. I don't know whether that is good but at least I respect myself now.

"France should have gone to South Africa on that tour. If we would go because we felt it was good to go. We could speak about everything.''

It is a viewpoint, of course, but it does not impress its opponents. Perhaps that is the great trouble with South Africa; it is a land which polarises people. You are for, or you are against; no in-betweens.

I recall the late Carwyn James walking stiffly out of his beloved sporting cathedral, Stradey Park at Llanelli, shortly before his club faced a Springbok touring team. That took pride, and a realistic assessment of the important points of life. Rugby football, even to Carwyn James, never gained greater credence than in the struggle between black and white in South Africa.

The South African reformists' lobby argues passionately on the subject. Yes, changes there have been, of that there is no doubt. Yet I remember the feeling of sickness in the pit of my stomach, when boarding a train in Johannesburg's suburbs. There was plenty of space in the white carriages; the few, tatty cars offered to blacks were overflowing and dirty. It takes a selective memory to forget such things, but Rives applies a tight tourniquet to prevent emotions coming into his mind. ''Surely, the only reason South Africa has moved at all in liberalising certain parts of life, is the boycott by the sporting world,'' I say to him.

''What do you mean?'' replies Rives.

''Simply this. South Africans love their sport; they are fanatical about it. The boycott which has ostracised them, in the main, from the sporting world has eaten into their souls, like a cancer. They have been forced to make alterations, in a bid to lure the world's sportsmen back. Can the world now turn to them and say 'It is enough. The boycott is finished'? Is that enough? Or now, as the pincer squeezes concessions, is it not the time to force greater privileges from their government. If the world plays sport once again with the South Africans, will that not be the end of the concessions?'

Rives replies: ''Do not misunderstand me. Apartheid is bullshit and I stand by that view. Always, I have felt that and always I say that. People in South Africa know I feel that about it. I hate apartheid, it is awful. But apartheid is everywhere. It is not just in South Africa. Apartheid is in your own town, your own city, in your own place. Apartheid is so easy to see. Each country has its problems, not just South Africa. In Britain and France, there is an immigration problem. It is not apartheid – but in a way it is. The best way to beat racism is to accept that people have different customs, a different way of living. Each country, each people have their own characteristics and we have to respect each and every one.

"Some people offer a flower at the cemetery, others offer food to the dead. Who is right and who is wrong? Neither. The best story about racism is a man in Japan. In a cemetery he saw a man bringing food to a tomb. Sarcastically he said, 'When are the dead people coming to eat your food?'

"And the other replied, 'When they are coming to smell your flowers'.

"That is a significant story – we have to respect each other."

But does the South African white minority have respect for its black neighbours? Agreed, in an ideal world, this would be so. But this is far from an ideal world.

Rives frowns. "We are living in a society which does not respect people. Not only in South Africa is that true, but everywhere in the world. Yet we have to respect ourselves if we want to respect someone else.

"Everyone fights for freedom in South Africa but Russia denounces that country. Yet look at their own problems they have. We have to fight for freedom in general, freedom everywhere.

"It is so easy to give £10 for a country and then say, 'I am so happy to give you that money, for food.' It is too easy. That is not enough. I don't know what more I can do. I went to South Africa and said I was against apartheid."

I said, "Is that not a minor inconvenience to the government. Is it not of greater value to them to have an international sportsman playing sport in their country. Is that not what they really want above all else, whatever the man says, within reason?"

A sigh. "Maybe, I do not know. All I do know is that when I go to South Africa, on TV as a Frenchman I denounce apartheid. But I say I am going because for me, sport is the best means to make people closer.

"And what of the people who say sport should be boycotted but not everything else. After all, governments still trade with that country, so why not sportsmen?"

Hands up in acknowledgement, point taken. I agree. But what of those like myself who believe all things should be boycotted, trade and everything, I ask.

"That is their view," says Rives. "It is hypocrisy for every country to buy and sell everything to and from South Africa but, when it is about sport, introduce a boycott. I don't want sport lumped together with everything. Sport must stay apart and you must go everywhere."

"How can that be practical in this modern world, for good or evil? Sport is, inevitably, involved in such affairs. It cannot be otherwise in this modern world, whether one approves or disapproves." I make my view with purpose.

Rives prefers to concentrate on the sporting aspect; fair comment from a sportsman. Neither of us is a politician, after all.

"When I go to South Africa, it is the only chance for me to speak freely with black people and everyone. In 1985, I went to Cape Town and I saw some black and white children training on the same rugby pitch. Maybe that is the only place in South Africa you could see that. It's the only place where people are the same.

"So I will continue to fight for freedom in sport – even in Russia. It is the reason I would always go to South Africa – to speak the truth. It is not the solution to put freedom in jail. The best way to make people closer is by maintaining links and keeping alive the contacts."

"We have to fight for this."

A pause for coffee. Our friendship is not bruised, but strong words on difficult subjects clear the mind by concentrating it. Coffee helps, too; hot, black and fresh in Jean-Pierre's Paris apartment, with the morning's chocolate croissants a worthy hors d'oeuvre to the day.

"Look," continues Rives. "Look at Ireland. The only time they can play together, be together is in rugby. It proves sportsmen can rise above these things.

"All the sportsmen in the world should stand up and say we want to be responsible; we want to make our own decision. I dream about seeing a team with one player from each country of the world, allowed to play together without trouble, and without boycotts. I would fight for that. But also I promise, if politicians want to make an Olympics of politics, then I would boycott it. I believe rugby should and could be played in the Olympics; why not? It is truly an amateur sport. Is that not the ideal of the Olympic movement? But not if politics is involved. Never should it be involved."

140

Rives wears the banner of players' rights and freedoms with both ease and compulsion. He reiterates the point, saying: "I am ready to offer a dialogue about South Africa but no-one can do that for me. You have to go there and decide for yourself, to make peace with your own conscience. Let me add this. If a small boy said to me, 'You coming to our country is bad for us', then I would never go back. But coming from politicians, no. I would not take their advice. I never let politicians have my mind. They cannot decide for me."

Right. Agreed. We both went and saw and we both made our decisions. Graham Mourie decided firmly too. In his mind, the oppression of the black man in South Africa far outweighed the natural eagerness of a sportsman to test himself against some of the best rivals in his field.

Naas Botha, Danie Gerber, Errol Tobias and Rob Louw were names of sporting legend, men to excite one half of New Zealand and agitate the other. Mourie, a shrewd, cool, cautious man both on and off the field, made his decision quietly and calmly – and simply walked away from the troubles. His, surely, was the wisest decision taken by all New Zealand in the winter the Springboks toured. Right or wrong, whatever your political viewpoint or persuasion, none could pretend that what followed was anything other than a total abortion of the spirit, ideals and friendships rugby was supposed to stand for.

Yet Rives will consider no criticism of his friend – for an estimable reason. "We are fighting for the same thing, all of us are doing that. OK, we believe in achieving that through different ways but the important point is, we are now on the same side.

"Graham Mourie was maybe the best captain I ever saw on a rugby field. But I respect his decision about South Africa and I am sure he would respect mine. I am fighting for freedom by going to South Africa and he is fighting for the same thing by not going there. After talking about it, if I feel that, for the sake of freedom, I have to stay in my country and never again visit South Africa, I will do that, I will stay here. But I don't want anyone to put my freedom in jail while they fight for another freedom. In other words, I do not think it right that politicians can say you must not go.

"I make no judgements about Graham not playing against the South Africans in 1981. I am sure he is right within himself. And that is the most important thing. I went to South Africa and I feel right within myself, too. If we are fighting for freedom, I am sure we are together on the same street. As a player, I went to Russia, Argentina, South Africa, everywhere. Because I want sport and sportsmen to be free. Politics enters sport too much, far too much.''

Freedom for all; it is a suitable toast to call with our refreshed coffee cups. Here in Paris, in a little backstreet where Rives seeks some sanctuary from the burden of publicity, we talk on about South Africa. A great land, beset by hideous problems. Our wish, our fantasy, is for peace and freedom for all, whatever colour or creed. There can be no deeper agreement, no more truthful joint communiqué between all those who look at the southern tip of Africa, and shake their heads sadly, in dismay and dejection.

But it is not the only problem that faces rugby. There is the question of professionalism and on this subject too Jean-Pierre Rives has his own, unconventional views.

''David Lord, the Australian entrepreneur, was good for rugby.'' Rives sucked in his breath through clenched teeth as if aware of the explosive effect. ''He created a lot of publicity around the game and made things move. He was controversial. I am not a controversial person but we need some people like that in rugby.''

David Lord, indeed, was persona non grata in the world's rugby union circles; a social leper, an outcast. Writers and administrators began firing away at this Billy Bunter type Aussie, who had a fetching kind of bounce in his stride but was disdainful of outraged officials. Perhaps the principal disappointment in the whole affair was its lame conclusion.

Lord boasted that two hundred players, from the leading rugby nations of the world, had signed up ready to join his professional circus. The first whiff of scandal had emerged during the British Lions tour of New Zealand in 1983, and it left the tour manager, Willie John McBride, puffing thoughtfully on his pipe, for what raised the rugby authorities' hackles was the scent of financial wheeling and dealing in this last bastion of amateur sport. The embarrassed look on the faces of certain players reminded me of the days when England was a smuggler's haven. What was the old saying . . . 'Watch the wall while the gentlemen go by, dear'. Something similar had been going on in Rugby Union circles for a long time. Specially designed training jerseys for the touring players in South Africa; mementoes for players visiting foreign countries, free shirts, give-away sweaters and the like. Others even had returned from South Africa bearing gifts for family and friends.

Rives, and his fellow players from around the globe, took a practical approach to David Lord's overtures; they indulged themselves in a little philandering which did no-one any harm. They listened to what the man had to say, did not sign anything, and waited to see whether the alleged gravy train, which Lord was riding Kerry Packer style, would ever reach service.

In the event, it became derailed before the first stop. As long ago as 1975, when Rives was starting his international career, whispers had been rife of players in Europe holding out their hands on Saturday mornings prior to internationals, like errant schoolboys, and having their palms greased to the tune of £200 a man, for endorsing certain products. No names, no pack drill, sort of arrangement – and, of course, there was no proof. But the stories persisted.

Rugby's chiefs were to tarry awhile for very nearly ten years, in fact – before making positive moves to help drag the carpet from under the feet of hard-nosed businessmen who were intent on driving a coach and horses through regulations in an amateur sport which they regarded as, at best, downright unfair and, at worst, hypocritical. It was a delay which proved almost fatal to the future health of amateur rugby.

The Kerry Packer affair in cricket ought to have sounded the alarm bells in Europe's rugby citadels, even if the men of the British Isles could not hear the sirens sounding from New Zealand and Australia. It was only a combination of David Lord's poorly organised train which derailed, and sheer good luck, that saved rugby from facing the same kind of upheaval.

Lord promised the earth to his players, and only a little less to his enthusiastic followers. The best players in the world drawn together in an organisation – titled, predictably, 'World Championship Rugby' – playing circus games in Europe and Australasia. Major industrial moguls, he bragged, were poised with pens at the ready. The start in London in January 1984 was timed to coincide with the opening of the European Five Nations Championship season, which France began by playing Ireland in Paris, and with Wales meeting Scotland in Cardiff. Rives, by this time a legend in his own right, was leading France in Paris.

But his astonishing admission now is clear-cut: "If David Lord had got the money and all the arrangements together, I would have joined him. I was ready to sign to play for him. I knew it would have been the end of my amateur career. But despite that, I was ready to go."

The French captain had made up his mind for one reason alone. If, as he believed, the world's best and most experienced players were to sign for Lord, he would want to go with them. But to dub Rives a dollar-hunter, intent only upon personal fortune, would be to misunderstand the man totally. The challenge, the search for projects which could fire honour and imagination, were what interested him, he claims. Money alone has always brought only a distracted shrug from Rives.

He says: "If Mr Lord had found the money to create a professional system, for sure I would have become professional. It would have cost a lot of money to do that. But the money did not interest me very much. I would have been prepared to sign for him because, to me, it was always important to play against the best players. You always want to test yourself at the highest level in any sport. If all the world's best players had signed for Mr Lord, and I believe that would have been the case, then I would have been ready to join them. I have always wanted to play with the best players in my sport."

The previous winter (1983–4) in Europe, France had achieved a share of the Championship, with Ireland. Only defeat in Dublin had prevented another French Grand Slam. Popular theory, the smart talk, alleged that Rives had nowhere to go, no further honours to achieve. His was a ship on which the party had continued for so long and been so successful, that its occupants had become bored. Nothing could have been further from the truth. But what upset him was the attitude of the sport's authorities, in refusing to budge on key issues which would bring rugby, albeit kicking and screaming, further in to the twentieth century.

The World Cup issue had been fudged again; great players, whom no game could afford to lose, were being banished into Siberian exile for writing books and articles about their careers. It was so ludicrous, it defied belief.

Rives says now: "If Mr Lord's plans had succeeded, the people in charge of rugby, the officials, would have been to blame for that situation. Why? Because they did not understand the way the players were feeling.

"When you are well and happy with your life, you do not want to change. But so many players said that they wanted change. It meant that things were not right. That is logical."

Rives remains convinced that the Lord incursion will prove to have been something close to divine providence. He says: "I think all this will help the game in the future. I hope, I believe, the mentality will change and that officials will become more aware of things. Rugby must change; the officials must change with it, too. Sometimes, the world and life changes quicker than you expect. We must be honest with ourselves, honest with our principles and honest with those around us. That may be difficult but it should be the way."

The Lord affair palpably influenced the International Board in altering its views. By March 1985 news was coming from the Board's meeting in Paris that, at last, a Rugby World Cup had been agreed upon, and would take place in Australasia in 1987. This was no coincidence; Lord's stab at exposing rugby union's suscepti- bility to a spectacle on a world-wide scale, had alarmed the ruling bodies. Creditably, Australia and New Zealand had seen it coming years ago, but their words of persuasion foundered on deaf ears. Only with Lord's intervention did officials see the danger.

So the belt, which had all but throttled the future health and invigorative nature of the game, was cautiously loosened. But not much changed prior to that decision. Back in 1978, Gareth Edwards wrote in his autobiography, "As long as the top rugby union players are paying their own hotel extras, and being denied a certain amount of privilege in a hugely sponsored game, then the ground is ripe for a Packer coup."

Rives sees value in the point today, especially with the South Africans still barred from participation in the world game. On that issue, he says: "I had hoped South Africa would play in rugby's first World Cup, but I fear they will not. South Africa should play because they are one of the best nations for rugby. A rugby World Cup without South Africa would be like the football World Cup without Brazil."

And again, on professionalism: "Writing books is not profes- sionalism. The professional is a man who is paid for playing, a man who is playing and being paid well for playing the game. That is the kind of professional system which David Lord proposed. He wanted to buy players. The only mistake Mr Lord made was that he did not have the money. But if he had found the money, the players would have supported him. With that money, maybe one hundred players would have signed to play for him. There were that many ready to join. I know, I met him. But I am still waiting for his call back . . . ! !"

Rives tackles the subject of sponsorship generally in rugby in animated fashion. He defends the value of sensible 'perks' for players lavishing great amounts of their time on the game. His is a realistic approach, he reasons, to a problem which has dogged the amateur game too long. The dilemma is sure to deepen before it is solved. "Let us have less hypocrisy and more pragmatism on this subject," he demands. "It is a difficult problem but the reality is there. I am for the sport of amateur rugby but today, even for players on tour, there must be help to make sportsmen secure after playing, because, when you are thirty, your life is not finished.

"Players give a lot of time between the ages of ten and thirty. So they must be helped in social, public or private ways. Or by their club or their own company. Maybe players should receive assistance with jobs. It is not the time to worry when you are still playing; it is afterwards, because you did not prepare for your future seriously enough while you were playing rugby at the top level.

"Most players just think about their passion for the game. But they should think also about the future, because life is short. The problem is, all sports people believe they live only until they are thirty. But you are still alive at thirty-five, so you must prepare and think about these things.

"When you are younger, you do not do that. So let's try to have positive action. It is not easy, I agree, but we must start to tackle the problem."

The choice: move with the times or incur an organisation which is out-dated, ineffective and ripe for exploitation. Rives believes there is scant choice, saying: "We have to do this. There is no need for fear; the game could still be only amateur if we choose a special sort of help. Social help from the club, from the public, from the government for jobs – that is the sort of special assistance which would be best.

"The economic system is becoming difficult and friends want to share the time of rugby players. If you are working, and after work you have training and also play rugby, friends and especially girls ask 'Why?' Women today want more time from their men."

"A Charismatic Nature"

"Be not drunk with wine, wherein is excess;
but be filled with the Spirit."
——————— *EPHESIANS 18*———————

Deep inside the concrete bowl of the Roland Garros tennis arena, the American, John McEnroe, was grinding an opponent into the clay court dust. It was not yet mid-day but the sun was already hot. Not far away, on the city's Périphérique motorway system, drivers trapped in hold-ups hit their horns and waved arms in the best traditions of Gallic frustration.

The refugees from the hot, packed courts who were taking a stroll outside, or other spectators still trying to get in, paid little attention to the plain, dirty black Renault 5, as it nosed carefully through the crowds. The car halted, a man with striking blond hair appeared.

Enter Jean-Pierre Rives, dressed in simple black casual jacket and shirt, and creased trousers, his hair as ever in no particular shape or form. But no famous tennis player or socialite could so have turned heads, brought youngsters rushing for autographs or sent grumpy gendarmes hurrying to move barriers and offer the Renault double parking, without a whistle of protest. Where Rives goes, doors are opened, unscaleable barriers are dismantled.

None of this distracted Rives from his task. His strong, roughly hewn hands were delicately lifting a crippled man out of his car and into a waiting wheelchair. Rives assembled the chair beside the vehicle and helped his friend into the seat. The car locked, he wheeled his friend up the road and out of sight, to the special entrance for the disabled.

It was a side to Rives' character few had seen yet, for the perceptive, it ought to have provided a vital key to unlock the real person. The gentleness inherent in such careful movement of his friend, belied one image. But it was only another side to a character whose complexity defies comprehension, even to his closest friends.

Rives the man or Rives the rugby player tells only half the story. One can, without difficulty, categorise and analyse radically differing aspects to his character – the rugby player, the man outside rugby, the gentleman, the whole enigmatic personality. Of course, the rugby image is the best known. The hair, very blond, gave Rives an image and a reputation: the blond bombshell, the golden helmet, the beacon for others to follow. Those engaged in the business of lyrical sobriquets reaped a rich harvest.

But none of these images began to tell of the real man, none scratched the surface of his character. But with the reputation came fan letters by the shoal, the approaches from businessmen, the close attention of sports sponsors and promoters, not to mention writers. France, as a country, takes its sporting heroes extremely seriously. Their value is extraordinary by the standards of other nations.

The Rives' figure, polished and adapted for public consumption, has been extensively documented. There is the easy adaptation to sponsors' events and the needs of the media men; the casual conversation with celebrities. Rives handles all with consummate ease: time for everyone, in a sense. And yet it is a strictly regimented timetable which keeps him moving, preventing the crowd closing his escape hole. The word on the international celebrities' circuits is: sign the autographs, clasp the hands, keep the smile ready and willing, but in all three disciplines, maintain movement; lest the blockage becomes impassable.

Rives' involvement with Pernod has made public presentation an aspect of paramount importance. Rives travels extensively. His easy-going nature impresses clients, likely to be in awe of this famous international sportsman. He had earned his reputation, but he enhances it with courteous manners and a pleasant bearing.

In France, it is by no means so straightforward for him. To a degree, he can claw some privacy for himself from the labyrinth of Parisian back streets. Yet once into the popular areas, his fame precedes him. Commendably he takes it in his stride but rather like a visitor to the Indian sub-continent coming to terms with the overwhelming poverty.

Imprison is too strong a word, yet public adulation has inevitably restricted his natural desires. When Stade Toulousain, his former club, reached the final of the 1985 French Club Championship, to contest Toulon on the last Saturday night of May, Rives astonished those who knew him only from afar by declining to attend. Instead, he sat in his Paris flat, sprawled across a bed, watching the television. Outwardly, he would tell you it was his wish to see the game that way. "I love to watch rugby, but on TV. Rugby is very good televised. You can see the faces, the happiness, the sadness. In the stand, that is difficult. You have to have a very good seat to see those things from the stand. So I like to watch on TV with a few friends. It is a different atmosphere but I am now a TV fanatic. And unlike some sports, rugby does not lose much on television."

A bland response. Pressed on the point, Rives concedes: "The fuss and all the people is perhaps the reason I prefer to watch on TV. To sign autographs is not disagreeable. But I am happier at home where I can see the match without too many questions and interviews."

The mask, having momentarily slipped, is hastily re-assembled. "Really, I don't see very well now with one eye, so television is better for me. In general, my eyesight is not too good."

His attendance, however, at France's 1985 European Five Nations Championship matches, at Twickenham and in Dublin, reveals the truth of the matter. Outside France, Rives feels better able to merge with the crowd. Particularly as his manipulation of the language barrier has been his ace joker in the pack for most of his career.

He himself tells a story about a visit he made to the United States of America, with his American friend, Jennifer Taylor, a model. When the pair flew into California, pressmen were gathered, ready to probe their future intentions.

"Do you have any plans for marriage at this time, Mr Rives," came the first question, loaded like a gun.

A brief pause, and then the automatic response, "Marrig – I am sorry, I not understand," said Rives.

"Well, what we wanna know is if you intend to marry Jennifer. Like, be husband and wife."

Another pause. "Please, really, I want to 'elp so much. But I no understand Eenglish so good. Ask, please, this question weeth Jennifer," was his crafty reply. Even the American journalists shrank from that challenge.

Rives tells the story now with enormous pleasure, the blond eyebrows jerking upwards in convulsive laughter. One suspects that the game, the pleasure of the hunter, is his delight. And something of the sort has been going on for years at rugby match press conferences all over the European countries.

'I no understand your question. But, for sure, eet ees going to be 'ard, vaire 'ard thees game. I ope we can win, but eet ees difficult for me. Also for my team. Eengland ees a vaire good side. Always at Tweeckenham, eet ees difficult for me."

Non-French journalists would splutter in frustration at the barricades thrown across their path. Rives, the epitome of charm, had been so helpful. He would listen quietly, intently to the publicised thoughts of the British captains and coaches, marking down particular quotes for his own use at some later date. But when the French contingent began their public inquest, so began the problem. Rives' English, abruptly, was lamentable. His friends in the French press, to a man, appreciated the joke and came to regard it as second nature.

Discuss Rives with one man and you will evoke images of the public figure: smoothly negotiating handshakes, deep conversations, a honeymoon full of kisses from famous and not so famous women, handling difficult characters with aplomb. But to others, there is only one character; the player of aggression and spirit.

Vibrant, live-wire, a person of great strength, courage and enthusiasm. On the rugby fields of the world, he forged one side of his reputation with remarkable feats of endurance, often far beyond expectation, a lively man who seems, almost magically, to come to life around the midnight hour.

He seldom touches drink, however, and claims abstinence for the greater part of the past three years. Nor does he miss it; he simply never became accustomed to the taste. He tells, with a hint of pride, a joke against his family. "My parents work in a bistro but neither of them drinks. My brother, Philippe, runs a bar in Majorca, but never drinks. And I work for Pernod, and do not drink!"

His restless urge for stimulus is the need he finds partially sated in the night clubs. In Toulouse, hidden away in a tiny alleyway off the Capitol Square, Rives spent many nights of his young life, in establishments like 'Club Ubu'. A darkened cavern, small yet elegant, where he entertained his hosts with great splendour and generosity whenever national teams played in Toulouse.

One person who would remember it, albeit with a grimace of pain, is that giant of a man from Perpignan, Jean-François Imbernon. Imbernon, a man as susceptible to injury throughout his career as a carpenter to torn hands, had suffered an excruciating blow on a leg during the first Test match of the 1977 New Zealanders' tour of France.

Hours after that match, as the players repaired to the club, I stepped across the darkened floor for a drink and struck his extremely swollen foot. There was a snort of pain, the rumblings of movement as he studied the injured limb with concern and fury. Handshakes and signs of reassurance dulled the fury, if not the ache. But Rives led the party ever onwards, with undiminished zeal. He was, almost invariably, a man transformed in the night clubs.

Rives' encounters with alcohol, in any quantity, have become little legends of their own. Gareth Edwards and Fergus Slattery both recall such rare nights with the Frenchman.

Edwards, the player whom Rives calls "perhaps the finest rugby player ever seen", remembers a long, gruelling night in Paris, after France had beaten Wales at Parc des Princes. On and on they went, from club to bar and back to another club, until the triumvirate of Welshmen – Edwards, Phil Bennett and J. J. Williams – could barely stand up. Rives, forsaking his usual Perrier, had joined the celebrations with a rare abandon.

"We were in a taxi, looking for one more bar, and dawn was almost breaking over Paris," said Edwards. "We had asked the taxi driver to stop but then we saw three Welsh supporters. Frankly, the last thing we wanted to do, after a defeat and then a night like that one, was to meet fans and start talking about the match. But the driver misunderstood our signals and stopped right by them."

Three weary Welshmen, far from home and wandering the streets of Paris, thought they were hallucinating as the internationals tumbled out of the cab. 'Look boys, it's Gareth, and Benny, and JJ.' As the players leaned uncertainly against the cab, Rives, his eyelids fighting a losing battle to remain open, keeled over and pitched into the gutter, vomiting away the night's excesses. The Welsh supporters applauded 'Don't worry boys; you lost the match, but we beat them at the drinking,' said one. Edwards remarked later: "They say you never beat the Welsh, even if you score more points than them. Here was the proof!"

For Fergus Slattery, that intelligent, articulate partner in a firm of Dublin auctioneers, who turned himself into a rugby player with as much potency as some of the whiskey his countrymen swear by, there was the memory of a long night in Dublin after one international. Exaggerating his own accent, he said, "Be-Jesus, it whirr loively, arl-roight. To be sure, Rives was taking the waters, that noight. A man who doesn't drink? Oi have other memories of him, oi'd have to say."

More revealingly, Slattery watched fascinated one night at an after-dinner gathering of the French and Irish players, as the charismatic nature of the French captain peeped out like the moon from behind clouds. "Some guy was playing the guitar, we were standing about chatting and it seemed a very convivial affair. But quite suddenly, Jean-Pierre wanted to go and said as much to all the French players. There followed the extraordinary sight of the whole French team following him on to the bus, like schoolboys off for a day's outing. It was remarkable. I would not have been able to find the players in the Irish team, still less get them to follow me. But Rives carried great respect from his players."

That esteem was created, initially, in the cruel, dangerous, hard world of French club rugby. Even the world's most hardened players baulk at what goes on in French club rugby. Far across the world from France, hidden away in the rolling hills which dominate the North Island of New Zealand, Colin Meads, a sheep farmer and a legendary All Black who became, to the world, plain and simple 'Pinetree' through a magnificent career which was extensive in tenure and awesome in power, shuddered at the incident which he believes was his worst on any field during his career. Inevitably, it came in France.

"I lay trapped by bodies, in a pile-up but my head was clear. I was aware of someone running towards me and then felt a boot kick me . . . in the head. Not light, deflected sort of kicks — full-strength boots. Christ, I lay there wondering what the hell was going on. It felt like my skull would break."

The culprit, a renowned hatchet man, played nine times for France during an era when sportsmanship had greater credence than in present-day sport. It was an indication of French readiness to accept such play which, even today, can pervade the club scene, and which remains a stain on French rugby.

"Jean-Pierre," said Michel Palmié, "was a player who would put his head where others would not put their hands. His bravery was unbelievable at times." Mark Loane's description of Rives taking bravery to the point of insanity, paints that quality best. As Rives dived in amongst the boots, so the blood seeped from his cuts; occasionally flowing in some quantity, but more usually plopping gently on to his shirt like a leaking tap, it became a symbol, a trademark of sorts. In reality it was far removed from the real person beneath the rugby jersey.

A third facet of Rives' character comes closest to revealing the man's true nature. On the rugby field, opponents such as the former New Zealand wing Stu Wilson would term him: "A true gentleman of rugby". And Wilson, although he may not have realised because he played against the Frenchman only rarely, came close to unravelling the mystery when he said: "I remember in 1977 a great day with Jean-Pierre when we saw two sides of him.

"Jean-Pierre invited three of us for a game of golf. It was a big thing for the club to have all these international rugby players playing their course, but Jean-Pierre insisted that we all had a champagne lunch before we started.

"There were literally hundreds of Frenchmen following us round when we eventually did get started, and it took us seven hours to play the eighteen holes. We were all pretty drunk and I recall our fly half Doug Bruce falling asleep with a bottle of champagne underneath a tree on the twelfth tee!

"By the time we had played a few holes, we were all feeling the strain a bit after such a heavy lunch but it didn't matter how badly we hit the ball, the crowd kept on cheering. On one hole, it took me five putts to get down and the Frenchmen clapped every one.

"After the game, we went back to Jean-Pierre's family house at Toulouse and he proved to be his usual magnificent host. Then, all of a sudden, he sat down at a grand piano and started playing beautiful classical music.

"I thought to myself: there he was – the blond terror – sitting there playing these gentle, soothing melodies like a concert pianist. I'd always thought that backs were the ones who could play the piano and forwards could only move them!"

That certainly was Rives; a man of paradox, a grand anachronism. Quiet, timid, courteous, charming, and concerned for others. When Bryan (B. G.) Williams, the All Black, dislocated a hip in the 1977 Test match at Toulouse, hospital doctors told him he could not be moved for at least forty-eight hours.

Williams was one of the game's greatest ambassadors and gentlemen, a splendid advertisement for his country. Few players rivalled his courtesy and manners. Williams said: "The rest of the All Blacks had already taken off for their next venue so I was feeling very lonely and sorry for myself. Lying in a hospital bed in a foreign country, with no-one speaking my language, wasn't much fun. But on the day after the game, Jean-Pierre came to visit me. I know some people would say that is the rugby fraternity anyway, but even so, it really impressed me. I suppose it was only a small thing really, but that is my most enduring memory of the man. He made me feel so much better that day."

Not only Williams would discover the extent of Rives' generosity. French colleagues used to tell the story of how, when Rives played for France in Romania, he was quietly appalled at the deprivation suffered by the poor people there. By the time the Frenchmen had concluded their tour and reached the airport for the return flight to Paris, they looked askance at the figure plodding along among them; few clothes left, and carrying hardly anything except his passport. Rives had given away most of his clothes. He returned to France with literally just the few items he stood up in. The rest had been given in friendship. "They needed them more than I," he told a friend.

In South Africa, Rives had forged a friendship with the Springbok player, Morné Du Plessis – and it was not difficult to see why. Both men possessed humility, alongside their popular public image.

Rives said of the South African: "A lovely man. He is a man of trust and great friendship. I found him friendly, helpful and always courteous. One of the nicest men I have ever known."

On tour, wherever he has been, for month-long visits to New Zealand or short weekend trips for internationals in the British Isles, Rives has faithfully telephoned home to his parents every day. Not through insecurity; rather, for the feeling he has for all his family. "We are such good friends," he says of his parents, adding with a smile, "but my telephone bill is always the biggest!"

Michel Palmié, sitting hunched over a large leather-top desk in his office behind Beziers' main square, gave a sketch of Rives, not the rugby man he played alongside for three years, but the character he came to know closely.

"Jean-Pierre is a man of showbusiness, he is always at receptions, on television. He is accepted wherever he goes. But that is not the real Jean-Pierre Rives. Jean-Pierre is an excessively shy fellow, rather close and uncommunicative. The real Jean-Pierre is the one who would be with me in the office alone. All around him is a certain 'aureole' (a halo or ring), which he is obliged to create for himself, which people know how to exploit, because the real Jean-Pierre is a friend, someone who, while I am drinking wine, wants some milk because he doesn't like wine. He is someone ordinary who does not have outlandish tastes. He is a great friend, always available; Jean-Pierre is a vagabond, a wanderer. He goes all over the world, he loves to travel but the real Jean-Pierre is the person alone, quiet, who lives in a sort of cloud at 5,000 metres."

And the shell?

"Perhaps it is a shell in which to isolate himself," continues Palmié. "I think he shows a certain image on the outside, but inside he is not at all like that figure. He is someone who isn't complicated, who hasn't problems, who lives his life to the full, who gets the maximum out of life."

And how many people know the other side of Jean-Pierre?

"I think only his friends, because you can create relationships with people; they like you or they don't, they know you well or they don't. But if they don't like you, you don't confide in them. I know Jean-Pierre relatively well because we often telephone each other. We have a good relationship although I haven't been in the French team for a long time. We don't see each other so often now, but when we do it's always good; we confide, we discuss, when he has problems he can phone me. It's a real friendship."

That is the hallmark of the Corinthian figure; the creator of deep friendships which last, surviving winds of whatever violence. Rives adopts an unobtrusive attitude to his friends, famous and unknown alike. His love of occasional anonymity, the company of only his closest friends is as emphatic as his dislike for pomp, arrogance and pretence.

His mother, Lydia has been quietly astonished at some of her son's aversions. During his career, Rives earned a treasure trove of awards, jerseys, plaques, portraits, and recognitions of all sorts. These, without exception, are locked away in a dusty old leather trunk which sits in the family attic like some outcast relation.

Inside his parents' Toulouse home there is not a single item, not a solitary picture or memento, to mark ten seasons of achievement for their son in the French national side. To them, it is as though Jean-Pierre is content to forget his past glories.

"We do not understand it, but we respect Jean-Pierre's wishes," says his mother. "If we put up a picture of him as a player, or one of his trophies, he will always say, 'Why is that there – please take it down', when he comes to see us. So there is nothing."

Withdrawn, secretive, the antithesis of his public image. In Paris, on a summer's day, you might catch a glimpse through the open window of the blond hair streaming in the wind. But the vehicle itself would never reveal the public man. His battered old Renault 5 is Rives' idea of vehicular comfort. "Why would I want anything better – it is only to take me from place to place," is his puzzled reply to suggestions of smart sports cars, or plush limousines.

Perhaps the final facet, the last piece of the jigsaw of Jean-Pierre's personality, is the most complex of all. A man who can be the epitome of friendship and courtesy can also appear to be unreliable and unpredictable, even exasperating. Roland Bertranne played with Rives, against him, and under him, and holds more rugby caps than any other French threequarter against International Board Countries. "If Jean-Pierre had a weakness," he jokes, "you would look for something in his private life, not on the rugby field. When you are in a group, in a team, you always have certain times and places for meetings. But Jean-Pierre was never there – never! He is a very charming fellow with an easy manner, but he is also a bit shy and sometimes elusive to grasp."

Others, who knew Rives better, develop the theme. Jean Michel Aguirre, a friend since they trained together at Toulouse University, says: "Always, Jean-Pierre was a very cool person. We spoke very often with each other because we had the problems of our ages, 20, 21 – of what we were going to do. But always Rives was cool; in his life and in his way of working. Always, he would arrive for meetings late."

Aguirre, straightforward, honest and intense, was sitting in a café in the town of Tarbes, not far from his home near the foothills of the Pyrenees. He pondered his current relationship with Rives.

"One of Jean-Pierre's characteristics was not to speak too much and sometimes not enough. For some years we were good friends, very good friends. We spoke about the same things, about similar problems. But after, I want to say what I feel, what I think. But maybe I speak too much . . . he didn't do the same.

"Even now, I do not know where we are. I cannot see. I have great pleasure in meeting him again from time to time but, for me, we are now on two different planets. We are different. Perhaps it is me, I don't know. I believe I was a good friend for him. We spoke of him and his problems and he had his problems at times. But later, my view of life was quite different to his. We would talk, and I said 'will you marry, and will you buy a house?' Like friends do. But I felt he did not like this; it seemed too much. To conform. These things were too conformist for him."

Unpunctuality is the essence of the man; you would never set your calendar by him, let alone watch. Aguirre goes on: "Very often on tour, we were invited, three or four of the French team, to some event. I would arrive, and the others and people would say to us 'Jean-Pierre – is he coming?'

"I would say, 'Surely, yes – he said he is going to come. He is coming.' But he was not there."

One of Rives' most endearing characteristics, when he does arrive, is his ability to put at ease all those whom he meets. Complete strangers, a shade sceptical as to their likely reception, cautiously approach for autographs or questions. But they all receive the warmth and friendliness which is the real man, and thus his popularity has reached astronomical proportions inside France.

Rives only occasionally eats in his Paris flat; it is simpler for him to cross the road and stroll a few hundred yards to a local restaurant where he is known. True, requests for autographs from waiters still accompany his quiet meal, yet such approaches are treated affably. Even the toot of car horns from total strangers passing in the street produce a distracted wave. It comes naturally to a man who has endured as much exposure as a President.

Yet the other side of his character is documented by Andy Slack, captain of the 1984 Australians' Grand Slam winning side in

Britain, and a visitor to France with Wallaby touring teams. Slack, no stranger to Rives for the two had played together in the President's XV as part of Welsh centenary celebrations and also met in Queensland on the French tour of that same year, found a curious anomaly in the Frenchman's makeup after the two countries had drawn the first Test match of the Wallabies' 1983 tour in France.

Slack said: "You wouldn't say we knew each other intimately or anything like that. But we had had a fair bit to do with each other on that 1981 Welsh President's side and I remember him out in Brisbane, playing with blood and guts coming out of him. He was absolutely everywhere against Queensland – we would have won by 20 points if he hadn't been playing. But when we played in France on that 1983 tour, it was as though there was a different man in his shoes. It wasn't a good tour socially because the French made no effort at all to socialise. I felt it was up to him as captain to get the teams together, but he didn't get involved. The worst part was outside the hotel after the drawn Test at Clermont-Ferrand. We saw Jean-Pierre there and were about to speak to him, when he just turned away. He didn't make any attempt to chat. He just went off with his mates."

Slack's opinion of the Frenchman as a rugbyman remained unimpaired despite that apparent snub. "Nobody in world rugby could be more respected as a player of bravery than him. When he played in Sydney with that busted shoulder, I never saw a braver piece of play in my life. He was in such pain but wouldn't go off. They kept putting water on it to help him. It must have been agony."

A bit of a loner, a mystery man; yet, conversely, the life and soul of the party, and the leader on the night-club circuit when the mood took him. Rives could be warm, friendly and approachable; equally, distracted, almost aloof and uninterested. Helpful, generous and charming – infuriating, annoying and remote.

Andy Dalton, captain of the New Zealand All Blacks in succession to Graham Mourie, said: "The most amazing thing about Rives was that he was such a Jekyll and Hyde character. So aggressive on the field, but such a quiet person off it."

The snub some felt was unfortunate, but more a cause of the man's natural shyness than of any malicious intent. He felt more at ease, more natural in the company of those he knew deeply; with others, there was a thin film, a layer of falsehood which no-one more than Rives enjoyed, peeling off to reveal his real self. But only to a handful of close friends. For the rest, the screen stayed firmly in place.

He still has the trace of a loner in him, perfectly happy to be pottering around his Paris flat. Yet, again in a reverse sense, he craves, at other times, the company of his friends, either in person or through his alternative lifeblood; the telephone. Yet even to his closest friends, there is, behind the exterior wall, an interior shell which none penetrate. Few would try.

Rives created the shell because he was a man often misunderstood. Some opponents, like the Welsh and British Lions prop forward Graham Price, might hint malevolently about the infamous Rives' trademark; the blood pouring out of cuts.

"When you are warm, blood flows more freely, anyway," said Price. "When it started to appear on Rives' face, the lads in the Welsh forwards would say 'Aye, aye – he's got out the sachet of tomato sauce, again, lads'. We felt he used to make the most of it all. After all, he sometimes had only a couple of stitches in the wound, afterwards."

To the Welsh hard brigade, like Price, France's captain invoked anger through his tendency to back-chat referees. Rives denies it, but Price said: "When we played France for the Championship, in Paris, in 1983, I certainly didn't think Rives was a sporting captain.

"He was always on to the referee, the New Zealander Tom Doocey, about our play. We had felt that, with a New Zealander handling the game, we could base our plan on setting up rucks – we decided we could get away with this. But Rives was constantly complaining to him, chatting to him. And Doocey changed just like that during the game – we suddenly got penalised incessantly. Rives talking to referees irritated opponents and certainly that day the referee was influenced. We felt it was unfair. He tried to influence the referee and although officials say they won't be influenced, they are. Rives seemed to be constantly barracking officials."

The other side of the coin. A figure who incensed some, charmed others. Misunderstood by most, a stranger to all except his closest friends. You know him and yet you do not. He remains a complex personality.

The Grand Slam
that never was

*"I am not arguing with you –
I am telling you."*
—JAMES McNEILL WHISTLER—
1834–1903

The dressing-room was silent. No-one moved. The bath water lay steaming, fifteen exhausted Frenchmen sat stunned. Those who glanced across at Jean-Pierre Rives, their constant source of inspiration these past five years, drew little comfort. The man who had encouraged his team the world over, lay slumped against the wall, his eyes closed. Only the usual weeping cut, its blood occasionally brushed into his hair, seemed the same. Rives could find no words of expression, still less some of cheer for his troops. Hope had flown the French cause, like the bird of freedom; and with it had disappeared Rives' grand reputation among the rugby fraternity of the British Isles.

17 March 1984 in Edinburgh was a watershed in Rives' career. By the end of a highly emotional, tense match Rives' name had tumbled badly from its exalted position in the game. Not in France; for the acrimony Rives felt at a naive referee, blatantly but unnecessarily controversial, was shared by his own people. In Britain it was different. But Rives had himself to blame.

As he studied the floor, the outward calm belied the inner rage. The French captain was contemplating eighty minutes of disaster for the French during which the Frenchmen had tossed away, like wealthy racegoers discarding dollar bills, a Grand Slam which should have been theirs for the taking. Rives knew his side was by far the best in the Championship, in terms of talent and potential, especially behind the scrum. His Corinthian values had denied him the egotistical thought of a Grand Slam, played in the style of the finest entertaining rugby, as a departure song for his career in the game. But at thirty-one, after nine years on the international stage, he knew it was almost time to call a halt.

Performing for nine years in international rugby is sufficient test for most men. For a player like Rives, with his frightening level of physical commitment in each game, it seemed an interminable period. Now after the Five Nations Championship in Europe, France faced another arduous venture, a tour of New Zealand. Rives had reached the peak of rugby back in 1979 when winning the All Blacks scalp in Auckland. What more had he to prove in New Zealand? Perhaps, more importantly, he had a considerable amount to lose. He had decided, at quite an early stage, not to make the trip.

Thus Edinburgh had assumed a greater importance, fortified further by both sides arriving for the match with unbeaten records in their three games against the other nations. Scotland had a Triple Crown stowed away in her kitbags for the first time in forty-six years. The last time she had won a Grand Slam, the Russian Revolution was only eight years in the past and the Great Depression lay five years in the future.

For Jean-Pierre Rives, the journey which had started in London, 1975, had been arduous yet exciting; physically demanding yet utterly exhilarating. Even the past two seasons, after the surprise 1981 Grand Slam, had been eventful. No sooner had French shares risen, phoenixlike, in the wake of that 1981 success, than their value collapsed the next season. France and Wales, for so long the exalted in European rugby, held last place in the 1982 Championship. Both countries lost three of their four matches, with Ireland winning the Championship with England, and Scotland hot on their heels a point adrift in joint second place.

France's poor scrummage that season had seldom seemed capable of releasing a talented threequarter line. It was a line of sharpshooters starved of ammunition. But perhaps France should have accepted that 1982 was likely to be a year to forget. Even early in the 1982–3 season, the Soviet Union had caused almost much heart-stopping down in the south of France when they met a French side at Bordeaux and beat them by 12 points to 6.

The President of the French Rugby Union, Albert Ferrasse, was shocked, but hardly vacillated in his thoughts afterwards. "Today, the Russians beat us by trying to play rugby. They ran the ball. They played the game with their hands as well as their feet. Russia has made far more progress in a much shorter time than Romania.'' The French side was not a full international team, yet the selectors were sufficiently alarmed by the portents to announce that they would, in future, choose sides of maximum strength against the Soviets.

In 1983, typically perverse and unpredictable, France won the Championship, in company with Ireland, and finished moral victors with a better points margin, although rugby officialdom, curiously, has never embraced the system of electing winners through the great number of points. But there was no mistaking the French style: the thrill of Blanco's refreshingly adventurous running from full-back, Estève's unrefined rugby skills but blistering pace on the left wing, Sella's youthful dash on the right and Codorniou's subtle skills in midfield. True, the French had dithered with their half-back combination all season but selectorial quirks, such as the dropping of Paparemborde the previous season, had been erased. There was a common accord, once more, in the French game and it focused on attacking rugby, intent on utilising the qualities of an outstanding threequarter line, which was unmatched in the Championship for pace, poise, skill and bravado. Even in defeat, 22–16 in Ireland, the quality shone; the Irish, 15–3 ahead at half-time, found themselves turned completely around, as though victims of the ebb tide, by France's storming riposte which gave them a 16–15 lead, courtesy of Blanco's genius. Irish grit and experience retrieved the situation, but it was close.

In Paris, one month later, however, there occurred another of those soured, embittered French–Welsh clashes which seemed to be so frequent at this period. Once more, too many individuals appeared unable to perform under pressure without resorting to foul play. If Wales won the match, they would finish the season as outright Champions for the first time in seven seasons. France required victory to win or share the Championship, depending upon the outcome of the Ireland–England match, in Dublin, the same day.

What the Paris crowd received was a degradation of a game, refereed poorly by a New Zealander insufficiently experienced in such battles. Dooccy had been less than impressive in handling the Calcutta Cup match at Twickenham between England and

Scotland. Then, the players had retained a reasonable grip on their tempers. This time there was no such control. Rives' head was split wide open in the brutal start to the match; French punches answered in a volley worthy of the Marquis de Montcalm, leader of the French at the battle of Quebec.

Doocey's refereeing may have altered the course of the game. Clive Rees, the Wales left wing, touched down over his own line after Belascain, the French centre, had charged down Ackerman's clearance kick. It had been close, Rees waiting to the last possible moment to see whether the ball would cross his line from the Frenchman's touch, rather than being forced to take it over himself, thereby incurring the 'penalty' of a five-metre scrum. In the event, the ball trickled over of its own volition yet Doocey signalled for the scrum. Rees, he said, had taken the ball over.

From the scrummage, France scored a try by Estève to take a 10–9 lead with ten minutes remaining. It was a significant moment to gain the advantage, for Welsh resolve was deflated by the decision. France went on to a 16–9 victory but Robert Paparemborde spoke for most people afterwards when he said: "That sort of game is very bad for rugby football. We were called a tough bunch in 1977 but we never did anything like the things Wales did to try to unsettle us here today".

The Welsh answered with their own accusations. Clive Rees said: "We felt that Jean-Pierre Rives made the most of it when he was cut. He would press his hand to the cut, it would bleed and then he would wipe his jersey over it. That spread the blood all over his shirt and it incensed the rest of the French forwards. That geed them up and they adopted a kind of 'We stick together now' approach".

But it was not only when the Welsh and French got together that the sparks started to fly. Early in the 1984 season, Rives had been caught up in a thoroughly unseemly row with his own French President, Albert Ferrasse, over the sending-off of the French prop from Lourdes, Jean-Pierre Garuet, against Ireland.

It was the first match of the 1984 Championship. On a dry January day in Paris, Ireland's old guard of Keane, Duggan, O'Driscoll, Slattery and Orr seemed to possess small chance of holding a French backline which threatened as much pace as the new TGV Rapide trains. The French team had an express of their own in the right wing, Patrice Lagisquet, an elegant, eloquent and courteous young man from the Bayonne club, credited with 10.8 seconds for the 100 metres. Opposite him, on the left, was the Narbonne flyer Patrick Estève, brusque on the field, highly emotional but dangerous when given the least space. At full-back was the galloping Serge Blanco, all dash and verve; in the centre, the quicksilver Codorniou, by now the experienced 'brain' who masterminded the backline, and the rugged Philippe Sella from the Agen club, a player in the mould of the competitive Bertranne. And, to light the blue touchpaper, Jerome Gallion, back in the international game after an absence of three years, due to disagreements with the French selectors. It was by far the best side in the Championship that year or in any recent year.

The steely resolve of experienced men in the Irish side made a contest of it, but when the French backs felt in the mood, the struggle resembled men against boys. Gallion and Sella finished scintillating backline movements with tries in the first minutes of the game, but the match was destined to be remembered more for the sending-off of Garuet.

The Welsh referee, Clive Norling, by some distance the firmest official on the circuit, dismissed the Frenchman apparently for gouging the Irish flanker, John O'Driscoll. The incident happened at a maul across the field from the main stand at Parc des Princes. Suddenly, with the ball as irrelevant as a bar of soap, O'Driscoll emerged from the cluster of bodies, flailing at an assailant. Garuet was taken aside by Norling and banished; the first Frenchman to suffer such an ignominious fate.

After France had completed a 25–12 victory, it emerged that Garuet's fingers may not have been in O'Driscoll's eyes, rather, attached to his nose and exerting some upward pressure. It mattered little, however, to the row which was about to break, for Albert Ferrasse condemned the player, calling him, in English, "an oaf". He went on: "The man is an imbecile. It was a terrible blow for French rugby and we will have to leave him well alone."

Rives took exception to this remark, and said so publicly. Furthermore, he vehemently defended Garuet even though the Lourdes man was now barred from playing for his country for the rest of that season.

Rives has since had time to reflect whether he was out of order in criticising his President. But he insists now: "I did what I had to do; I have no regrets. What I did was controversial because it was against Ferrasse. But if I were in the same situation today, I would do the same thing.

"I defended Garuet because of what he told me. I know that when a friend does something bad you have to support him even if it is difficult. But this was not like that. Garuet said he did not intend any damage and that made it different.

"Only two men know the truth of what happened; Garuet and O'Driscoll. Garuet said to me he did not do it intentionally. And for me, that was enough. Because if he did not mean it, I accepted what he said. Even to this day, I believe that what he told me was the truth.

"I don't believe Ferrasse felt angry at what I said. Maybe he did not understand, I don't know. But I understand him. He had his position to think of; I had mine too, which was different. I am at peace with myself over what happened. Garuet is not a dirty player and I knew that. I knew about his spirit, about his heart, too, and that was why I fought for him. He has never had a reputation for dirty play. For some players I have known I would not have spoken in defence. With Garuet, it was different."

It could perhaps be argued that prudence was as familiar to Garuet as the workings of the Soviet Politburo. He had already been penalised twice for deliberately collapsing scrummages. Any further misdemeanour was not likely to go unseen by so zealous an official as Mr Norling. He never missed much. Garuet should have realised that.

France did not play again for a month, which ought to have allowed tempers to calm. Instead, there was once more the spectacle of Welsh and French players extracting revenge upon each other. The match at Cardiff was Rives' final opportunity to beat the Welsh in their own backyard, which he had been trying to do since 1976.

The match, however, although exciting in the later stages as Wales threw youthful backline enterprise at the tiring French and all but snatched a win, was an unedifying struggle. The *Daily Express* reported: "The way Richard Moriarty (Wales) and Jean-Pierre Rives conducted themselves in the international was bad enough to make an orang-utan lose its hair."

Rives was incensed by some of the Welsh tactics and, in his eyes, blatant obstruction. The Welsh, for their part, alleged that French line-out tactics badly transgressed the laws. Again, the international referees board had selected a southern-hemisphere official, the Australian Dick Byers, to handle the match. Such clashes were notorious; it seemed to any astute observer, that a Scot, Irishman or English official would have been a more knowledgeable choice. Byers admittedly coped better than had Doocey in Paris a month earlier; but it seems unfair to appoint an official unaccustomed to such clashes.

France led 12–3 at half-time, fortunate so to do because the Welsh tight five forwards proved an excellent combination. Only some crafty obstruction of the high-leaping Norster ensured some decent ball for the French, while Lescarboura's kicking was in sharp contrast to the Welsh who squandered five goal attempts.

The second half was close. 12–3 became 12–10 but then 15–10 and even 18–10. Welsh resolve stiffened. Full-back Davies added a try, which he converted, to two earlier penalties, to cut the French lead to 18–16. But Lescarboura, upright, strong and usually uncannily direct, placed another penalty goal like the vintage Nicklaus chipping close to the flag. It was decisive; France held on for a 21–16 win.

Rives joked later: "Billy Beaumont told me he had a dream. He wanted, more than anything else, to beat Wales in Cardiff, in the last minute, by a single point. But I was not like that, oh no! Me? I wanted to beat Wales in Cardiff by two points, by scoring in the last two minutes. That was all."

But at the time Rives was a far from happy man. He rushed off from the field and was in the dressing-room within seconds of the final whistle. The next morning, he was stalking through the departure lounge of Cardiff airport to board the flight for Paris, still unhappy. "He went through here," remarked an airline receptionist, "with a face the colour of thunder. He wasn't taking any messages from anyone."

Rives later talked about the affair and admitted: "That match was not played in a very good spirit. It was always difficult against Wales and especially in that game because they were a little nervous, maybe because of the results before. All their famous players had retired, they had lost some matches in Cardiff and badly needed a victory.

"It was my first win in Cardiff and my last. It was a special feeling to win there because it is a ground of such tradition. So many great players have appeared there for Wales; they have produced marvellous teams over the years. That means that, if you win in Cardiff, it must have a special feeling. But on this occasion it was not a match to enjoy. Just a result achieved. But generally, I have an enormous respect for Welsh rugby.''

The season was developing in so contentious a manner that it looked as though Rives' doubts about playing at all in the international team that year had been justified. Jo Maso, his friend and counsel, explains: ''Jean-Pierre asked me whether I thought it would be a season too many if he played again for France in 1984. He was not sure whether to start again or not. But I told him, if he possessed the will to play and he wanted to play, then he should go ahead and make himself available. Otherwise, I felt, he would feel a void and always wonder afterwards whether he should have carried on.''

Maso insists Rives made the correct decision. ''In my opinion, his last season was a very good one for him. Certainly, he had lost a little speed. We all lose speed as we get older. But look at Fergus Slattery. He carried on and was magnificent until he was 35. Jean-Pierre was only 31 when he made his last international appearance. Particularly in France, people question your ability to continue at that age. When you are past thirty you are old here. But it is not true. If players train as necessary, they can go on.

''I played in South Africa for the centenary and one of the Springboks was 35 or 36 years old. But he was still amazing. Certainly Jean-Pierre lost speed after 25 or 26 but he was still the best player in his position when he played his final season.''

That view is supported by Jean Michel Aguirre. ''Jean-Pierre's last season was one of the best he ever had for France,'' he said. ''He was certainly better balanced in his mind through his profession and in his work. Before, he had always been between Toulouse, Paris and everywhere.

''In 1984, he was settled in Paris and perhaps in his mind too. He knew it was his last season. I felt that the time when he did not have so good a season and was nowhere near as effective was when he had problems with changing clubs, from Stade Toulousain to Racing Club de France. He was not the same dominating player that season (1982–3).''

Maso added: ''Jean-Pierre Rives' great qualities as a man – physical, hard in training – he kept until his last match. He was always present at important moments. He had such an influence on the field that he was always respected, by his teammates and opponents alike. He was recognised as a player who was always very correct. His prime quality is his intelligence, his good approach to the game and to life. He knew how to talk to men. His human qualities were above the norm. That is why he was a great captain and a great player.''

Controversy, however, had begun to run in Rives' shadow, like an assailant in a darkened alley. In 1982–3 he had incurred the displeasure of the national authorities in France by changing clubs, leaving Stade Toulousain for the Racing Club in Paris for the simple reason that he was now living and working in Paris. The Federation promptly banned him, however, from playing Championship matches for his new club, under the ruling which restricts movement between clubs.

To this day Rives resents that decision. He says: ''As far as I was concerned, it was a simple move. I had moved to Paris, I was working in Paris; I wanted to play for a club in Paris. So I telephoned to the President of the Racing Club and said I would like to play for his team because I was moving to Paris. He said 'fine'. That was the only arrangement. But the FFR said I had changed clubs so I was made an example. I played only six games that season; four internationals and two minor games for Racing.

''OK, I accept it was the law by strict interpretation of the rules. But all the time the law is moving, and people should remember that. The law must be adaptable and keep up-to-date with modern life and society. The law is changing all the time for the players. Everyone must have the same freedom.

''If we are playing amateur rugby, I do not understand why they should make such a fuss. In an amateur game, we seem to be more strict than professionals. I do not understand that. Nor do I think it is right. Certain safeguards are correct, yes, but not such tight restrictions that the amateur is penalised for no good reason. The authorities knew I did not get any money for changing clubs – it was only because I had moved to Paris.''

So Rives played the entire season for his country in the International Championship, from the unlikely basis of fitness achieved in a Parisian gymnasium. As for match fitness, he acquired it during the international matches! He defended the situation, especially as it was not of his own making. ''I kept fit, I trained hard in the gym. And I don't think I was the worst player on the field in any of those matches. Boxers fight only once or twice a year, preparing themselves for a peak at a certain date. They are not fighting every day in matches. So why not rugby players, too?''

It is essential, in order to understand Jean-Pierre Rives, that one factor is grasped: his sheer love of playing the game. At the close of his career he said: ''I enjoyed all my ten years and, if I could have played for ten more, I would have loved it. Some players say they were glad to finish when they did – but not me. I would have liked to go on if it had been possible. I was still like a youthful enthusiast the day I finished.''

A man of character and great determination. It was always the same as a player, as a man, as an artist or poet. Fierce resolve smouldered in his mind. When Rives sets his mind to achieving something, he invariably succeeds. As, for example, with his decision to give up smoking at that time. Rives explains: ''You are offered cigarettes and when you smoke, you always take them. But one day in 1982 I was next to a man who was offered a cigarette and he said, 'No, I am sorry, I am not a smoker. I don't want one'.

''I listened to that man and felt admiration for him. I felt I would love to do the same and say to people 'I am not a smoker'. So I stopped and it felt great afterwards, saying the same thing when people offered me cigarettes. I was very proud I had stopped. After all, you have to respect yourself. I missed smoking in the beginning but I tried to keep to what I had promised myself. It was like a game for me. Now, I feel healthier without smoking.''

Healthier. And fitter too to expose English deficiencies once again. In 1984, it was no different; England were systematically taken apart but this time by a rampant French threequarter line, every member of which scored points. The result, a 32–18 win for France, in no way flattered French supremacy. Rives had played ten times against the English during his career, winning on seven occasions and losing only three times. Such was France's superiority over England during the mid-1970s and early 1980s.

Even so, Rives refuses to castigate English rugby. ''You have a lot of players, many good players. Do not lose heart. France, too, has been through a bad period. But a good team is not just about good players. It is something different. It is not a problem of players in England; it is a problem of a team. The first condition of a team is confidence; if you change the team all the time, it is very difficult. France, too, has been guilty of this. In 1982, when France lost three of the four Championship games, constant changing did not help to build any team spirit.

"But to give confidence you need to get results, you need to *have* confidence. It is very difficult, a circle really. That is why Wales were so good through those years; a settled team, players with confidence who started to achieve good results and continued getting them. They expected to win when they went out to play and that makes an enormous difference. Because when you put a doubt in your head, it is the worst poison in rugby. Even if you have a very good player, he will find it hard."

So France beat Wales to retain their one hundred per cent record, and Scotland won in Ireland to clinch their first Triple Crown in forty-six years. Two matches remained in the Championship; England against Wales at Twickenham – an irrelevancy since neither side could win the title and Ireland were already holders of the Wooden Spoon – and Scotland against France in Edinburgh to decide the Grand Slam winners, assuming there was a win for one side or the other. Death or glory, all or nothing. If this was indeed to be the climax, and the conclusion of Jean-Pierre Rives' international rugby career, it could not have arrived at a better time. It was pure Hollywood to contrive so dramatic an ending to Rives' record in the game. Edinburgh, surely, would provide a suitably gracious occasion for Rives' swansong . . . if such it was to be.

In the event, Murrayfield saw one of the worst displays of petulance by an international rugby captain ever witnessed in the game. It reflected so badly on Jean-Pierre Rives that, in many people's eyes, his behaviour soured a glorious career. It was a tragedy for a man so in love with the game and the spirit in which it ought to be played.

But if Rives was in the dock after France's defeat, by 21 points to 12, then another man joined him, the Welsh referee Winston Jones. Jones appeared, courtesy of a grossly insensitive and inefficient decision which ignored the obvious dangers in giving a man, making his debut as an international referee, a match in which the stakes were so high. Both teams were unbeaten; a Grand Slam was to be decided. Experience, on the part of the official taking charge, was surely the very least that players and spectators could expect. Instead, a man was handed the game who had never known the pressures exclusive to the European Five Nations Championship.

Rives was seen as the villain of the piece, but without doubt he and his players suffered unacceptable provocation. Mr Jones had done his research in one respect, ascertaining all there was to know about French indiscretions in the line-out and other phases of play. He refereed the French like a sergeant-major handling new recruits. The minute any Gallic hand or boot strayed across the dividing line between misdemeanor and acceptable error, he blew his whistle.

Excellent in principle; many spectators felt that the French had escaped too lightly all season. But Mr Jones seemed to be assuming that the Scots were as innocent as choirboys. The fact of the matter was, Scotland could have been penalised almost as heavily in many phases of the play but particularly for offside play. Without that authority over them, the Scots exploited the situation to the full. The French found themselves caught in a Catch-22 situation. They were being watched, as a hawk follows its prey, by the referee but the Scots seemed free to infringe whenever and wherever they pleased. French frustration boiled up like trapped gas.

The explosion did not come until the second half. Before then France proved conclusively which was the finer team by dominating the Scots. The home side could attempt little, was forced merely to hang on and hope that the storm would abate. In that period of ascendancy, France should have put the game beyond their opponents' reach, but strangely they failed to do so.

They had nine attacking scrums close to the Scottish line before the interval but scored from only one. Gallion, the classiest performer on the field, scored the one try, burrowing over on the blind side of a scrum five. Lescarboura, the Dax giant, converted, giving France a 6–3 interval advantage, Dods' penalty being the only score Scotland could make before half-time. Such a paltry advantage was poor reward for a French side which had outplayed its foes. And as the crisis deepened for France after half-time, accentuated by Gallion's departure through injury, French discipline began to crack, like dried-out clay. Rives, as captain, lost his temper completely.

The referee continued to penalise the Frenchmen; David Leslie, the Scottish flanker, continued to frustrate them by hunting the loose ball in the most predatory style. Leslie, angular, correct, committed, and toughened like shatter-proof glass, ignored the studs that ripped open his flesh, in order to protect the ball from the speedy French threequarters. His was an essential contribution to Scotland's triumph.

So, too, unqestionably, was Gallion's loss, heavily concussed in a crunching collision midway through the second half. Berbizier, his replacement, offered France nowhere near the same strength or subtlety, intuition or daring, behind the pack. His absence was more keenly felt than would have been the case with any other player on the field. Gallion was not captain but his was the general's role; assessing, plotting and executing the strategy. Rives had his own problems as he attempted to control his growing fury at what he saw as discrimination by the referee.

Rives' reflections from the distance of an armchair, twelve months later, were tinged with regret at what had transpired. He knew there was no excuse.

"After that match at Edinburgh, I knew I had not been a good captain that day. I know I should have kept my mouth shut. One time the referee penalised us and we did not understand why . . . but it was OK. Two times, well again, . . . OK. Three times, maybe, but I do not see why . . . but OK. Four times – again, can this be right, but . . . OK. Five times, it was still OK, maybe. But six times, I became nervous, agitated. Why only us? What had we done? Why this? However that night in Edinburgh, I slept well. Maybe some other people, whom I shall not name, could not do that.

"We could have had a chance to win the Grand Slam. Of course, the Scots could win, too. But with the referee, there was only one side which could win that match and it was not France. I do not know whether we would have won with a different referee, but at least we could try. We would have been able to fight in the right spirit and we could play. As it was – well, we were stopped from playing in the match. Anything we did, we were penalised. It became too silly.

"I am not prepared to say we would have won with a different official. It would not be fair to the Scottish players to say that. They won and I am happy for them. But we shall never know what could have happened. A referee is on the field to referee, not to be a President or a personality.

"If you ask me whether I enjoyed the game, I would say 'Yes' –

until the first whistle went. It was fine until then. We cannot blame other things which happened. Gallion was injured; I was afraid for him because it was a shocking blow. Yes, he was a great player but I do not believe it was decisive when he went off.

"The point wwas, I do not know how we could have won that game – I could not see a way for us to win it. No way at all, whatever happened. It was too difficult. I want to say I am sorry for all the trouble with the referee. I admit I spoke too much. But I tried not to say anything and for a long time I did not. But it continued, always us penalised. I had to ask why."

Rives concedes now that his actions were seen as unsportsmanlike and ungentlemanly. But he defends, sternly, his countrymen against the overly hysterical accusations which trailed in the wake of the Edinburgh affair. "Some British people think too badly about the French and that is not right. They think we are all like thieves, robbers and we have bad spirit. But we are not that – we also have and deserve a lot of respect and have good spirit, too. The truth is not only in the confines of Welsh rugby committees – they do not have a monopoly on great spirit. That I want to say."

Some opinions on Rives allege a prima donna, an aloof, mysterious, moody, unpredictable Frenchman. It was a popular view round the time of the Edinburgh match. But to insult Rives in such a way reflects on his detractors, for they ignored the man's great contribution to the game and, more essentially, the spirit he epitomised in which it should flourish. Those who doubt such a view ought to study the words of men like Salut. Certainly, the man had his faults, and he was wrong to react as he did in Edinburgh. But perhaps the real culprits were neither Rives nor Winston Jones; rather, those who put an inexperienced man into such a potential cauldron for his baptism in the international refereeing world.

What is clear is that French play simply disintegrated. But we should remember that this had peviously been France's traditional weakness; their instability, and susceptibility to crack under pressure. During Rives' captaincy, however, this tendency had been all but eliminated in the French international sides. No longer did they panic; they maintained their resolve and quietly, determinedly clawed their way back into contests. But this did not happen at Murrayfield; it was like watching the brittle French sides of the past, exposed to pressure and quickly confounded.

France's 9–3 lead vanished in the face of Dods' two penalties; 9–9. Lescarboura dropped a mighty goal before Dods nullified the advantage with another penalty; 12–12. Rives' arguing had conceded vital yards at penalties, affording Dods an easier target. Then Calder dived over for his side's only try from the back of a line-out. Rives' face, haggard and ashen, was captured in a photograph taken the instant the try was scored, the look of a frustrated, foiled man at the end of his tether, weary from the exertions of ten seasons in the international game, and shattered at the injustice he and his side felt.

Dods converted the try and added another penalty goal, following a late tackle by the French. It was Scotland's Grand Slam, by 21 points to 12 and those who saw it, never mind played in it, streamed away drained and exhausted, both mentally and physically.

The furore which followed was understandable. To a man, the French closed ranks behind their captain. Some conceded Rives had become more aggressive on the field, particularly in the business of talking with referees, but all pointed an imaginary finger at Mr Jones as the cause of the trouble.

Jerome Gallion said: "For a start, I do not agree with some people who said Jean-Pierre played for one season too many. After all, we played in the Grand Slam decider – that is like the European Cup final in football – and it is very difficult to blow the whistle on a player's career. He knows best when to finish. As for Edinburgh and that match, I had no respect for such a game. What was most lamentable was that we did not have a proper chance.

"I believe that Jean-Pierre, like every French player, thought we could not win. Rives had a stature as a captain such that each personal intervention was automatically discussed and always criticised. And when sometimes he appealed for calm or watchfulness from the referee, it was always interpreted negatively. Sometimes, Jean-Pierre wanted no more than to ask the reason for a penalty, not to argue. But automatically he would be penalised for disobedience. He was just asking 'why'."

Jacques Fouroux, French coach, said: "At the end of his international career, Jean-Pierre became more aggressive. Usually he was aggressive in the game but at the end he set about talking with referees. But it was because the context was difficult. There was suspicion through the French team and so it was for him to defend a good cause, that of his team. I would say that for ten years Jean-Pierre was a model player, extraordinary throughout his career, except perhaps near the end when he argued a little too much with some. But in Edinburgh, it was very difficult not to do that.''

Others talked along similar lines. Michel Palmié considered that Rives did not have any weakness in his game as a player, but added: ''His only fault came at the end of his career. Then, he spoke a lot with foreign referees. But he was obliged to look after his teammates because he was the only Frenchman who could speak English properly.''

Jean-Pierre Bastiat stoically defended Rives and elucidated at some length the differing opinions of some members of the British rugby fraternity. ''To begin with, I do not accept Jean-Pierre was wrong to question certain decisions in Scotland that day. Jean Pierre was a winner. He was a fellow who supported his team and his country; he wore his shirt for victorious rugby and, as he was captain, he did everything possible by means of whatever person or player to obtain this third Grand Slam in Scotland that year. Now, may I say, you British have one fault which is that you like the losers and you like the winners, but you really like people who are actually good sports. And when people win too much, you don't like it so much. It was the same in London when we played there in 1977.

''I think Jean-Pierre discussed with the referee certain matters. But, personally, I am convinced that the Welsh had had a little too much of Jean-Pierre Rives.''

Intriguingly Bastiat wondered aloud whether Rives had been in Edinburgh through choice, or because of a patched-up compromise with his employers from the Pernod company. He speculated: ''Jean-Pierre is a professional man in public relations with Pernod and I think he could no longer play at the level he had been playing. And so I think what happened was that Jean-Pierre signed for Racing Club but played very few matches because of his injuries, because he had a bad shoulder, and because of his professional commitments all over the world for Pernod.

''And so he could not train normally with his club. It was convenient for him to play for the Racing Club simply so that he could play with the French team. Because in the French team, people would talk about him for another year knowing Jean-Pierre was with Pernod.

"So I think that, although his rugby career was at an end, he prolonged his career a little bit to assist his professional life. So well that, now he has finished his sporting life, you still see him so much on all television channels, whether it is a political programme, cultural, sporting, variety, whatever it may be. Because it is necessary to see him on the screen, in the papers too. Because always behind Jean-Pierre is Pernod. His face is so well known."

Did commercial considerations therefore come before feelings about whether Rives was really good enough to play a final season, in 1984? The Pernod President Daniel Hémard strongly refutes the suggestion. "Certainly, Jean-Pierre's strong personality is fine for the company," he says. "We didn't take Jean-Pierre on just to play around; he takes his job very seriously. But the priority was rugby; he had to play rugby as long as possible to be well known.

"The ideal would have been for France to win the Grand Slam in 1984 and then for him to retire. That would have been perfect. But nothing in life is perfect. Jean-Pierre came to us and asked whether he should play in the 1984 season. We told him the worst thing to do would be to try to play if he couldn't, if he was not physically fit. We said 'If you don't feel well, then stop'."

So Rives' decision was his own, founded on his belief that he could play a final season. And there is no real evidence that he made the wrong decision. He led France to the brink of a Grand Slam; under his leadership, the French team played some of the finest rugby seen in Europe for years, full of spirit and adventure. Rives was no passenger in that side; rather, a source of inspiration, a venerated figure in the eyes of his team. Only a misguided choice of referee possibly prevented the Grand Slam which would have crowned Rives' career.

What had occurred by now, however, was that certain officials in authority within the French rugby hierarchy had begun to jettison their links with the national captain. First, Rives' reign was ending; quite possibly, a new style would accompany his replacement and he was sure to be a totally different character to Rives. After all, France had not had so charismatic, yet so much a playboy type as Rives for a rugby captain in her whole history. Those who had hitched their stars to the Rives caravan now started to jump off.

Jean Michel Aguirre explained the point. "I don't know whether the star system was accepted by some in French rugby, and Jean-Pierre was a star. Of course, some liked it but others never fully accepted it. With his looks, his frequent appearances on radio and TV, Jean-Pierre was a high-society figure, very different from the traditional rugby type. Jet society is not the character of rugby in France. Perhaps there was a problem between rugby and the image of Jean-Pierre. It was not accepted by some players, by some members of the public or by some officials. After all, it was not so long ago that Jo Maso was excluded from the French side because he had long hair.

"Also, Jean-Pierre created so big an image. French rugby did not like that, it was too much for some people. There is room for only one Ferrasse in French rugby."

Michel Palmié endorsed that opinion, saying: "Jean-Pierre had a well-known image. I think personally he was exploited by certain people. I cannot say who but certain people made use of him and I think Jean-Pierre was like a balloon which was inflated, inflated, inflated. One day, he disturbed certain people too much. Then, these people persisted in trying to bring him down to the ground. They made plentiful use of him and then, once he became too important, he inconvenienced and embarrassed them.

"Jean-Pierre is someone who doesn't expect problems; he lives as if in a dream. Now he is beginning to have problems. But for five years of his life he lived in a dream. He had the life of a star with all that brings in a superficial way."

Robert Paparemborde suggested that the increasing criticism of Rives hastened his departure from the game. He claimed: "In France, Jean-Pierre is like a film star, a real personality. But the people in rugby started to criticise him towards the end of his career.

"That was because in France people do not like those who succeed so much. They were a little bit jealous of Jean-Pierre and it was a pity. That criticism pushed him into stopping. I am certain of that. But, in fact, he did well to stop.

"Jean-Pierre and myself have been friends for many years, so that he is more than a friend. In fact, more like a member of the family."

Fergus Slattery pays tribute to Rives, the man who could feel comfortable even within the circles of French rugby politics. "I don't believe Jean-Pierre went on for too long because he made a different kind of contribution from when he became captain. It came to him at the right time, too and he enjoyed that new contribution. To survive in French rugby, you have to have a good relationship with people and Jean-Pierre had excellent relationships. He had the confidence to do things other people would not have had the confidence to try.

"Albert Ferrasse rules rugby in France. He is a very strong figure. He has a nucleus of trusted acquaintances around him, people like Guy Basquet who is also from Ferrasse's home town, Agen. Jean-Pierre Rives could have trodden on certain toes and got away with it because he had Ferrasse and Fouroux behind him. Others would not have survived had they done so. Jean-Pierre was good for French rugby. As a player, he was first-class although in more recent years I felt Jean-Luc Joinel was very much the master of the French pack and certainly of the back row. The best player in the French pack is Philippe Dintrans but he should not be captain."

On the matter of Rives' injudicious querying of refereeing decisions, Slattery said: "Any Frenchman can play the innocence of the language. He always has that advantage. Referees would take more stick from French players, they would be more conciliatory towards players from France because of the language difference. Rives got away with more than players like Gareth Edwards or myself."

But, as happened in Edinburgh, that can work in reverse, to the detriment of the French side. It happened frequently because the side involved tends to find its concentration on the game completely or even partially disrupted. And in such moments, international matches can be resolved. Earlier in his tenure of the captaincy, however, Rives was at his peak. He possessed a knack, a capacity to settle his players down, unlike his successor Dintrans, who found it hard to keep his own cool, still less the heads of others. Ireland, 1985, was a classic illustration of the point and it cost the French dearly in the final reckoning for that season's Championship.

Slattery continued: "As he got older, Jean-Pierre would chat to referees a lot more; complaining and moaning. But in the earlier days, he was not involved in those things. Perhaps the trouble was, the ideal reign of a captain is two to three seasons. After that, you go sideways and then downhill. You cannot maintain it; you lose the enthusiasm. You are either building up a side or having to maintain it at the top. If you stay on too long, people get tired of listening to you.

"Perhaps Jean-Pierre did stay too long as captain. For the last two or three years he was talking of retiring. I heard that from him several times and then, there he would be out on the field again. When you are thinking that way, you get out; you should not hang in. He might have pulled out two years earlier as captain. As a player, he played his best in the first five or six years in the French team. And that is nearly always the case. He was a very, very fine player and a very fine captain but like all good things, they come to an end. Perhaps he was pressurised by Ferrasse and Fouroux – that is possibly what happened."

A very, very fine player? Without question. Men of all nations, whatever their position on the rugby field, saluted Rives' outstanding abilities as a player. The New Zealander Stu Wilson said: "He revelled as a player and a captain and he could destroy you almost single-handedly in a match. But probably his best attribute was that he was so good at keeping the game moving. He hardly ever killed the ball. That sort of thing cannot really be coached. It's a question of something a player is born with, a real, natural instinct to attack and be positive."

Andy Dalton, All Blacks captain of the early 1980s, added: "I have the highest possible regard for Jean-Pierre Rives. The French loved him and he had the ability to lead a side by example. The players looked at him as a man prepared to sacrifice everything for his country."

Others spoke of Rives' impressive behaviour on the field. John Rutherford, fly half for Scotland in the 1984 Grand Slam decider, said: "Rives would never try to intimidate you, as a flank forward to a stand-off half, unlike the Welsh wing forwards who believed in such methods. Rives was different, no matter how important the game." And Mark Loane, the Australian, added: "I always had a great regard for him. He was one of the most respected players and captains ever known. You couldn't speak too highly of him. The harder the conditions, the more he liked it.

"It wasn't possible to intimidate him; he had such a very high pain barrier. He was one of those players who almost went looking for pain and suffering. The more they take, the better they feel after the game. They live on pain. After matches Rives used to look like King's Cross station. They used to drop some fibreglass on his back in the end to fill up the cracks!''

How others see him

*"The purest treasure mortal times afford
is spotless reputation; that away,
men are but gilded loam or painted clay."*
From *Richard II* by
———— WILLIAM SHAKESPEARE ————
1564–1616

The little man clutching the steering wheel, his grip as tight as though he were on a roller-coaster at the seaside, lifted his eyes almost to the heavens and waved an arm in frustration. 'Mon dieu'; and 'C'est impossible'. A grunt of displeasure came from the back seat of the vehicle, too.

Jacques Fouroux, all 5ft 5ins of him, resembled a truant schoolboy on some illicit venture. Beside him, Jean-Pierre Rives looked a trenchant character, inspired by the crisis at hand. In the back, sat the man regarded by Rives as the finest scrum half ever to play rugby union: Gareth Edwards.

The scenario was unusual; the problem, nothing different. Time, a commodity Rives uses as frequently in his life as the weather reports for shipping and coastal stations, was desperately short. Edwards' jet back to Britain was threatening to leave Paris without him.

Escaping from the Parisian evening rush-hour without delay is as simple an exercise as wing forwards found stopping Edwards scoring tries from five-yard scrums. But Fouroux had an idea. With a bump and a lurch which suggested a safari trip across rough, open country was imminent, he guided the car on to the pavement and started plotting a course through the rush hour crowds. On they went, past astonished commuters and shoppers. Until the motorway system, choked, polluted and impassable. A sudden conference produced another route to the motorway further towards the airport. Through more city streets, weaving all the while like poplars in the wind, above a French country road.

And then, an emergency stop. Out jumped the two Frenchmen and dashed into a shop. Edwards was mystified, incensed. 'All this traffic, so little time and they go shopping,' he mumbled beneath his breath. The chaos, meanwhile, inside the car had moved to the shop interior. Strong, brawny arms grabbed bottles of fine wine, tins of pâté de foix gras, some soft, creamy cheeses, and two bottles of French cognac. Money fluttered on to the pay-out counter; the two hurried out, not bothering about change. Breathless, they struggled to open the car door.

'What on earth ... where have you ...?' Edwards' voice, unmistakably tinged with protest, tailed off in surprise and embarrassment. 'For you,' said Rives, as the two unloaded their haul into the Welshman's powerful arms. 'A souvenir of Paris.'

Edwards, rendered speechless, spluttered his thanks. He was still ruminating at his hosts' great generosity as Fouroux once more steered the car past unlikely obstacles, this time along the hard shoulder of the périphérique. Eventually, open road and a race for the airport.

Rives flung open the door and ran for the departure gate. Fouroux, ignoring the vehicle's security, hurried Edwards inside. 'Quickly, quickly,' called Rives, having manipulated officers in sufficient authority to put through a call to the plane, asking for a brief hold.

Edwards continues the story. ''I had a bag and all this great food and wine. When Jean-Pierre came up to me, I'd checked in and was running to the passport check area. Jean-Pierre stuffed my boarding card into my mouth – it was the only way I could hold anything else because my arms were laden with all these goods and bags. Jacques picked up a tin of pâté I'd dropped and both waved me through. I ran, half stumbled down a long approach to the plane, staggered on board and they shut the door. Off we went. That was my last memory of Jean-Pierre and Paris.''

Yet it was by no means his sole recollection. ''Poor Gareth,'' said Rives. ''He almost ended his career prematurely in Paris. But not on the rugby field; in a Paris street. A friend of mine was driving Gareth, in an English car, and he was so impressed by Gareth, and was saying how he was a great fan of his, that he didn't see a bus coming and he hit it. Much damage to the car but not to Gareth – he is indestructible.''

But rugbymen the world over would vouch also for Rives' indestructibility. ''I can remember going in to tackle him in one particular match,'' said the Scottish hooker, Colin Deans, ''and finding myself going backwards. I wasn't used to that sort of experience. You could feel the momentum, the force propelling you backwards.''

But should we judge Rives in a wider perspective than merely his qualities on a rugby field? After all, did he not aspire to, and has he not reached a pinnacle, far beyond the confines of the sporting field?

He leaves you baffled, bewildered at times. Thus some people, like Jean Michel Aguirre, feel it is impossible to dissect the true Rives. ''I feel he has been insecure for a long time. He is very complex or perhaps very simple. He has been made by the media and by society, not by himself. At present, he lives in a superficial world, it is something of a superficial life. Perhaps he is very deep, we do not know. I do not believe anyone knows him for he does not know himself. In a few years we will see a clearer man, I believe. But not yet – in a few years when he is beginning to be a little forgotten in rugby.''

Former adversary of Rives, and occasional colleague in Barbarians and Invitation teams, Fergus Slattery plots a similar course in assessing the man. ''I have not yet made up my mind about him,'' says the Irishman. ''I would say he is totally interested in what he is interested in and nothing else. I would question his sincerity. But that is my suspicion, not my conviction. He is a mystery man.

''He stirs it up the way he has been known to parade around the place. He doesn't care about things, doesn't care what people think. People would shout the most outrageous things at him on rugby grounds around the world. 'You're a – – – – – poof' and 'You've got woman's hair, Rives'. He would have got a lot of stick playing with Toulouse. You tend just to put your shirt on for your club. In reality, you are trying to stay alive for the next international.

''Against that, however, there is the other side. He is a bit of a loner and likes to keep very much to himself. He can be very polite but he won't get stuck into a conversation with you for half an hour. He doesn't want to be with you that long. He likes to keep moving; he doesn't like to stop on the one spot for very long. But he has a good sense of humour, is good fun and because of that it's very hard to make a clear, conclusive judgement on him."

Claude Dourthe, although conceding that this connection with Rives was during the formative years of his career, provides objective assessment: "When I first knew Jean-Pierre, he was a very nice boy but I didn't think he was destined to be the superstar he became. In my opinion, he was very shy, very intelligent, very engaging, very nice. But he has suffered from the image of the superstar that has been made of him.

"He took perhaps a little badly all the popularity he had later on but when you meet him again on his own, he is always very engaging and it's a pleasure to see him. He is a very sensible man with whom you can discuss things.

"Unfortunately, I think he is rather too big a star to devote enough time to his friends and to be natural in certain circumstances. That's rather a pity for him and a pity for his friends. You don't benefit from it. You have a good time if you can see him as a friend ... but as a friend, not a star. But since he became a superstar he is no longer free."

This judgement comes remarkably close, I suspect, to the truth about the man. Away from the crowds, the fuss, the accolades, the constant attention, Rives is a different creature; quiet, shy, humorous, courteous and kind almost to excess. One has the feeling he is the quintessential friend; busy, perhaps too much so and too much a victim of the lunatic demands of his schedule. But if one were in trouble, Rives would almost certainly assist, discarding the less important affairs to find the crux of the problem. To him, friendship is deep and important. Talk to him quietly, seriously and at great length about himself, his life, his thoughts and it is as though another man is emerging from behind the mask. In public, the mask remains firmly in place, allowing only a peep through the slit eyelids to the real man hidden away inside. That real man has his faults, of course; what man has none? Rives can be astonishingly naive, occasionally grossly insensitive and appallingly unreliable, to the point of creating frustration and anger. He can appear cunning and at times hardly scrupulous. But under the veneer is a man of great warmth. If he were given time to think before his actions, it is inconceivable that others could question his sincerity. But it is a mistake of Rives' own making, caused, one suspects, through the continual rush which is his life. Without the opportunity to assess the man at close range over a period of time and at prolonged spells, it is all too easy to assume that he does not care. That image is Rives' own fault.

In Perpignan, in the Catalan region of south-east France, Jo Maso is another modern-day legend from the rugby field. Visit Maso and you find your faith in humanity restored. There he sits, quiet, charming, friendly, the epitome of courtesy. Maso resembles Rives in certain respects: a laid-back, cool attitude to life, an elegant flat, yet far more conventional than Rives'. His beautiful wife, Annie, has made their home a haven of comfort and graciousness. The chief difference between Rives and Maso is unquestionably the latter's greater maturity, emanating probably from his marriage.

Maso provides, in my view, the best analysis of Rives because he comes closest of any man to portraying the true figure. "I would say that few people know Jean-Pierre. He has such a profound nature that those who don't know him well judge him superficially. You have the image of him as a star of rugby who appears on TV, because of his blond hair, etc. But he is a marvellous man. All the people I saw at a match quite recently, such as Gerald Martinez, respect Jean-Pierre. I said to Gerald, "How are you. How are things in Paris, with Racing Club de France?" and he said, 'It's good because Jean-Pierre is there. He is so good to us'.

"But all of Jean-Pierre is like that. You can call him about any problem, for anything. He has a fantastic nature, very generous. But not many people know this side of him because they do not know him well enough. Because Jean-Pierre is shy, very shy, and he is afraid of people. People all around frighten him. I am a bit the same. He always has a shell around him. And people don't know him well because of this.

"He has a poet's spirit. He has, too, an agreeable approach to life; casual and free from care. He is not a matter-of-fact type. He is one of those people I like very much. He loves the simple life. He loves nature, simple and easy things. He likes his games of golf, lunching with friends.

"In rugby, I believe he suffered through being captain. Because it is difficult at that level. It is true that the people who manage French rugby are the people who want to make the decisions, who want everything followed to the letter. But when there was a problem with Garuet and the President of the Federation, Jean-Pierre said, 'No, I don't agree.' This proved Rives' character.

"But it's not obligatory always to be in disagreement with the Federation to have personality. I think that Jean-Pierre, as he is intelligent, knew how to manage both, to shout when it was necessary and to know how to smooth away problems. It's a proof of intelligence. But when it was necessary he knew how to bang on the table and say, 'No, I don't agree about Garuet or about this referee'.

"Jean-Pierre is a man apart in rugby. There are few like him. He approaches rugby differently from most rugby players. Above all, he always played rugby for pleasure. That was the important thing. He was there to play for eighty minutes. This is a bit like the British attitude. That is what made him the player he was.

"His qualities as a man, from his heart, were recognised by players with him and against him. He achieved enormous stature in French rugby which he deserved because he never cheated. He always played   and I saw him from when he was very young – with the same fervour, the same enthusiasm for the game of rugby.

"Not everything which surrounds rugby interests him. It's the media who made him a man of rugby but, for him, it was the game for the game's sake.

"French rugby owes him a great debt. He was one of the players who made a real mark on the game in France, on the same level as Jean Prat, Lucien Mias and Michel Crauste, the great captains of France. Like Crauste, Jean-Pierre is a holy monument to French rugby. He had a personality strong enough to influence his teammates and you have to take your hat off to him, for that."

Gareth Edwards also pays tribute to Rives' influence on the mental attitude of the French teams. In a sense, reasoned the Welshman, Rives revolutionsed the French character by his example and demands.

"The French became very disciplined and almost British in their attitude," he said. "They were very structured. Before Rives' captaincy, their natural game was stifled and I was very disappointed in that sort of rugby. It was not typical French rugby, the kind I had grown to admire.

"Before Rives' influence, they used to be ill-disciplined and therefore easier to beat. But Rives gave them flair and discipline and that is why they should be potentially the best rugby country in the world.''

Rives' legend in the French game has not been remotely dissipated by his retirement. Jacques Fouroux, his captain and then coach, says: ''Since Jean-Pierre Rives, I have never seen a player on any field with his ability. I have seen some bigger, some stronger physically, some faster, but I have never seen one player who gathers together so many rugby qualities – only him. He is the player who has impressed me the most in all my rugby career. I always saw him at his peak. Quite objectively, I have no memories of having seen Jean-Pierre play a bad game in the national team. With his clubs, Stade Toulousain or Racing, I don't know, I don't really remember. But he wasn't the great, great Jean-Pierre then. But the moment he put on the French shirt, he was another man.

''He made his mark not only on French rugby but on international rugby. Many boys and adolescents ally themselves to Jean-Pierre Rives; they want to be like him. That is the best reward for a player. It exists normally in other sports like tennis and football. The players are stars and children dream a little through them. But Jean-Pierre is the only example in France. He has a very positive image and that is how he has marked his era.

''He was *the* great rugby player of France. But he still remains the same man and that is important. Even his friends do not know Jean-Pierre really well. He is the only person who knows him. You think you have discovered him but it is another Jean-Pierre who has appeared. That's disconcerting, but I believe at heart, because I think I know him, that he is an extremely sensitive person. Very, very sensitive.''

The Englishman John Scott, winner of thirty-two caps between 1978 and 1984, the bulk of them from his base with the Cardiff club, faced France's international side seven times during his career. He provides a shrewd assessment of Rives' value to the French, a fact recognised by the story of Rives' special holiday on the way home from a sporting trip to Argentina.

Scott said: ''I understand Rives telephoned Albert Ferrasse and asked if he could stop off in Rio de Janeiro for a few days. It was six days holiday paid for by the French. They have a nice cut-throat attitude. If you were in, you were definitely in . . . and Rives was.''

But Scott had no doubts about Rives' abilities on the field. ''It is hard to lead, especially the French side, when it is going backwards and under pressure. But Rives held them together and they would have had a lot more selection changes and problems without him. He could knit the players together.

"In a sense, he was very typically French . . . very emotional. But he played on that a lot. The speeches I heard him make were very emotional in getting the French players and hierarchy into the right frame of mind. He is a very clever bloke. He was always diplomatic, a good ambassador. He is like a god in France.

"Towards the end of his career, he started standing off. That tends to creep into your game. Whether it was because of injury, I don't know. Perhaps he was frightened and was trying to do everything for the players. But he was at his best when he was handling the ball. However, his qualities of leadership cannot be disputed. In 1981 when France won the Grand Slam, they were a competent team but not outstanding. Rives was a bloody good captain; he offered the French team far more than captains in the past. Towards the end of your career, other roles take over, like leadership. The 1985 season proved the French were not as effective without Rives."

But what of the man's surely astonishing decision to walk away from rugby, without even the briefest glance back over his shoulder? What are we to make of such an act? The game made him; did he not owe it a deep debt, once his playing career had ended?

Many were surprised by the action, but not Roland Bertranne. "That is the other side of Jean-Pierre. It didn't surprise me at all. After his decision to stop, he went away, no-one saw him anymore and that was altogether Jean-Pierre. It is because rugby was not his sole preoccupation. He had other things which he wanted to do. He took a great deal of pleasure in rugby but he's going to get pleasure elsewhere now. In life, there are two sides of Rives – the rugby player, and then the poet, the man who likes to travel, loves music, plays golf."

The old international Walter Spanghero agrees. "I, too, felt when I retired that I wanted to get completely away from rugby. For ten or more years, I had known nothing else. I wanted to find other things, forget rugby, have a total rest from it. But now, after a spell of a few years, I want to be involved again, in coaching or something. Maybe Jean-Pierre will be the same, in time. It is a natural process."

Three other playing compatriots – Michel Palmié, Jean-Pierre Bastiat and Jean-Claude Skrela – pay tribute to Rives' honesty, his achievements and the mark he left on French rugby. Skrela admitted: "At certain times, Jean-Pierre became annoyed with the adulation, all the fuss, because he was so talked about. He wasn't so much bored as annoyed because people said a lot of things about him. But he remained capable of analysing what he would do and what he wouldn't do. He let the media have their say and then he made up his own mind. But, in addition, he had a quality on the rugby field of honesty. He was always honest and people reacted to that, they saw that and followed him because of the respect that created."

Palmié believes Rives to have been the best ambassador for French rugby the game has known. "When he was captain, he was a marvellous ambassador for our game. On the field he proved his quality, and off it he created, through the media and through his life in Paris, a new image of rugbymen, of rugby players, which previously had been bad in certain ways. In fact, he was an ambassador. That's to say, everyone saw and heard him talking about rugby in his own style, and I think he paid a great service to the French game and even now, when he doesn't play anymore, he is still a leader. He is a man of show business, he is always at receptions, on television. He has done so much to popularise rugby, to raise it from how people used to think about it."

Palmié talks quietly yet with animation. He has the look of an overweight, over-grown schoolboy, tie loose at the collar, hair slightly scruffy. But two factors dispel the illusion. He is an enormous man who seems to tower over everything and everyone. And he has a nose which looks as though an old Parisian tram has knocked it sideways.

On the western side of the Pyrenees, in Dax, there is a curious little hamlet, a tiny pocket of rugby intensity . . . all in one street. Claude Dourthe shares his dental practice with Jean-Pierre Lux, his co-international rugby centre of the late 1960s, through to the mid-1970s period. Downstairs in the same building, Jean-Pierre Bastiat runs an insurance company. A few doors down stands 'Hotel Lescarboura'. The perfect rugby side, I thought to myself as I waited in Bastiat's modern office. Bastiat to win the ball at the back of the line-out; Lescarboura to link and kick the goals; and Dourthe and Lux to run in the tries. And with a street bearing the name of 'Foch', you wouldn't have to go too far for a President.

Bastiat, his giant hands threading intermittently together and apart to illustrate his points, says: "Rives did not have just one success in rugby. Everything he accomplished since 1975 was a triumph. We had the Grand Slam in 1977, the second Grand Slam in 1981, and his great captaincy. But maybe his greatest success is that all the rugby nations, whichever they be – the Fijians, Australians, English, New Zealanders, South Africans – all ask him to come and play a match with them. I believe that is the most rewarding success Jean-Pierre ever had."

All agreed on one point – Rives, by uniting many qualities such as a special appearance, certain intellectual qualities, above-normal intelligence and courage also out of the ordinary, was a man apart. "Only Jean-Pierre has become the superstar of rugby. And I do not believe there will be any others like him in the future," said Dourthe.

The New Zealand All Blacks lock forward Andy Haden smiles broadly when asked for his favourite memory of Rives. "I have in my mind the memory of Jean-Pierre throwing one of the biggest tantrums in his life. It was a few years ago in a special challenge match. The Sydney team was playing a World XV, in Australia, and Jean-Pierre was one of the players recruited to play. I remember it particularly because I was looking forward to teaming up with Rives. The game started and after about twenty minutes Jean-Pierre got his usual cut down the side of his forehead. I remember he was always a great bandage man and he left the field and disappeared into the dressing-room to put a dressing on his injury. But when he came back about five minutes later, he was furious to see a replacement already on the field. What had happened was that everyone thought he was going off injured and so another forward was brought on. The look on Rives' face was something else. He was screaming at the referee and his team-mates but of course there was nothing anyone could do about it. Looking back on it, I suppose it's quite funny that Rives should come 10,000 miles to play twenty minutes rugby but at the time he was absolutely livid."

Such a glimpse of Rives was rare; he was one of the most modest of international sportsmen. He was injured, but continued to play, taking risks without thought which others would have deemed unacceptable. Yet he listened to the praise and adulation although preferring to leave at the earliest opportunity for the company of his colleagues. Rives, of course, was as recognisable off the field, in a city street, as in his bloodied shirt of the French national side. But the idea of enhancing that fame was anathema to the man. Nor was it cultivated. For a start, it did not need to be, it flourished of its own making. For another reason, Rives enjoyed too much his private, quiet moments away from the prying eyes. He cherished, often craved, his freedom.

Rives was expected to attend functions, shake hands, exchange back slaps and suffer the most interminable bores which seem, appallingly, to congregate around the best sportsmen. The John McEnroes of this world usually despatch such characters with little regard for human feelings. The courteous variety, like the golfers Nicklaus and Palmer, swallow the talk and make their excuses to leave. Rives selected the latter method and was all the more respected, spoken more highly of, for being polite.

Rives had found the company of older, more mature people, of greater stimulation than most people of his own age group. It is so with only a handful of young men, and invariably they are of strong character and personality, well used to thinking for themselves and leading individual lives, without recourse to the shelter or protection of large groups. One man, a close friend of Rives, but, aptly, from almost a generation before him, watched the young man's progress, in rugby and in life. He provides a particularly revealing picture of Rives because he was so much like him; Rives' mentor, Jean Salut.

We were searching for him all over Toulouse. Without success. No answer on his telephone at home; no response at work. He is a masseur in the city, clearly part-time.

At last Pierre Villepreux provides the key. We meet him at six and wait until after training outside Stade Toulousain's head-quarters. Then, a twisting car ride down to the TOEC tennis club. Inside, as the bar is closing, Salut is about to leave.

So he sits in the cool early summer evening, the wind whistling through the tennis courts, where friends play with energy, as much to keep warm, one suspects, as to clinch points. He looks, for all the world, like football's Tony Currie, the former Watford, Leeds United and Queens Park Rangers international midfield player, whose value was scarcely recognised, still less utilised by England. Salut also won only a handful of caps. He played in the

Currie mould, too: individually, unconventionally with the hint of rebellion never far from the chunky frame. Salut wears grey boots, black trousers, a white shirt. His long hair is slicked and combed back and a baggy sweater is draped over his shoulders beneath a long white knitted scarf. He bears the unmistakable look of a tough cowboy in those leather boots, with his very light hair. The soft, delicately pale blue eyes seem incongruous, for there are no more soft features. A face full of character; a ruggedly handsome man.

What was his special relationship with Jean-Pierre Rives?

"We were very, very good friends. Despite the gap in our ages because when I played in the French team, he was only a junior at TOEC. But he preferred to associate with people older than himself. Also, he was blond, like me, but more so. He played in the same position as me, we had many similarities. He liked me, often came to see me. In him, I saw myself the way I had been when I was young. And even now, years later, I still see him often when he comes to Toulouse. We meet together as much as possible. It is always a pleasure to see him again. But when we meet, we talk very little about rugby. We talk about anything else, depending on who is at the table with us. We talk about amusing things but in a serious way."

Salut's views on the game are very much mirrored by Rives. A fantasy rhetoric, some might assert, yet commendable and perfectly feasible given the collective will to succeed. He says: "There is too much pressure on rugby players nowadays. It was not like that for me. There were fewer journalists then, television was less important than it is now."

Would he like to be a player now? "If I were fifteen years younger; and like Jean-Pierre. When you are a champion you can get big-headed. But he is very modest, therefore a unique personality in the world of sport.

"My philosophy was probably like Jean-Pierre's. In my opinion I had a very British attitude. I never took a penny for playing rugby, I always played for pleasure. I went out in the evenings; I smoked, I drank, I trained not a lot. It was only for the pleasure of the game that I was involved in rugby. I played four years for France but had disagreements with some of the selectors. But that was not important. Taking pleasure from the game is the fundamental element. I have talked much with Jean-Pierre about playing for the pleasure of it. I believe that if he had not played like that he would not have played so long. He did not do it for the money."

Salut believes his was the purer era, in comparison with Rives' time in rugby. "I am certain I was better off playing when I did. It is much too serious now. I only go to matches from time to time; like Jean-Pierre, I prefer to watch on television. I am short-sighted now, and do not see very well.

"But Rugby today is not the same. I dearly hope it will re-capture the great days of not too long ago. If that were to happen, there would be more people in the stands. In the semi-finals of the 1985 French Championship, half the stands were empty at the two matches – Stade Toulousain against Mont-ferrand, and Lourdes against Toulon. In my day, there would have been no room. Many people prefer the rugby of my era because it was much more attacking. There are not enough tries now."

Salut's opinion is that Rives' sterling defensive work compromised his attacking functions. "To my mind, he wore himself out too much, tackling and defending. He had less strength afterwards to play the ball. But he found that the modern game demands that. He could be a very strong attacking player like when he played for the Barbarians. But here in France there is too much demand for defensive work and that is a bit worrying. And the half empty stands show it."

Pierre Villepreux takes up Salut's point about Rives changing from being an attacking player: "When he was captain of the French national team he was only on the ball on the ground, or in the mauls. OK, the game changed, but Jean-Pierre changed his way of playing completely. I think that was partly because of the responsibility of captaincy; you have to be where the ball is, to show your players where to follow . . . Maybe Jean-Pierre followed the evolution of the game. He was a wonderful player, intelligent and with a good technique. But maybe too he was a victim of the way rugby changes in the mid-1970s. OK, he had a big career as a captain and player, but I believe he could have had a more complete game than he had eventually."

It is in his testimony to Rives' qualities as a leader, however, a man who took French rugby away from its often ugly image towards a reputation for better behaviour, that Jean Salut paid his greatest tribute. "Jean-Pierre changed rugby here and that reputation. How did he do it? It was natural. Because he had a good education, then he became captain of France. He was a person of distinction. There were great players like him before but they behaved badly. Now, since Jean-Pierre, rugby players are much better behaved and more polite.''

If that was the finest achievement of Rives' career as leader of his country, which game stood out in the memory of those who played with him through the major part of his career? Jerome Gallion highlights Auckland 1979 as an obvious peak, saying: ''It is difficult because he played so many times at a very high level. But I think that game in Auckland will remain engraved on our minds, strong in our memories. Because it was a victory against the All Blacks, and because it was the first time the French side had carried away victory on New Zealand soil. To be captain of that team, must have been fabulous.''

Gallion endorses the view that Rives was probably the finest captain France has known. Certainly, the most influential. He remains an important figure in the game, inside France, even today, long after his retirement. Men like Fouroux and senior members of the FFR hierarchy pay heed to his words, expressed with great thought and concern for the correct image of the game in France. It seems almost inconceivable that Rives will play no part in the future of the game in his country. Fouroux says: ''I do not know in which capacity Jean-Pierre could be involved but I cannot think he will stay forever outside the game. He is too valuable a figure for French rugby to lose forever.''

Rives as a decision-maker in the game is, however, a notion which rests uneasily in my mind. He shows no sign of desiring such a role, nor does his character suggest any easy adaptation to so structured a part. But in his own particular brand of leadership, he showed great skill and judgement. Such qualities cannot be ignored. As Bastiat says: You become a good captain like Jean-Pierre was, when you have been captain twenty or twenty-five times. You take first of all the measure of your responsibility and then have to supervise the game as a whole, as well as playing yourself. That is difficult, very difficult.

''But Jean-Pierre became a good captain, an excellent and extraordinary captain incorporating all those factors, after he had won five or six caps as leader. That was phenomenal. Jean-Pierre Rives is a monument to rugby. He had two essential qualities.

That was to be the person he is with the temperament he has, and to have the desire to play rugby as he did."

Rives' boss at Pernod, Daniel Hémard, is another to express satisfaction and respect for Rives' temperament and personality. Hémard's decision to engage him, in 1981, was something of a gamble for his company; they had no history of employing leading personalities from the sports world. The measure of Rives' success in the job was that Pernod decided, within a couple of years, to extend the experiment, taking on another great man of rugby, Serge Blanco, to work in their south-west region.

Hémard says: "Jean-Pierre is a very sensible man with a very large heart. He took to his job naturally and went along very well with all the people inside the company. That was very important. We were not sure whether he could work successfully in the company but we felt he was very wise to create an easy relationship with other people. Jean-Pierre knows everybody, in the cinema, in politics, the arts, and of course in sport. He has friends everywhere and that is very useful."

Hémard still chuckles at the Rives stories which have become legendary in the company. Like the time he was driving in Paris and stopped at traffic lights. "Some people saw him, despite the late hour – around four o'clock in the morning – and waved to him, calling: 'Hi, Vitas, how is the tennis.'

Rives, ever ready to fall in with a joke, replied: 'It is hard. I must play later today.' And then he was gone.

That afternoon, in the Roland Garros championships, the American Vitas Gerulaitis beat Jimmy Connors. And people all over Paris were saying after reading the story in a newspaper, 'That Gerulaitis, what a man. He was in the nightclubs until 4 am and then still got up to beat Connors. He must be some player, some man!' "

Another occasion was in London. "We had been to the British motor cycle Grand Prix and arrived at Heathrow Airport early on Monday morning, for the 0730 flight to Paris," said Hémard. "As we were having breakfast in the airport, an elderly lady serving us said to Jean-Pierre, 'I know you'.

'No, no, it is not possible,' smiled Rives.

'Yes, you are a very famous rugby player in France,' replied the waitress.

"It was amazing. An elderly lady, maybe sixty years of age,

recognised Jean-Pierre. I don't think many ladies of that age would recognise any other foreign rugby players.''

Rives' humour is as appealing as his humility. As Hémard says: ''He realises he has had many things but he doesn't behave like someone who thinks everything is due to him. He is not spoiled, probably because of his intelligence. He is a man of culture. That helps him to face life, and it helps us too.

''If Jean-Pierre were rude and badly behaved, he would have been rejected by our company. But he is very polite and knows how to behave. I have been surprised by his approach. He has kindness in his heart and understands politeness. All those things make it so easy to work with him. Many people when they saw him here for the first time didn't realise he was so modest. We didn't think he would be like that.''

But what of Rives himself and the men he respected? Which players left an impression on the French captain, for their charm and quality? Graham Mourie – ''so polite a boy,'' said Rives' mother – has become a close friend of the Frenchman. Rives says: ''Graham was so humble, so gentle in victory, when we played in New Zealand 1979. He is a great example of New Zealand people. For me, New Zealand is the best tour you can make; a real rugby country, nice people, good spirit and great rugby. Their hospitality is magnificent. Their rugby is terribly powerful, always the greatest test. But away from rugby, their country is so very beautiful and I like the people especially.

''South Africa is a hard tour, Australia, too. But they are different. Perhaps the Australians are known best for their desire to move the ball, something I respect greatly. It is, I am certain, the way the game should be played. In South Africa, there is such interest and love for the game. The matches are all hard, no matter which team you play against.

''But New Zealand is the toughest of the tours. Their attitude to the game dictates that. But what a wonderful tour to make, to New Zealand.''

Into the reckoning in recent years, in terms of world ranking, have come the Argentines. Inspired by their wonderfully deft, creative stand-off half Hugo Porta – a man with a reputation for strong kicking but, unlike many of the ilk, aware that such a style is no simple panacea for the problems of the game – their international side has earned universal respect.

197

Even with Porta now at the veteran stage, so immaculate a player was able to demonstrate his timeless skills when the French team toured that country in 1985, by helping Argentina defeat the French in one of the Test matches. A French win in the second Test levelled the two-match series, but there was not a single member of the French party who returned to Paris harbouring any illusions as to the Argentinians' credentials in calling themselves one of the world's most improved rugby nations.

Rives has known Porta for years, and although the 1985 tour came ten months after his retirement, he still keeps in touch. "Hugo is a great, great player and a fine man who has the best spirit it is possible to see in the game," says Rives. "We talk on the telephone sometimes; we write to one another, too. He is one of the best stand-offs there has ever been. Very clever and a great general on the field. Argentine rugby has come up so much and Porta has had a lot to do with it. He, especially, has helped to create such a good spirit in the game in his country. They have good ways; they are good players on the field and fine people off it, away from sport. I have no doubt in my mind that Porta has helped that; he carried a lot of spirit, as a player and as a man."

Any others?

Andy Ripley. "Rugby needs people like Andy. Like Laurent Pardo, the Montferrand and French international. You can still meet people like them in the game and that proves to me that rugby has kept the same correct spirit. I have a lot of respect for Andy; he is such an interesting man. A great man with a great soul. People say you must have a certain image, which is very strict, to play good rugby but that is crazy. Take seriously some things but don't take yourself seriously. Through all the humour, he always said very important things for those who cared to listen carefully. Rugby needs people like him, but the world needs such people, too. People like him are very rich in spirit and friendship."

Fergus Slattery. "Ah, Fergus, a great man. We have had so many battles, many fine matches together, but more than that. Friendship away from the rugby field. He is like a big piece of fighting spirit; a lovely man. I love, too, his country – it is a wonderful place to be. Such warmth and friendship from the people."

Gareth Edwards. "Maybe he was the best rugby player of all

categories, of all time. Certainly, the finest scrum half I ever saw. He had such strength yet such skill. Oh, tackling Gareth was almost impossible, he was so strong. And he was like so many, filled with the best spirit for the game. It is a great credit to rugby that all the good players, the fine players with the best spirit, are so nice. They are such a good advertisement for the game, as people.

"Now, other countries have come up to the standard of the established nations. Look at Romania, Argentina, Fiji. Argentina has had very good results in France and at home against us, and also against the South Africans. Rugby deserves a good team like them, and the others, not just ten strong countries and nothing else. That is why the World Cup is such a wonderful idea because countries can come together, in the right spirit, to test their progress, to learn, and to create friendships. The World Cup should have been in existence for years but London is very far from the rest of the world in its mind!!"

In Rives' own mind, he sees a World Cup as the ideal opportunity to enhance the spirit of the game, much as the splendidly organised 'Cathay Pacific Hong Kong Sevens' tournament has done in recent years. That event has become a great celebration of the Sevens game and a meeting place of friends from around the world. It evokes harmony, understanding and friendship, yet it is still regarded with suspicion in some official British quarters.

However, the idea of nations such as Sri Lanka or Western Samoa or Tonga meeting and playing against powerful rugby nations like New Zealand and Australia can surely only help the development of the world game. Such tournaments are to be commended and encouraged.

In August 1984, Jean-Pierre Rives toyed briefly with the idea of playing one final season in the International Championship. He still felt he could contribute, still loved the game and the involvement, and planned, if all went well, his retirement for the end of the 1984/85 International season in Europe. But fate was to decree otherwise.

Playing for the French Barbarians against the London club Harlequins in a match to commemorate the famous former Harlequin and England international, Wavell Wakefield, meant much to Rives. It was the first time the French Ba-baas had ever played a full, fifteen-a-side match in England. The honour of leadership fell to Rives, something he cherished.

But during that match, on the first day of September 1984, Rives injured the cap of his left shoulder. Already his right shoulder, damaged against the Australians, was less than perfect. Now in a friendly match, came serious damage to the other one. It was the last straw, the final injury he was to suffer. More than three months of rumour followed, while Rives sought with increasing frustration and urgency to find effective treatment to solve the problem. It was not to be.

On 14 December, eleven days before Christmas, Jean-Pierre Rives sat at a Paris press conference, all but blinded by the television lights, hemmed in by pressmen from every kind of organisation. He brushed away the suggestion of a tear as he announced his retirement from the game at the top level.

''I am not fit enough to play in this weekend's club game for Racing and therefore not fit enough for the Five Nations Championship early in the New Year. So that is it – goodbye.'' *L'Equipe*, the French sports paper, said simply: 'Goodbye Mr Rives'.

Rives had won 59 caps and captained his country a record 34 times. He led France in 30 of the 47 matches he played against International Board countries, a unique record. To the end, he promulgated a policy of modesty, the proper spirit and courteous behaviour. Self-aggrandisement was as strange to Rives' mind as the actions of those who, by their tactics on the field and poor spirit off it, soured the image of a glorious game.

Once, when asked to explain his dislike for trophies or mementoes, he replied without a trace of mendacity, ''Because I am not an African hunter. I do not hunt trophies. I do not want to hear about that. I do not want to put pressure on people around me with this. I do not want my house or my parents' house to look like a rugby museum. So I gave away most things to my friends; jerseys and things like that. That is better because I know they are happy with such things. Happier than me, that is for certain.

''It is not that I am ashamed; I was ashamed a little at the beginning, at all the fuss. But not now. I prefer to have everything around me which is of good spirit, given me by my friends. Everything in my flat is from my friends, presents to me from people I like. That reminds me of the friendship of life. I do not need my own things around me. I would rather have these gifts and nice things on display than pictures of me playing rugby. I do not consider myself attractive, in an aesthetic way, on the wall.''

By 1985, Rives had been sharing his life with his constant friend, Jennifer Taylor, for several, years. An American model who speaks fluent French, she travels the world in pursuit of her job, as does Jean-Pierre. Their lives are as hectic as the aeroplane schedules they constantly scrutinise to whisk them to their next assignment. But they snatch time together in Paris whenever possible.

What of the future? It cannot be known, especially for a man such as Rives. None can forecast it, for even he cannot tell. All his life Rives has been a man influenced by his will, spontaneous in his actions, brave and bold in attempting fresh projects.

He left rugby the richer, the greater for his presence. Perhaps some day he will return, in another role, to enhance the virtues he gave the game. Increasingly in our modern world, such qualities are needed to counterbalance the greed, the cheating, those who embitter and destroy the image of the game.

All his career Rives has fought to enshrine a special spirit, a joyous approach. He will be remembered as a man who cherished such spirit, in himself and in others. His lasting testimony to the game is not of tries scored or matches played or jerseys swopped: such are peripheral matters. It was always 'spirit' which motivated Rives, that is a love for the game, played in the finest traditions with love for those involved, even one's fiercest opponents. These words from Shakespeare's *Richard II* could almost have been written to sum up this quality in him:

> A jewel in a ten-times-barr'd-up chest
> Is a bold spirit in a loyal breast.
> Mine honour is my life; both grow in one;
> Take honour from me, and my life is done.

Bibliography

Rothmans Rugby Yearbook, 1975 to 1984, Rothmans Publications Ltd.
'La fabuleuse histoire du XV de France', by Jacques Carducci, Editions Odil, 1976.
'De la vierge rouge aux anges blonds,' Cepadues-Editions, Toulouse, 1984.
'Fran', Fran Cotton: An Autobiography. Queen Anne Press, 1981.
'Graham Mourie, Captain'. Arthur Barker, London, 1983.
Stade Toulousain Revue Annuelle 1983/84, 1984/85.
The Daily Telegraph, The Daily Express, The Sunday Telegraph; various issues,
    1975 to 1984.